Financing Higher Education: 1960 - 70

Contributing Authors

Robert D. Calkins

Harold F. Clark

Philip H. Coombs

Raymond Ewell

Clifford C. Furnas

Seymour E. Harris

Harlow J. Heneman

John D. Millett

Gordon N. Ray

Willard L. Thorp

Sidney G. Tickton

W. Homer Turner

Dexter M. Keezer, *editor*

Financing Higher Education

—————————— 1960-70

The McGraw-Hill Book Company 50th Anniversary Study of the Economics of Higher Education in the United States

New York

Toronto

London

McGRAW-HILL BOOK COMPANY, INC.

1959

FINANCING HIGHER EDUCATION: 1960–70

Preface

The purpose and scope of this study are admirably described in the following introductory chapter by my colleague, Dr. Dexter M. Keezer. It only remains, then, for me to give McGraw-Hill's thanks to all who have had a part in it.

First, I want to express to Amherst College and the Merrill Center for Economics, and especially to the Director and Assistant Director of the Center, Willard L. Thorp and Clarice Brows Thorp, our deep appreciation of their generosity and hospitality in co-sponsoring a two-week conference at the Merrill Center on the subject of our study.

Next, we are very grateful to the members of a Steering Committee who gave invaluable advice and guidance in planning the study and the conference:

Thomas R. Carskadon, *Associate Director, Twentieth Century Fund*
Philip H. Coombs, *Secretary, The Fund for the Advancement of Education*
Seymour E. Harris, *Chairman, Department of Economics, Harvard University*
Willard L. Thorp, *Director, The Merrill Center for Economics*
Herman B. Wells, *President, Indiana University*

Most of all, we must, of course, thank the authors themselves. Without their hard work and patient dedication to their assigned topics, neither the conference nor this volume would have materialized so successfully.

Finally, our grateful thanks go to the following additional participants in the conference, to whom we are greatly indebted for their unflagging interest, their objective criticism and appraisal, and their many substantive contributions:

William G. Avirett, *Executive Associate, Carnegie Endowment for International Peace*

Sarah G. Blanding, *President, Vassar College*

Edward E. Booher, *Executive Vice President, McGraw-Hill Book Company*

Frank H. Bowles, *President, College Entrance Examination Board*

Charles W. Cole, *President, Amherst College*

Edmund P. Joyce, C.S.C., *Executive Vice President, University of Notre Dame*

Nancy D. Lewis, *Dean of Pembroke College in Brown University*

Ralph F. Lewis, *General Partner and National Director of Management Services, Arthur Young & Company, Certified Public Accountants*

Morrough P. O'Brien, *Dean Emeritus, College of Engineering, University of California*

Theodore W. Schultz, *Chairman, Department of Economics, University of Chicago*

Frank H. Sparks, *President, Council for Financial Aid to Education*

John N. Stalnaker, *President, National Merit Scholarship Corporation*

W. Blair Stewart, *President, Associated Colleges of the Midwest*

J. Cameron Thomson, *retired Chairman of the Board, Northwest Bancorporation*

H. Edwin Young, *Chairman, Department of Economics, University of Wisconsin*

We hope that all concerned with the production of this volume can feel that its content and potential influence are ample rewards for their generous efforts.

Curtis G. Benjamin
PRESIDENT, McGRAW-HILL BOOK COMPANY

Contents

1

Introduction

Dexter M. Keezer

How much substance is there really in the estimate that the number of students in our colleges and universities will almost double in the next ten years?

How much of the cost of his college or university education is it wise to call upon the student to pay?

Are loans to students going to be a major source of funds for higher education in the years ahead? If so, what effects will this have on higher education for women? Will mortgaged brides be alluring?

Is Ruml right?[1]* Can our colleges and universities make big savings without cutting quality by simplifying their curricula and increasing the ratio of students to faculty members? If so, what is the way to get the cooperation of trustees, administrators, and faculty members necessary to get the job done?

Is there much financial nourishment for higher education in more extensive cooperation between institutions—in joint use of laboratories and libraries and joint registration for some courses?

Will the publicly sponsored colleges and universities be able to get enough tax support to keep their tuition charges low?

Can government agencies bearing research contracts get universities into financial troubles?

Can gifts by business corporations be made a major source of support for higher education? If so, is there danger that educational policy would be dominated by business?

Does anyone in Washington have a clear idea of all the ways in which the Federal government is supporting higher education at present? If not, what should be done about it?

If there is to be more Federal support for higher education, should it be

* Superscript numbers refer to notes collected at the ends of the respective papers.

1

given in the form of help for students or help for institutions? And if for institutions, should it be grants for capital equipment or grants for operating expenses?

Will institutions outside the conventional framework of higher education, such as those conducted by business firms, handle much of the load of higher education over the years ahead?

Where can the prospective consumer of higher education get the information needed to be reasonably sure of getting into the right institution for him, thus avoiding waste of time and money?

As the result of a most extraordinary collaboration, this volume throws light upon questions such as these, light focused directly on problems of financing of higher education. In the process it makes a pioneering contribution to the scanty literature on the subject.

Upon the successful financing of higher education could depend our successful survival as a nation. Upon such a solution surely depends the avoidance of great expanses of intellectual slums masquerading as institutions of higher education.

Higher education in the United States is poorly financed at present. This is most strikingly attested by authoritative findings that its faculty members—who are its most crucial element—are on the average only about half as well paid as they should be.

But the present financial plight of higher education is only half the problem. The other half is created by the clear prospect of a doubling of the demand for its services over the next decade. Where there are about 3.6 million students in our colleges and universities today, it is confidently to be expected that at least 6 million students will be in something called an institution of higher education ten years hence. Whether it will actually be such an institution in anything except name will depend in major degree on how well the job of financing is done.

At present the annual expenditure on higher education in the United States is about $4 billion. Careful calculations, amplified in this volume, indicate that ten years hence the annual expenditure (in dollars of their present value) must be about $10 billion if (1) higher education is to be put squarely on its feet financially and (2) the surging demand for higher education is to be met with a product generally worthy of the name.

In terms of the nation's total resources, $10 billion is not a staggering sum. In fact, it is not much more than 1 per cent of the total dollar value of goods and services which the United States can reasonably be expected to be producing, and consuming, a decade hence. Also it is only a small fraction of what is being spent and presumably will continue to be spent for the physical provision of national defense, of which, in large measure, higher education is the intellectual counterpart. But it is a fraction of the nation's resources that must be increased at relatively high speed if higher education is to have a fair chance of performing its crucial role properly. It is this double-barreled problem of getting it out of a deep hole at the same time that it is being expanded rapidly that adds peculiar difficulties to the job of financing higher education, and also adds urgency to the question posed at the outset.

In the collaboration on this problem which resulted in this volume, the first step was to enlist the cooperation of the best people who could be found in preparing papers on the various phases of the financing of higher education. Then, over a period of two weeks, these papers were successively subjected to detailed discussion and criticism by a group of the nation's leading authorities on the subject matter, selected to give representation to varying points of view on some of its more controversial aspects. No less than fifty hours, spread over sixteen sessions and two weeks, was spent in seminar discussions focused on the papers under review. These discussions were extended by a myriad of individual and group conversations. The scheduled discussions were led by Dr. Willard L. Thorp, Director of the Merrill Center for Economics. In a most generous collaboration, the spacious quarters of the center, an adjunct of Amherst College donated by the late Charles Merrill, at Southampton, New York, were made available for the two-week seminar.

In the light of the critical discussions of them at the Merrill Center, the authors revised their papers as they saw fit. In most cases the revisions were substantial, and in some cases they were complete. That author was not unique who wrote, "I have completely revised my chapter as a result of the discussions at the Merrill Center. Needless to say, I think it is vastly improved." It is.

Now the papers, as revised, are embodied in this volume and to them is added a paper by Dr. Thorp, giving his impressions of the sessions at the Merrill Center as viewed from the head of the conference table. Dr. Thorp's paper both highlights the discussions at the center and develops points made in the discussions in addition to those covered in the papers under review.

"With so much talent so diligently applied to the problem, you must have come up with the right formula for financing higher education in the United States." This is one phrasing of a not unusual reaction to an account of the sustained and searching collaboration involved in producing this volume.

But the reaction misses a key point, underlined again and again in the course of the collaboration. It is that there is no single "right formula" for the successful financing of higher education in the United States. To get the job done tolerably well, many different methods must be used to meet the problems of an enormous diversity of institutions with widely varying academic and financial requirements.

Higher education, as the term is commonly used and is used in this volume, includes institutions ranging all the way from university post-graduate schools, which test the far upper reaches of intellectual capacity with complicated and costly equipment, to certain junior colleges conducted on a shoestring in borrowed buildings, which in some cases can be called institutions of higher education only because those attending them have completed some kind of a four-year high school course. In such a diverse array of institutions there are obviously great variations in financial requirements.

Also there is a wide array of different methods of getting these institutions adequately financed. Some of them are designed to make more effective use of existing financial resources by better educational organization and use of more effective teaching methods, thus decreasing the financial requirements to be met. Other methods, which must be very extensively exploited if the financial problems of higher education are to be adequately handled, are directed to getting more financial support —through tuition payments, gifts from friends and alumni, taxes, etc. Still another method of formidable proportions is that of having more of what is in fact higher education provided by institutions which fall outside the conventional framework of higher education as at present conceived.

In this volume you will find some new methods of financing suggested and some old methods reexamined in a new and more revealing light. You will also find some disagreement on the proper emphasis to be placed on different methods of financing, for example, on the relative loads appropriately placed on the consumer—that is, the student—and the taxpayer.

Disagreement of this sort is quite in keeping with the spirit of the undertaking which resulted in this volume. It was not designed to lead to a "Now be it resolved that this is the right and proper way to do it" conclusion. Neither was it designed to produce an encyclopedic account of all aspects of the financing of higher education in the United States. Rather, it was designed to open up new vistas, stretch imaginations, and offer new and inspiring insights into the vastly difficult and complicated business of financing our institutions of higher education properly.

This general purpose is reflected in the rough outline which the contributors were asked to keep in mind in preparing their papers on various phases of the financing of higher education. Since it had a formative role in shaping the final product, the original outline is reproduced in the Appendix.

While the seminar at the Merrill Center was the antithesis of a series of me-too sessions, broad ranges of agreement on right and wrong ways to get ahead with the financing of higher education were uncovered. One on which there was virtually vehement unanimity was that it would be a certain route to disaster all around for institutions operating under different kinds of sponsorship, such as public and private sponsorship, to divert energies badly needed for a common assault on their financial problems to slugging each other.

There is, it was agreed, much room for constructive competition between institutions of different sponsorship. In this connection it was observed that the competition among many of the leading institutions, both publicly and privately sponsored, to enroll the best students available is even more lively than the general public understands the competition for potential All-American halfbacks to be. But when, as it has on occasion, this rivalry descends below a plane of fair competition toward mutual questioning of educational *bona fides*, there was complete agreement that mutual disaster is also being courted.

There was also full agreement that the great surge of students set to descend on our colleges and universities is not a statistical mirage but is just about as certain to materialize as tomorrow's rising of the sun. Right now the youngsters shaping the surge are extant and are, indeed, making their way through the lower schools with a determination, at least on the part of their parents, that they shall have the advantages of higher education. And seeing higher education "as a way of giving reality to their dreams," they clearly have the staying power, economic and political, to get exposed to something so designated.

So the issue is not whether the added millions headed for our institutions of higher education can somehow be discouraged or detoured, but how they can be provided with something that really is higher education at the same time that the urgent business of upgrading the existing product quite generally is going forward.

Naturally enough, the papers dealing with various financial facets of this problem and the critical discussions of them ranged almost all the way from the kindergarten to adult education for those not far from the grave, with comparable scope for disagreement along the way. But perhaps remarkably enough, the tendency in the discussions was quite consistently toward more rather than less agreement when the discussion of a particular phase of the general problem under discussion was concluded.

"I came to get my prejudices polished," was the introductory confession of one of the participants in the Merrill Center seminar. But at the end he cheerfully conceded that he had actually failed even to keep some of his prejudices in the face of discussion of the problems of financing higher education by those who approached the problems from positions that provided a perspective that had not been available to him. For example, most of those who arrived with a disposition to look to higher tuition payments as the most promising main route to financial salvation for higher education left with greater appreciation of the powerful case to be made for maintaining low tuition charges, and vice versa. And in the process it came to be agreed that this, along with almost all phases of financing higher education, is a case not of either or, but of more of all.

While agreement was not the goal, here are a few of the propositions about the financing of higher education, in addition to those noted, on which you will find a substantial measure of agreement reflected in the various papers or in the report of critical discussions of them:

The financial problems of our colleges and universities start in the high schools, and they can be eased by helping the high schools do a better educational job. The requirements for advanced university degrees are much higher than they were a generation ago. There has been no comparable upgrading of the requirements for graduation from most high schools. The result is that the load of the colleges in preparing students for graduate work has been greatly increased, and so has the expense of carrying it.

There is much expensive hit or miss in fitting the needs of high school graduates to colleges with the best chance of satisfying them. A good consumers' guide to colleges and universities would do more than save mismatched students a lot of money and valuable time; it would spare the colleges the waste of money and the loss of enrollment due to students getting into the wrong school in the first place. The cost of higher education is commonly calculated as the amount of money devoted to it; the calculation of cost should include the value of the time the students devote to it. Such a calculation would further underline the financial importance of doing a better job in guiding students to the right schools.

Most colleges can ease their financial problems very substantially, without reducing the quality of their instruction, by increasing the average ratio of students to faculty members ("There is a great deal of bunk in the folklore about small classes") and vigorously exploiting modern mechanical supplements to face-to-face teaching ("From a fourth to a third of the undergraduate courses are susceptible of substantial mechanization without sacrifice of quality"). Most colleges won't get much done along these lines soon, however, if the job is assigned to the trustees. Neither can the president—now generally an outside man who, busy with his begging cup, has little time for educational matters—do it. The job calls for active faculty leadership and cooperation. This might be stimulated by channeling some of the savings made to increased faculty salaries, as Beardsley Ruml suggests. So Mr. Ruml has a good idea in his book proposing a higher ratio of students to faculty members than generally prevails, but he gets it off to a rough start by presenting it in a volume entitled *Memo to a College Trustee.*

If they will, colleges and universities can, to their financial advantage, learn a lot from business enterprises about the effective management of their physical facilities and long-range planning of their operations. In the planning of new colleges and universities, of which many will be established in the years immediately ahead, application of market research as practiced by business firms can help to avoid bad mistakes in location and type of educational facilities. There have been many such mistakes in the past, and they have aggravated the financial headaches of higher education. Although not run for profit, colleges and universities can, if they will, learn a lot from profit-making enterprises about increasing the efficiency of their housekeeping operations.

Research, much of it financed by the government, will in the years ahead play a part in financing higher education even larger than the one it has come to play today. But unless there is careful planning of it, including integration of research and teaching programs, and careful cost accounting, research can add burdensome complications to the financial problems of the institutions involved. Research done on a project basis can leave an institution with a financially painful set of commitments when the projects are concluded, unless there has been careful planning for that eventuality. The liberal arts colleges have potentialities for cooperative research which have scarcely been tapped.

No one is going to win any sort of a clear-cut victory in the argument over whether higher tuition charges to students should be the principal reliance in meeting the financial problems of higher education. Tuition charges will continue to go up for students in both publicly and privately sponsored institutions. But the publicly supported institutions will receive sufficient tax support to continue to provide instruction at relatively low prices, and those prices will be much lower than most privately supported institutions can match. Under such circumstances, some privately sponsored institutions would be well advised to turn away from the idea of price competition with publicly supported schools and instead emphasize a high-quality, high-priced product for which there is a widening market in the United States.

There is great need of a device to stimulate saving for college education. Studies show that families planning on college education for their children and endeavoring to make some advance provision for it are actually saving at a rate far less than that which promises to be required to meet the prospective college costs, given the most optimistic assumptions about subsidies to be available to college and university students.

Loans to students, by both private and government agencies, are going to play an increasingly important part in the financing of higher education. They can be arranged on terms which, compared with prospective postcollege and postuniversity incomes, their recipients should find relatively easy to manage. When made available by government, they have the virtue of involving no direct control of the institutions which their recipients elect to attend. However, expansion of loans to women for higher education is likely to lag relatively because of potential matrimonial complications. This presents the women's colleges with a special financial problem.

Contrary to the widespread view that income taxation has largely dried them up, private sources of financial support for higher education remain large and are getting larger. This is notably true of financial support from business firms, which has increased $2\frac{1}{2}$ times in five years and, if well cultivated, will continue to increase rapidly. One of the most important elements of good cultivation is a clear and convincing statement of what the institution seeking support is trying to do and why. The fear that business firms will accompany gifts to higher education with attempts to control educational policy is out of date.

It is a waste of time to debate, as a matter of principle, whether or not the Federal government is going to finance higher education. The fact is that the Federal government is up to its ears in providing that financial support right now. More Federal support will be provided in the years ahead. However, the financing operations involved at present are so chaotic and disorganized that a first step toward consideration of further Federal support should be a systematic lining up and assessment of what is being done now. If further support should take the form of direct support of students, it would involve risks of the same political pressures for expansion which have characterized benefits for large groups of individuals such as farmers and veterans.

Although higher education is commonly conceived as something purveyed by colleges and universities, there is about as much of it conducted outside those institutions—by industrial firms, units of government, and a large variety of organizations—as there is inside them. Closer coordination of the two general types of higher education could advance the successful financing of college and university education. With a working lifetime of independent study a requirement of success in more and more occupations in the United States, there is need of further developing independent-study courses in the colleges and linking the courses with occupational requirements. Success in such operations would have an important bearing on the financing of higher education as a whole.

There is no reason to be discouraged about the possibility of financing higher education in the United States successfully. It is a very formidable, but by no means impossible, undertaking. With their sputniks, the Russians have helped to speed success, primarily by creating pressure to get things done in the field of higher education that we have known needed doing, but about which we have been laggard. General appreciation of the crucial importance of higher education has increased greatly in recent years. If those responsible for financing it respond by devising comparably imaginative devices and incentives to do it well, the job can be done successfully. The hour is dangerously, but not fatally, late.

In the papers collected in this volume key phases of the financing of higher education which have been quickly passed in review here, and many others, are subjected to searching and meticulous exploration. In the nature of the subject matter the exploration must range widely over a lot of rugged and complex terrain. But the ultimate objective is simple and clear cut: It is to make a constructive contribution to the successful financing of college and university education in the United States, which in very basic terms is the successful financing of the future of the nation itself.

This has never been put more bluntly or better than it was by Alfred North Whitehead, in 1916, when he wrote:[2]

> In the conditions of modern life the rule is absolute: The race which does not value trained intelligence is doomed. Not all your heroism, not all your social charm, not all your wit, not all your victories on land or at sea, can move back the finger of fate. Today we maintain ourselves. Tomorrow science will have moved forward yet one more step, and there will be no appeal from the judgment which will then be pronounced on the uneducated.

Why should the McGraw-Hill Book Company have selected the study of the financing of higher education, reflected in this volume, as a key part of its celebration of its fiftieth anniversary?

The answer is quite simple. As a publisher of their writings and for their courses, the Book Company lives much of its life with college and university teachers. So it has a special degree of knowledge of both their academic and their economic problems. And it also is in a peculiarly good position to appreciate the fateful importance of having these problems adequately handled.

Acting on this understanding, the Book Company, in association with its affiliates in the McGraw-Hill Publishing Company, has done some editorial pioneering on the financial problems of our colleges and universities and the ways to move toward solutions of them.

In graphic form, here are two of the findings reported in a series of editorials on financial aid to higher education which has appeared, over a number of years, in the McGraw-Hill magazines and, as paid editorial advertisements, in metropolitan newspapers. Requests for reprints of these editorials have numbered in the hundreds of thousands.

What's happened to college faculty salaries*
INDEX (1940=100)

* Real income before taxes
SOURCE: Council for Financial Aid to Education: U.S. Dept. of Commerce: U.S. Dept. of Labor. (Published in January, 1956)

The McGraw-Hill program of financial aid to education also includes sponsorship of twenty-two National Merit Scholarships. In addition, the company matches the gifts that its employees make to colleges and universities. In an effort to see that they are fully reimbursed for their services, the company makes supplemental tuition payments to institutions at which its employees take approved self-development courses for which the company pays one-half of the tuition fees.

Against this background of concern about the financial problems of higher education, it was easy to decide that it would be particularly fitting to celebrate the fiftieth anniversary of the Book Company with a special effort to speed the successful handling of those problems.

In this effort, resulting in the collaboration that has been described, we have received a measure of cooperation which far exceeded our most optimistic hopes. For that we are profoundly grateful. But all of us who worked together on this enterprise will be much more gratified if, as it

In the field of education......
Who are today's capitalists?

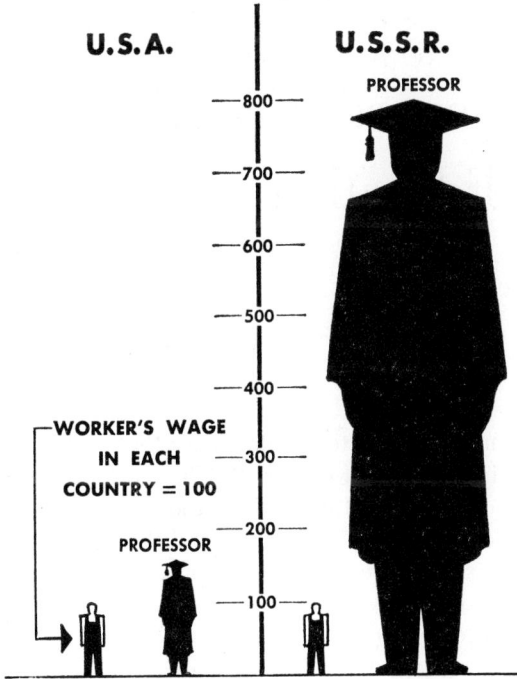

U.S.A. | **U.S.S.R.**

PROFESSOR

—800—

—700—

—600—

—500—

—400—

WORKER'S WAGE
IN EACH   —300—
COUNTRY = 100

—200—
PROFESSOR

—100—

Published in September, 1957. (A report of the relative, not absolute, economic positions of college professors.)

was solely designed to do, it makes a consequential contribution to the crucially important business of getting our colleges and universities squarely on their feet financially.

Notes

1. Beardsley Ruml and Donald H. Morrison, *Memo to a College Trustee: A Report on Financial and Structural Problems of the Liberal College*, McGraw-Hill Book Company, Inc., New York, 1959.

2. Taken from the report of the President's Science Advisory Committee, *Education for the Age of Science*, May 24, 1959.

2

An Economist's Overview of Higher Education

Philip H. Coombs

Higher education in the United States faces the most formidable assignment and grueling test of its career. But it also faces an unprecedented opportunity. A confident public expects the colleges and universities to double their enrollments by 1970—to expand their output, in other words, by as much in a single decade as in all previous history. In addition to this great expansion in *quantity*, the times call for a sweeping improvement in the *quality* of higher education.

Almost any other industry in the American economy would respond with enthusiasm to a guarantee that its market would double in ten years. But the responsible leaders of higher education are far more worried than elated by this prospect, and with good reason, for theirs is a peculiar industry with a unique set of problems. Higher volume in most industries means lower unit costs and larger profits, but for higher education larger volume promises larger deficits and possibly poorer quality. The colleges and universities even now are economically hard pressed. They are plagued by a shortage of good teachers and adequate facilities, a shortage of money with which to secure more of these, a shortage of almost everything except students.

It is tempting to assume that all of the problems of higher education could be solved by a great infusion of additional money, but unfortunately the need is not that simple. Far more money will certainly have

12

to be provided from every source, public and private. But along with increased financial support of higher education from the outside there must be far-reaching changes and improvements from within. The internal improvements will require the intensive application of creative brain power by the colleges and universities to their own internal affairs. The knowledge and analytical skills of such academic fields as history, psychology, political science, economics, accounting, and administration which in the past have been applied so fruitfully to the affairs of mankind in the larger world must now be applied, with great intellectual interest and advantage, to the affairs of the academic world itself.

Also required are more facts, more rigorous analysis, and more general understanding of the needs and processes of higher education. It is astonishing how much of importance we as a nation do not know about so large, so expensive, and so critically important an enterprise as education. Moreover, the techniques of reporting basic data on a rapid and accurate basis which have been developed in such fields as agriculture, manufacturing, banking, horse racing, and baseball must now be applied to education in the interest of knowing how we are doing, where we are heading, and how we can do better.

Almost daily, under the pressure of circumstance, great questions of policy and program are decided in individual school systems, colleges and universities, private foundations, professional organizations, and at all levels of government. These decisions are shaping the course of higher education for years to come, yet they are often made by hunch or compromise, without benefit of adequate facts and analysis.

Before embarking upon an examination of some of the economic dimensions and problems of higher education, it may be well to emphasize that the whole object is to search out better means by which colleges and universities may effectively pursue their ends. Economic analysis and economic resources are important only as they enable these institutions to carry out their mission of advancing the frontiers of human knowledge, enriching culture, and developing the intellectual powers, skills, and moral strength of individual young people each in its own particular way.

It is not the purpose here to delve into the complex subject of the aims of education, but it is important to bear in mind as we consider the economic aspects of higher learning that the aims of different colleges and universities, while having much in common, vary enormously in detail. This diversity of specific objectives befits a highly diversified system of higher education which seeks to prepare young people for a variety of careers and for a good life in a free but pluralistic society. An engineering school, a school of business administration, a medical

school, a school of agriculture, and a liberal arts college are all concerned with developing the individual potential of young people and
making of them good citizens, yet each has its own specific and unique
aims. A Catholic-sponsored college, or a Methodist, and a publicly
sponsored institution may have curricula that look very much alike in
the catalogue, yet obviously and desirably provide quite different envi-
ronments and influences and have different specific aims. Indeed, each
institution, regardless of its affiliation or category, tends to develop its
own personality, its own peculiar strengths and characteristics, which set
it apart from all others. And it is this freedom of each to be different
that lends great strength to the unique systems of higher education in
the United States. Moreover, it is the freedom and aspiration of every
college and university to be better than it is that nourishes the fundamental dynamic of the system.

Colleges also vary widely in the types of clientele they serve. Some
serve a local or regional and others a national clientele. A relatively few
are highly selective and serve only students who rank in the top 1 per
cent of the intelligence spectrum, whereas many others, fortunately,
keep their doors open to young people lower on the ability scale, yet
motivated to advance themselves. The saying goes that, "There is a
college in the United States for everyone."

This diversity, with its great advantages, also has disadvantages. For
one thing, it forces many consumers to make uninformed choices, because it is exceedingly difficult for a youngster and his parents, or even
for a reasonably proficient high school guidance officer, to have a well-
informed appraisal of any particular college or university. College cata-
logues are little help in this regard; they often confuse more than they
clarify, and there is no independent agency to which one can turn for
competent and objective advice.

There are two main reasons why the foregoing comments are relevant
to the discussion that follows. First, the role of the economist is not to
judge what is "good" education or "poor" education; his task is simply to
help each college pursue its own aims, its own concept of a good education as efficiently and effectively as it can within the limits of the resources available to it. Second, one cannot talk sense about the economics
of American higher education without recognizing at the outset that
this large industry is made up of nearly two thousand relatively small
"firms" which are exceedingly diverse in their specific characteristics and
purposes. It is, moreover, an industry which has long been undergoing
considerable change of structure and character, and whose rate of change
promises to be greatly accelerated during the next ten years.

A Burgeoning Demand for Quantity and Quality

Recent estimates by the Office of Education suggest that total college and university enrollments may rise from 3.5 million in 1958–59 to approximately 6.4 million by 1970. This projection, like so many before it, may well prove to be too conservative.

The dramatic increase expected in college enrollments in the next ten years is explained by two factors: the sharp rise in births since 1943 and the continuing rise in the proportion of young people going to college. Annual births averaged 2.9 million in the 1920s and 2.4 million in the 1930s. The annual average jumped to 3.2 million in the period 1943–49 and moved up still further to 4 million in the period 1950–58. A rough index of the proportion of young people going to college is the ratio of total college and university enrollments to the total population of eighteen- to twenty-one-year olds. This ratio rose from 16 per cent in 1940 to 30 per cent by 1950 and reached 39 per cent in 1959. The Office of Education projection shown above assumes that the ratio will reach 44 per cent by 1970. There is a good chance, however, that it will reach 50 per cent or better.

A broad-based survey conducted for the Ford Foundation in the spring of 1959 by Elmo Roper and Associates revealed that 69 per cent of the children presently below eighteen years of age are expected by their parents to go to college. This figure must be discounted to allow for parental pride and optimism, but it does demonstrate that a college education has come to be widely regarded in our society as the *sine qua non* of personal success, just as the high school diploma did earlier.

The continuous rise of educational aspirations of American parents for their children is dramatized in the historic correspondence between the percentage of one generation going to high school and the percentage of the next generation going to college. For better or for worse, the present generation of young American parents appears to have already made its decision that half or more of its youngsters are going to college.

It is not a particular year, such as 1970, nor the accuracy of a particular statistical projection that is important; what matters is the general magnitude of the enrollment increase which clearly lies ahead. Most analysts, while differing in their precise projections, would agree that somewhere between eight and twelve years from now the colleges will have to handle twice as many students as the 3.5 million they enrolled in 1958–59. This rise will occur whether or not the colleges and universities receive enough additional resources to maintain and raise their quality, just as in recent years many public schools have been forced to absorb far more students than they really had enough resources to handle well. But when educational resources fail to keep pace with the rising enrollments, something has to give. What does give, of course, is quality.

Thus, the really central question about the future of American higher education is not what precise number of young people will be going to college during the next decade or so but what quality of education they will receive when they get there. In other words, the qualitative dimension of future demand is more critically important than the quantitative dimension; for it is largely with respect to quality that American higher education may fail to meet the challenge it faces. If external support and internal improvements lag behind the need, the result will be a subtle erosion of quality which may go undetected by the general public until it is too late.

Quality is a difficult dimension for both economist and educator to deal with, especially in the absence of objective means for measuring and comparing it. Educators are often tempted to judge it by such measures as expenditures per student, the student-teacher ratio, and the number of books in the library. But that is like judging an automobile or a suit of clothes not by performance, but by the factory conditions under which it was produced. Education, like any other productive process, must ultimately be judged by the performance of its end products, the students.

Despite certain charges to the contrary, most informed observers would probably agree that by and large, the quality of American education today—school for school and college for college—is better than it has ever been. That, if true, is encouraging. But it is not good enough; for it seems equally clear that in the last twenty-five years or more the quality of education in the United States and the magnitude of our educational effort have not kept pace with the expanding educational demands which the changing world has imposed.

The adequacy of an individual's formal education and the adequacy of a society's educational effort cannot be judged by some fixed standard for all time, except in a purely static world. They must be judged in relation to the demands and choices, the problems and opportunities, which press upon individuals and whole societies in any particular era. In our own time the conjunction of powerful forces—the explosion of population and of knowledge, the revolution of human aspirations, the eruption of great political changes and rivalries on a world-wide scale—have multiplied the educational requirements of every individual and of our whole society. What was a good education for an individual fifty years ago is not good enough for his counterpart today, whether he is a doctor, teacher, political leader, or an unskilled worker. And what we may regard as a good education for today will certainly not suffice for the youngsters now in grade school who will spend many years of their adult lives wrestling with the complexities of the twenty-first century.

In short, the essence of this nation's educational problem is that we have allowed a potentially disastrous educational lag to develop, a gap between our mounting educational requirements on the one side and our educational effort and performance on the other. Even in a stable and peaceful world this gap would hamper us seriously in moving toward the highest goals of a free society in which every individual would have the opportunity to develop his potentialities to the full. But the world is not stable and peaceful. The Soviet Union is making a much greater educational effort than the United States and the whole free world in pursuit of goals which are hostile to a free society. The central task for the United States, therefore, is to close this educational gap and keep it closed.

The Resources Required

The central task identified above will require an enormous outlay of money and human energy, but if it is viewed as an investment, and not merely as an expense, it is evident that the yield will be high.

Total expenditures on higher education in the United States must more than double within the next ten years. That conclusion of the President's Committee on Education Beyond the High School, the Rockefeller Panel on Education, and most recently, the Killian Committee on Scientific Education, has not been seriously challenged. Later in this book, Prof. Seymour Harris develops an estimate that current expenditures of institutions of higher education, excluding board and room and auxiliary enterprises but including student aid, must rise from the 1957–58 level of $3.8 billion to $9.8 by 1969–70 (assuming no further inflation.)

Such an increase is well within the economic capabilities of the United States. To double expenditures on *all* formal education in the next decade would require only a small fraction of the increment in national income that can reasonably be expected over the same period. That would require no sacrifice of present living standards, though it would obviously mean less *additional* funds available for other purposes in the future than would otherwise be the case. There is no way to get more and better education without paying for it, but the price for the United States is entirely feasible. Moreover, not to make a greater investment in education might very well retard the future rate of economic growth, not to mention other undesirable consequences.

The central question of public policy, therefore, is not whether as a nation we can afford more and better education but whether we can devise an acceptable combination of fair and effective fiscal means by which to channel a sufficient proportion of the rising national income into the educational enterprise. This raises, of course, such controversial issues as state and local taxes, tuition increases, and Federal support of education, which are dealt with elsewhere in this volume.

Meeting the resource requirements of higher education, however, involves much more than raising and spending more money. The money is important only as it gives the colleges and universities effective command over manpower, facilities, equipment, and other factors required to produce education. It should be noted, moreover, that a large cost of higher education which is not included in dollar figures such as those used above is the earned income forgone by students who enter college instead of the labor market and the corresponding production forgone by the nation. Altogether this is probably a larger cost than the direct expenditures on higher education.

If sufficient funds were available, there would be no serious problem about physical facilities and equipment; once authorized, they could be expanded rapidly. But the supply of good teachers *cannot* be expanded rapidly. That is the most essential resource required for good education. To be sure, any one institution, by lifting its faculty salaries and fringe benefits above the prevailing market level, can draw and hold good teachers. But if there are not enough good teachers to go around, which is clearly the case, then quality can be maintained in some institutions only at·the expense of others. The production time for a good teacher is a matter of years, so that improvements in fellowships, faculty salaries, and the like will have a relatively slow effect upon the total supply of teachers. Meantime, the demand is expanding rapidly.

The shortage of good teachers is part of a larger, national shortage of highly developed manpower. The broader shortage results not from a decline in supply, but from a large and continuing increase in demand on the part of industry, government, and the major professions, including education, for the kinds of able and well-educated people needed for teaching. In contrast to others, however, the colleges and universities are in the unique position of being both producers and consumers of such manpower. As producers they are being pressed to turn out more and better graduates to serve the needs of others, but as consumers they are being outcompeted by the others in their efforts to hire enough good teachers to get the job done.

The teacher-shortage problem, all through the educational system, is not a problem primarily of getting *more* people to enter teaching but of getting *better-qualified* people to enter teaching. As a nation we have allocated our best-qualified manpower poorly and unwisely, at least in this respect, by allowing the attractiveness of teaching to decline relative to other career opportunities for able and well-educated people. In the short run the results may not be serious, but in the long run they could be disastrous. Unless the schools and colleges can command the services of a sufficient proportion of their own finest products, the nation's future supply of well-educated manpower and well-trained specialists will suffer seriously. It is a disconcerting fact that college and university campuses all across the country are fairly crawling with financially well-armed recruiters for almost every occupation but teaching. There have been times, it is said, when these eager fellows, having picked over the seniors and the faculty, have even resorted to recruiting one another.

There is serious question whether a good many of the specialized people hired by industry, and especially by major firms handling large government contracts, are not being wasted and might not serve themselves and the country better in teaching.

A substantial rise in faculty compensation, relative to competing occupations, is certainly a prerequisite to correcting this imbalance. It is encouraging that, after a long period of erosion, faculty salaries have lately been rising at a fairly rapid pace. According to studies by the United States Office of Education, faculty salaries rose only 20 per cent in the seven years from 1947–48 to 1953–54, but they rose another 20 per cent in the four years from 1954–55 to 1957–58. Then in 1958–59 faculty salaries rose 7.6 per cent, which reflected a still higher annual rate of increase.

There is good prospect that the pressures of competition and the strenuous efforts of the colleges and their friends will lift the general structure of faculty salaries by 1965 to at least twice the 1955 level. The time has come to stop convincing every undergraduate that a teaching career requires a vow of poverty.

Even with great improvement in faculty compensation, however, the manpower problem of the colleges and universities will be far from solved; it may simply get worse at a slower rate. The central fact is that the total output of the graduate schools, and the fraction of their graduates going into teaching, are much too low to sustain the present quality of the nation's college faculty over the next ten years as the size of faculties expands. The graduate schools will undoubtedly enlarge their output, though probably much less in the next five years than from 1965 to 1970. But as things presently stand it seems highly improbable that they will expand nearly fast enough to keep up with the needs of the colleges. The colleges as a whole are likely to find themselves, despite higher salaries, increasingly unable to fill their ranks with first-class teachers, especially if they try to preserve today's student-teacher ratios as enrollments expand.

A number of practical steps could be taken with greater vigor by the colleges and universities to expand the supply of teachers, though most of them would require a change of entrenched habits and attitudes. For one thing, a far stronger effort must be made to encourage able undergraduates to consider a teaching career, partly by giving them a chance to participate in the teaching program of their own institution. Better guidance must be given them in choosing an appropriate graduate school, and they must have greater financial assistance for pursuing graduate study. The graduate schools, in cooperation with strong undergraduate colleges, must take more initiative in improving and expanding their programs, giving greater emphasis and respectability to preparation for teaching and not simply for research.

Relatively untapped sources of teachers must now be developed more fully. The widespread and long-standing academic prejudice and discrimination against women as faculty members, except in a few women's colleges, has deprived the colleges and universities of a great reservoir of brain power. Colleges and universities will do well to search diligently among business firms, among retiring military officers and well-qualified government officials, and among the retiring teachers of other institutions for able people to add to their faculties.

The college-teacher shortage need not be attacked exclusively on the supply side of the equation, however. The demand side very much needs investigation with respect not only to teachers, but also to physical facilities and all other educational resources. The future requirements for all these factors of production depend not simply on the number of students to be educated but upon the efficiency and effectiveness with which the resources are utilized as well. There is abundant room in the colleges and universities for improving the efficiency of resource use, and in ways conducive to the improvement of educational quality. It is very doubtful that as many teachers are needed as the projected requirements show. The productivity and thus the salaries of well-qualified college teachers could be raised substantially and the quality of education could be improved—as Beardsley Ruml and Donald Morrison have argued in *Memo to a College Trustee* and as many college teachers and administrators have lately been demonstrating—by adopting a more efficient pattern of teaching and learning arrangements, including a less overburdened curriculum, and without resort to any stretch-out system.

Closing the Financial Gap

The financial problems of colleges and universities derive largely from unique pricing policies and a tradition of operating on the principle of deficit financing. Colleges and universities have always had to be concerned not only with financing their own operations as producers but with the financial needs of their customers as well, and their budgets have had to bear both burdens.

Privately and publicly supported institutions alike have traditionally pursued a below-cost pricing policy in order to keep their services available to the children of middle- and lower-income families in the interest of equality of opportunity and in the belief that higher education benefits all society and not merely the individuals who are educated. This means that all college students, including the children of wealthy families, are heavily subsidized by private gifts, tax funds, or both. But the student and his family usually share a good part of the cost, and so the subsidy is far from complete. Rarely has tuition been set at zero, and it is customary in residental institutions to set the charges for board and room at approximately the actual cost. Thus, despite the tuition subsidy, the cost of going to college, including a tax-supported one, is too high for many families to afford. To a degree this problem has been offset by scholarships, loans, employment opportunities, and similar student aid programs, but there are still serious financial obstacles to going to college, and especially to the most appropriate college, for many able young people.

The financial gap between the actual costs of running the college and the revenues received from students must be made up annually by income from endowments, current gifts, tax revenues, and other sources. With the rise in costs in recent years, closing the financial gap and raising capital funds has commanded an increasing proportion of the college administrator's attention and has led to a greatly increased emphasis on fund raising and public relations. The deep concern over finances, reaching at times an almost neurotic preoccupation, has on occasion provoked unfortunate tensions between public and private institutions, to the benefit of neither. It has also led at times to a public relations strategy, born of financial desperation, which has contaminated the atmosphere of intellectual freedom which is essential to true liberal learning and scholarship.

Another peculiar handicap of higher education is its lack of ready access to capital funds for expansion, despite its booming market. The assurance of expanding markets would make it easy for most industries to raise capital, but there is no organized capital market for education, and tradition prevents many colleges from even considering the possibility of loans. Plant expansion by private institutions is often dictated by the fortuitous timing of a donor's death rather than by a carefully considered plan for growth. This is one major reason why many private institutions are not contemplating substantial expansion today and why a disproportionate share of the burden of increased enrollments will have to be assumed by tax-supported institutions.

Increasingly, however, the tax-supported institutions are also encountering serious financial obstacles to physical expansion because of the tight fiscal position of most state and local governments and the strong competition of other public services. Education is severely handicapped in competing for limited state tax dollars against highways, hospitals, and the like for which Federal matching funds are available. Shortage of capital funds has had the effect in some state universities, when applicants have outstripped available dormitory space, of stiffening admissions requirements very substantially and raising barriers against out-of-state students. While a case might be made on education grounds for more stringent admissions standards, it hardly seems appropriate to have such a basic decision made indirectly and fortuitously by a capital shortage.

There is need to develop ingenious new arrangements by which higher education may tap the nation's capital funds on a parity with industry, highway programs, and other activities. The Federal College Housing Program, though limited in size and applicable thus far only to dormitories, dining facilities, and other self-financing structures, has been useful to a considerable number of institutions. There are encouraging signs that private banks and insurance companies are beginning to view the colleges and universities as a promising field for investment and that college trustees are modifying their traditional aversion to borrowing. Obviously a private college must be prudent in borrowing or in using its own endowment funds for capital construction, but there are probably many instances in which the over-all economic and educational position of a small college could be strengthened by breaking a particular facilities bottleneck. The construction of a new dormitory or lecture hall, for example, might make possible an expansion of the student body and the more productive use of existing faculty and facilities. If the marginal cost of serving additional students is less than the additional tuition income received, the college's financial position will be improved. Moreover, an expansion of the student body without increasing the faculty may be the most practicable way to raise the student-teacher ratio and thus make possible an increase in faculty salaries.

The financial problems of higher education which arise from below-cost pricing and lack of access to capital are considerably complicated by a lack of adequate systems of accounts, budgets, operating data, planning techniques, and general budgetary discipline in most colleges and universities. College and university accounting, though better than it once was, remains a relatively primitive art—even in institutions that offer a Ph.D. in accounting—and is better suited to the purposes of auditing than to effective management and decision making. Most colleges have only the roughest notion of the actual costs of rendering various educational and noneducational services and therefore do not really know the relationship between cost and price. Oftentimes such items as utility costs and pension costs are lumped together rather than allocated to instruction, dormitories, and so forth, thus giving a deceptive picture of costs. Many colleges make no regular allowance for depreciation, amortization, or repair and maintenance of physical plant, with the result that their costs are higher and plant value lower than they realize, and eventually a large repair bill catches them with no reserve.

In the interest of getting funds to raise faculty salaries or for some other important purpose, colleges often make tuition increases without even an effort at market analysis (except to determine whether their closest competitors plan to make comparable increases) and without taking steps to ensure that the additional revenue actually goes where it was intended to go. Two years later, when another tuition increase seems necessary, it is difficult to determine where the additional revenue from the last one really went, how it affected the composition of the student body or the market position of the college, or just where the college is heading with another increase.

Attention is usually focused on this year's budget and the next, but most colleges seldom pause to see where they have been over the past ten years and where they hope to be ten years hence. It often comes as a shocking surprise to discover that great shifts have occurred in such critical factors as the student-teacher ratio, the faculty work load, the number of courses being taught, the distribution of classes by size, the utilization (or underutilization) of physical facilities, and the proportion of the budget going into faculty compensation or into general administration.

There is a strong need for better tools for fact finding, planning, operations analysis, and reporting so that the president, trustees, and faculty will have a clearer frame of reference within which to make program and management decisions and check progress against predetermined plans and goals, all in the interest of getting the best possible educational results from the resources available.

A large number of colleges are already in deeper trouble than they realize, both economically and educationally, and are heading for still more serious trouble. They are insufficiently aware of the large shifts which have occurred over time in their internal use of resources, in the composition of their student body and faculty, in the quality and character of their educational services, and in the career choices and performance of their graduates. They have been so busy, day after day and year after year, with making specific decisions and meeting each pressure and problem as it arises that they have not taken time to assess the implications of the course they are traveling. That course may well be headed toward educational insolvency.

Colleges and universities do not lack for a great many detailed facts about their operations; indeed their budget statements and accounts are often very imposing in size and complexity. What they especially lack is (1) an analysis and ordering of those facts to provide an overview of the institution and its many related parts *as a whole* and (2) a view in perspective of the road the institution has been traveling and the alternatives that lie ahead.

Better Use of Resources

A college or university obviously cannot be run as if it were a steel mill or a drug store, but neither can educational decisions be made in an economic vacuum. Yet the most important decisions of a college are often made with no conscious reference to the economic limits that surround the enterprise. The net effect is that faculty salaries are lower and educational results poorer than they need to be, even within the limits of resources already available.

Whenever there are economic limits and alternative ways of employing available resources, choices must be made. The choices made by colleges and universities are often more wasteful, and less effective in advancing the priority educational goals of the institutions, than is generally realized, mainly because of deficiencies in the decision-making processes.

Among the costly practices whose educational virtue (as distinct from mere convenience) should be carefully reconsidered are these: the five-course plan, with students typically spending fifteen hours a week in class; the scheduling of most classes in the morning, with a peak at 11:00 to 12:00 P.M., and most laboratory and athletic periods in the afternoon; the 8½-month college year; the accumulation of numerous small courses which are infrequently reexamined for merit; inadequate provision of secretarial help to professors; drill sessions in foreign languages that use highly paid faculty members as drillmasters; large numbers of discussion sections and small to medium-sized courses which often are taken up with ill-prepared "vest pocket" lectures and little if any true discussion.

Much of the problem arises from the fact that the quality of education is too largely judged by input factors and too little by output and performance. In the folklore of education, quality is judged especially by the smallness of the student-teacher ratio. But if in order to keep

POPULATION INCREASES
1959-1970
BY SCHOOL AGE GROUP

5 to 13 Age Group

14-17 Age Group

18-21 Age Group

Millions

40

35

30

25

20

15

10

5

0

1959 1970

1959 1970

1959 1970

UP 20%

UP 44%

UP 57%

U.S. Bureau of Census

the ratio low, available funds must be devoted to hiring the statistically correct number of teachers at salaries too low to attract real competence, "all that is accomplished," in the words of the late President Charles Johnson of Fisk University, "is to enable the teacher to communicate his mediocrity in an intimate environment." The student-teacher ratio, taken by itself, is a poor indicator of quality. The mere physical proximity of teacher and students, regardless of the size of the group or the frequency of its meetings, does not guarantee learning.

Great good could come from a systematic and honest effort by any faculty to expose and reexamine critically the long-hidden premises about the nature of the teaching and learning process which underlie the conventional practices and logistical arrangements of our colleges. A number of plausible alternatives, when tested out, might yield considerably better educational results along with a more efficient use of available resources.

Higher education, in contrast to most other sectors of the American economy, appears on the surface at least to be an increasing-cost industry, in the sense that expenditures per student on a constant-dollar basis have risen substantially over the years. At least three major factors help to explain these rising costs. First, the services, both academic and non-academic, which a college typically provides to a student today have become considerably more extensive and more expensive. Not only has the curriculum been broadened and deepened, but many student services such as guidance, recreation, and health care have been introduced or expanded. Second, higher education by its very nature is a high labor user, and its wage and salary bill has been forced up by rising productivity and consequent increases in real wages and salaries elsewhere in the economy. Finally, and of special relevance here, relatively few cost-reducing innovations and improved technologies have been introduced in higher education. On the contrary, there has tended to be an accumulation of "built-in inefficiencies," such as practices which result in low utilization of space and low productivity of faculty.

A recent survey of more than a hundred colleges and universities revealed that, on the basis of a forty-four-hour week, the institutions used their available classrooms at only 46 per cent of capacity (only 25 per cent when measured in terms of student stations) and their laboratories at only 38 per cent of capacity. If more productive use were made of plant facilities and the student body expanded, the additional tuition revenues could be devoted to higher faculty salaries rather than to additional brick and mortar.

A Midwestern-college president whose institution is hard pressed for funds said recently: "We run our college from 9:00 to 12:00, 1:00 to 4:00, five days a week, eight and one-half months a year—and we like it that way." Perhaps so, but this underutilization of an expensive physical plant may pave the road to educational insolvency for his institution. Soon it will be forced to double faculty salaries or settle for mediocrity, and much of the college's economic strength is frozen in idle buildings.

It would be prudent for any college or university, before investing additional funds in buildings rather than faculty, to examine carefully the possibility of making fuller use of buildings already available.

The economic wastes in the curriculum are probably much greater than the waste in idle buildings. There are, of course, sound reasons for adding new courses to a curriculum, but there are also reasons, sound both educationally and economically, for removing some that are already there and for resisting the addition of certain others. When any faculty, in the exercise of its jurisdiction over the curriculum and other academic affairs, proceeds over a period of years to proliferate the curriculum out of deference to individual and departmental interests, to tolerate the accumulation of small courses of dubious importance, and to insist upon "convenient" teaching hours—all in the name of academic freedom and good education, it not only holds down its own salaries but, what is much more serious, hobbles the institution's ability to be first class in the future.

Blame for collegiate waste of resources rests not with individual faculty members but with the system by which decisions that determine the use of available resources are made. It is an illusion to think that a college can do its best when responsibilities are divided down the middle, with "academic affairs" in the hands of the faculty, to be decided without reference to economic considerations, and with "financial and management affairs" in the hands of the president and trustees. The most important *economic* decisions—the ones which determine how effectively a college's available resources will be allocated and utilized —are actually made by the faculty when it decides upon the curriculum, upon teaching methods and schedules, and upon other aspects of the educational programs. Once these decisions are made, the task of the president and trustees is to try to find enough money to validate them. But if no one—either the faculty or the administration—is obliged to evaluate the educational *and* economic viability of the arrangements, the college may be using its resources very largely to support various conventional forms which enclose and obscure relatively inferior educational substance.

There must be a better kind of internal governmental system than that which prevails in most colleges, one that provides for decision making within a more realistic context and which inherently tends toward the pursuit of educational excellence rather than its opposite. The political scientists and economists who have studied and made recommendations to improve all other sorts of decision-making and governmental systems could usefully turn their attention now to the unique and intriguing one in which they live and work.

Structural Changes

Our discussion thus far has largely concerned the internal affairs of colleges and universities, but note should be taken of the important changes which are occurring in the total structure of American higher education. These changes have a considerable bearing upon the character, quality, and economics of higher education.

A half century ago "going to college" usually meant leaving home for four years to pursue a full-time course of study toward a degree, most likely at a private college or university. Today "going to college" means, for more than half the students, going to a tax-supported institution, and for a rapidly increasing number it means living at home and taking courses at a nearby junior college, community college, or state university branch. It may also mean taking college courses on a part-time basis, perhaps in the evening, while working at a paying job on the side.

These basic shifts in the structure of higher education are likely to continue, probably at an accelerated rate, because they fit the pocket-books of a majority of Americans who are seeking a higher education.

An important factor in raising college enrollments has been the increased accessibility of colleges to students living at home. The junior college is especially worth watching; for it is mushrooming across the country in response to an insistent demand, yet it has not yet fully found its rational place in the total structure of American education. There is reason to doubt that the junior college will forever remain a "junior." It may, like the old two-year normal school, evolve into a four-year institution, while at the same time more and more four-year colleges move toward offering graduate courses and conferring the master's or doctor's degree.

For the next ten years it seems likely that nonresidential commuter colleges will account for a disproportionate share of the total increase in college enrollments and that the proportion of part-time students will increase. But in the longer run the pendulum may swing toward a heavier emphasis upon residential institutions. Many of today's students who are attending local junior or community colleges, or local branches of the state university, come from parents who did not go to college at all and may not even have finished high school. Attending a local non-residential college is a major upward step educationally for the children of such families, but their aspirations for their own children when they come along are likely to be higher still, and their notion of "a *real* college education" may revert to the older concept of a four-year experience on a full-time basis at a residential college or university. By then, also, the prime issue of public debate may no longer be, "Who and how many should go to college?" but "Who and how many should go to graduate school?"

Another major trend of the past which is likely to continue is the incorporation into the formal educational system of many types of training which earlier were gained through apprenticeship or on-the-job training. The great expansion of courses in business administration, real estate, journalism, and professional education in the last forty years are cases in point. While it is true that large business corporations are developing impressive training and educational programs of their own, they will still rely heavily upon the regular schools and colleges to develop their future employees. Small businesses will perforce rely even more heavily upon the formal educational system.

In any event, American higher education, already very diversified in character and quality, is becoming even more so, and its structure is bound to be in a dynamic state of flux for years to come.

The fate of the independent liberal arts college in the midst of these structural changes has become a matter of doubt and concern. Some predict that it will follow the path of the independent school and become a relatively unimportant "vestigial remain" in American education. Others surmise that many small private colleges will become publicly sponsored ones. The share of the market of privately sponsored colleges and universities has declined in a few generations from a majority to a decided minority position and will surely decline further. The role and influence of independent colleges in American education may conceivably decline in like measure, but that seems far from necessary or inevitable. The choice rests largely with the liberal arts colleges themselves. They will need external help, but their future strength and significance will be determined primarily by their internal vigor, ingenuity, and sense of mission.

Meantime, it will serve no useful purpose for the privately supported and the tax-supported institutions to pit themselves against one another in a destructive battle for increased funds and institutional prestige waged in a smoke of pious rhetoric. Clearly there is room and need for both types of institution, and they can lend strength to one another, as they are doing in such states as Indiana.

It cannot be ignored, however, that the shifting structure of higher education is bringing about important economic changes for both producers and consumers.

Financing a college education, despite rising incomes, is becoming a serious problem for more and more families, with college fees rising, with larger families, and with larger numbers of students coming from lower- and middle-income families. For the typical middle-income family, the total cost of a residential college education for two children approximates two years of income. Payment of the full amount out of current income during a four-year period is often impossible, especially when more than one child is in college. The solution does not necessarily lie in cutting student fees; for that merely shifts the problem to someone else or reduces the college's operating income. For many families, especially in the middle-income brackets and higher, much of the answer may lie in spreading college costs over a longer period of income, forward and backward, through savings and loans.

American consumers have been well taught how to spread the cost of automobiles, television sets, houses, and other consumer investment goods over a long period of income, and great ingenuity has gone into developing and promoting convenient financial instruments for the purpose. But most Americans have not yet learned how to finance what is perhaps the most important investment they will ever make, a college education, and surprisingly little ingenuity and effort has gone into the invention and promotion of effective instruments for the purpose.

Student loans are becoming more popular, especially since the creation of several state plans to encourage private bank loans to students and the Federal student loan program under the National Defense Education Act, but loans are still a minor element in student finance. There are, of course, a variety of conventional methods by which families can save toward college, but they are not well tailored to the purpose and, even if undertaken, they are easily forced to a low-priority position on the family budget by more immediate and pressing items such as mandatory payments on the car, the TV set, and the house.

There needs to be undertaken a major effort to educate American families on how to finance a college education and to develop more convenient and effective means for helping them do so. A single instrument which combined savings, investment in equities, and term insurance on the family breadwinner, which had built-in rewards for continuity, and which could be contracted for conveniently and without payment of heavy sales costs would be highly attractive to many families. A special government savings bond specifically for college education, with a premium interest rate if held for a long enough period and cashed by a bona fide college student, would in itself be very useful and might also help create a favorable climate for greater ingenuity and initiative by private financial institutions.

Better instruments for consumer savings and loans will, of course, only contribute to a solution; they will not provide a panacea. There will still be need for more scholarship aid to able and needy students and more job opportunities that will strengthen and not handicap a student's educational efforts. With the approach of a time when half the young people in the United States will be seeking an education beyond high school, the whole subject of financing a college education needs to be given fresh and imaginative reconsideration. The old attitudes, slogans, philosophies, and practices have been rendered obsolete by a vast change of circumstances.

The shift in the structure of higher education is also producing significant changes in institutional cost patterns. A two-year, nonresidential college with a limited curriculum, for example, can have operating costs per student closer to those of a high school than a four-year residential institution. Typically the four-year college has considerably higher costs per student for juniors and seniors than for freshmen and sophomores because of the larger number of small and specialized courses in the upper two years. To the extent that they draw student traffic away from the lower division of four-year colleges, junior colleges may tend to impair the economic position of the four-year colleges by taking away their lowest-cost students. But on the other hand, many four-year colleges can improve their cost position by admitting more junior college graduates to fill out the excessively small courses in their upper division.

At the graduate school level, an increase in enrollment in many departments in which courses are now too small will, within limits, reduce average costs per student, but such gains may be more than offset by increases in research or by curriculum expansion.

This whole matter of the economic consequences of rising volume and the shifting structure of higher education warrants much more study. It seems clear, at least, that the future economic requirements for handling twice as many college and university students cannot be computed, even within a wide margin of error, simply by multiplying the *status quo* by two.

It seems likely, also, that the next ten years will witness an absolute growth in virtually every existing type of higher educational institution, large and small, public and private, residential and nonresidential, but that a disproportionate share of the total growth will occur in those institutions whose costs to the student are lowest, notably the nonresidential ones, and in tax-supported colleges and universities. The structural pattern of American higher education is bound to change substantially in the next ten years and to become even more varied and diversified in every respect.

The Future Role of Government

For a nation deeply committed to the importance of education, the people of the United States have been singularly reluctant to acknowledge their commitment in relevant national terms. There exists nothing approaching a declaration of national policy, and there is no definition of the role of the Federal government in this area of admitted vital importance to the national interest. Instead there is a confusion of activity and rhetoric. Over the years we have developed a public rhetoric which pretends that the Federal government has never really entered the field of education, and annually we conduct the same fruitless debate over whether it should or not. The debate is highly unrealistic, however, despite the passion that accompanies it, because over the last hundred years the Federal government has in fact initiated a wide variety of programs which directly affect higher education—ranging from the land-grant college legislation signed by President Lincoln to the current programs of the National Science Foundation, the Office of Education, and better than a dozen agencies.

It would take the Bureau of the Budget's best team of analysts to put together the whole picture of Federal activities affecting higher education, and no one has tried. But even very superficial search will show that the Federal government, through a wide range of programs whose administration is scattered over many separate agencies, is deeply involved in the nation's higher educational system. A considerable number of these uncoordinated and often competitive programs impinge especially upon the graduate schools of the universities with enormous effect upon their present behavior and their future shape. No agency of the Federal government and no committee of Congress had responsibility for bringing together an over-all picture of these diverse Federal programs, for assessing their probable impact, and for encouraging coordination until recently when the Office of Education was given some such responsibility in a relatively obscure section of Title X of the National Defense Education Act. Moreover, the Federal government's program of gathering and disseminating basic facts about education, initially provided for in the legislation of 1867 which created the Bureau of Education (now the Office of Education), is far less adequate to the need than the Federal statistical programs covering manufacturing, labor, agriculture, banking, transportation, and other fields. Without adequate facts and analysis, it is difficult to make good policy, whether in an individual college or in the Federal government.

There is little doubt that the pressures of national need and duty will bring the Federal government increasingly into the field of education in the next ten years. But if it is done in a haphazard way, as it has largely been to date, the Federal expenditures involved will certainly be less effective than they could be, and at times they may seriously distort and handicap the educational system. A number of temporary presidential commissions over the past fifteen years have underscored the need for more effective Federal organization for dealing with education; yet the situation has, if anything, grown worse. It might prove salutary if leaders in higher education themselves undertook a searching examination of Federal organization and administration affecting education and made positive proposals for improvement. The colleges and universities, and the whole nation, have a large stake in such improvement.

Apart from the question of organization, there are, of course, a variety of major issues of Federal policy and program in higher education which are bound to come in for serious discussion and perhaps legislative action in the next few years. They include:

1. The review and possible modification of the National Defense Education Act

2. The size and scope of federally sponsored research programs and their impact on the programs and financial position of colleges and universities

3. The size and variety of Federal fellowship programs and their impact on the national supply of specialized talent

4. Construction loans and grants to colleges and universities

5. Federal scholarships and student loans

6. ROTC programs

7. Federal support for the expansion of educational television services

8. International assistance and cooperation in higher education and the international exchange of students and scholars

9. Improvement of teaching in science, mathematics, and foreign languages

10. Training of specialized civilian personnel for service abroad

The Federal government is already involved, at least to a degree, in most of the foregoing activities, and it is likely to become more involved in them. Every one of them is bound to affect, for better or worse, the future pattern and quality of American higher education and the internal economics of individual institutions. The cost of these programs to the taxpayers and their influence on the Federal government's fiscal position is, of course, important. But far more important in the long run is the question of how each of these activities will affect the performance of higher education and the opportunity of young people to get a good college education. There is need for far more rigorous analysis and appraisal of the likely educational and economic consequences of Federal activities in education to provide a better basis for policy and program decisions and to ensure that the actions of the Federal government will serve to strengthen and not handicap American higher education in accomplishing the priority tasks which have been imposed upon it by the forces of history in our time.

Conclusion

This overview of American higher education—of the tasks it faces and the needs that must be met if the tasks are to be accomplished—has merely opened up a number of important topics. It has left many others uncovered. It has not considered, for example, the important development in recent years of extensive educational programs of a collegiate and university caliber beyond the borders of the formal system of higher education, including those sponsored by industry or carried on within the armed services. (These are dealt with in Prof. Harold Clark's paper.) Likewise, we have not dealt with the mushroom growth of sponsored research in the universities, the developments in professional training in various fields, or promised developments in communications technology —such as instructional television—which have far-reaching implications for the quality and economics of higher education.

The central theme has been that higher education in the United States, viewed as an organic whole, has entered an era of unprecedented growth and change fraught with exceedingly complex problems and unparalleled opportunities.

There will be growth and there will be far-reaching changes in any event, but whether the growth will be in excellence as well as in quantity and whether the changes will be for better or for worse depends heavily upon two factors: the extent to which our society is willing to invest sufficient additional resources in the educational enterprise, from bottom to top, and the extent to which educators themselves, including scholars, teachers, administrators, and trustees in all disciplines and at all levels, apply their energies and talents to achieving the most effective use of the new resources in behalf of *better* and not simply *more* education.

What is required, in short, is a financial break-through to new and much higher levels of external support for higher education generally and a sweeping break-through within the colleges themselves to improved forms of internal organization, teaching methods and techniques and curriculum arrangements which will make the whole enterprise more efficient and effective, both economically and educationally. The conventional premises, procedures, and folklore of education must be subjected to critical scrutiny and change. New approaches must be tested out, new technologies introduced, many old habits abandoned, but always with an eye to the improvement of learning and the advancement of knowledge.

All this will not be easy; for colleges and universities are among the most conservative—the most resistant to change—of all our human institutions. But change they must—and very quickly and radically —if they are to meet the demands imposed upon them by our times.

There is already discernible throughout the country a new ground swell of critical self-examination, experimentation, and constructive change in many colleges and universities. If it continues to gather force, higher education promises to be one of the most exciting frontiers for scholarship, innovation, and individual creativity in our society during this and the next generation.

But the colleges and universities cannot meet the need by themselves. As a nation we must raise our sights and our assumptions very considerably with respect to how much we need to spend on higher education and how much we can afford to spend.

3

Financing of Higher Education: Broad Issues

Seymour E. Harris

My task is to give an over-all view of the financing problems. My colleagues develop some aspects of these problems more fully in other papers of this volume, and I devote all of a forthcoming book to them. My wish is to interest the reader, not frighten him; hence I put the tables upon which this analysis is based at the end of the paper. But a brief statistical summary here is the price that has to be paid for an understanding. I hope the reader will bear with me and consider the dull statistics in the next page or two.

The Budget

In the note at the end I present a budget and projected enrollments for the years 1929–30 to 1969–70. This is a budget of $9.2 billion by 1969–70, and $9.8 billion if allowance is made for the rise of scholarships. The educational and general budget for 1957–58 was $3,650 million. Hence the increase is $6.2 billion, or about 170 per cent. Since enrollment is expected to rise by about 90 per cent, it can be assumed that more than one-half of the rise is to be associated with increased enrollments.

These statistics of needs are basic material for other papers in this book, but my sources of income should be compared with those presented by President Millett.

Even the estimate of $9.8 billion may well be too low, first, because we are discussing operating budgets only. The capital budget may well be of the order of $1.5 billion per year, an amount roughly double current capital outlays. Economies may cut this figure. At any rate we should keep in mind the point that we may need for capital purposes in the next ten years about one-half billion additional over and above what is now available per year. Second, we have assumed no inflation. A more realistic estimate is a 20 per cent inflation in ten years and hence a total operating educational and general budget of $11,760 million.

But let us revert to the $9.8 billion budget on the no-inflation assumption. Where is this money to come from? Table 1 gives the picture.

Table 1. Sources of Funds, Institutes of Higher Education

	1957–58		1969–70	
	$ million	Per cent	$ million	Per cent
Tuition......................	904	25	3,800	40
Government..................	1,752	48	3,700	38
Endowment income and gifts.....	578	16	1,200	12
Other (scholarship fund from various sources, etc.)..........	416	11	1,100	11
	3,650	100	9,800	101*

* Percentages do not add to 100 because of rounding.

SOURCE: See note.

In general the relative contribution of tuition is likely to increase, that of government to decline, that of endowment and gifts also to fall. Yet the dollar incomes from government and philanthropy will more than double.

Resources of these proportions may not be forthcoming. If they are not, then enrollment may suffer; but as we all agree in this volume, the net effect is more likely to be a decline in the quality of the product. I am also aware that, although increased cash resources are required, the rising flow of cash may largely yield inflation rather than genuine resources if, for example, the flow of personnel of ability is not accelerated.

This is not a forecast of what is going to happen; rather, it is an attempt to estimate what the sources of income should be if the budget rises from $3.6 to $9.8 billion in twelve years. Many will contend that I am relying too heavily on tuition—as does President Millett in his paper. Government may make larger contributions than I estimate; if so, the rise of tuition need not be so large as I here suggest.

I have argued frequently on the practicability and equity of higher tuition fees. The rise of $2,900 million from tuition is explained in the note at the end of the paper. This increase of $2,900 million in tuition income seems less frightening if allowance is made for the $800 million associated with rising enrollment at current fees and the $530 million of additional scholarships.

The major part of the rise in government funds projected is in Federal government funds. But of this increase about a billion is for research, with research income from Federal government accounting for 13 per cent by 1969–70 as compared to 5 per cent in 1939–40 and 12 per cent in 1955–56. State and local government income is to rise by about $600 million, or 60 per cent, and endowment income and gifts would roughly double. (More will be said on these estimates later.)

Expenditures rise primarily because of the doubling of enrollment and of salaries and related instructional outlays. With a trebling of costs, it is assumed that administration's share would drop from 12 to 10 per cent and research's share (government-financed and other) would rise from 5 per cent in 1939–40 to 18 per cent in 1955–56 and 23 per cent by 1969–70. The assumption here is that research is going to play a much larger part in university activities and that, as currently, almost two-thirds of it will be financed by the Federal government.

In earlier versions of these estimates I included as a factor making for higher outlays the sharing by higher education in the gains of the economy. That is, if the average standard of living of the population improves by 30 per cent in ten years, similar gains should be allocated to higher education. In a sense that is what I assume here.

Average Cost per Student, Assuming No Inflation

Year	Cost
1957–58	$1,070
1969–70	1,520

The above table reveals that unit costs rise by more than 40 per cent. That, despite the large increase in faculty pay assumed so far, unit costs have not risen more may be explained in part by the failure of other costs to rise as much and by the tendency of students to shift to low-cost institutions. This is indeed a large rise of unit costs, especially when it is realized that there are likely to be large relative shifts to low-cost institutions. But the trend is consistent with our history, and especially so in view of the current underpayment of faculty now to be corrected.

Economies, as we shall suggest later, may well yield gains of $1 billion to $2 billion per year by 1970. If that should happen, then the quality of the product might improve further or the demands made on the student and taxpayer might be reduced below our projections.

We should perhaps distinguish between economies and savings. An economy might, for example, be better use of classrooms or elimination of unnecessary or high-cost courses without any serious effect on the quality of the educational product. A saving might result from the trend toward two-year colleges, for example; not that they are necessarily cheaper than the first two years of a four-year college, but rather that a much larger proportion will be in those institutions. (We have already allowed for this type of saving.)

But there are other types of savings. For example, with the large rise of demand for teachers in the next ten years, the colleges are likely to command disproportionately young and non-Ph.D. teachers. Hence, a doubling of salaries might result in an over-all increase of salary costs of 75 per cent in 1970. Such savings might amount to as much as $600 million. The result is a likely deterioration of product, but $600 million less resources would be required. I consider this a saving because I assume that the younger teachers would do a less effective job. If the product is identical and expenditures are cut by $600 million, there is a genuine economy.

Economies

Economies require further discussion. In his excellent paper, Mr. Tickton assumes a substantial increase in the student-faculty ratio to be achieved in an actual plan well advanced. Here is a sample illustration of the possibilities of economies:[1]

Current Situation, Data of 1955–56

Full-time enrollment equivalent	2,300,000
Full-time equivalent faculty	152,000
Student-teacher ratio	15:1

Proposed Rise in Student-Teacher Ratio

Increase the ratio to	20:1
Needed teachers at 20:1 ratio (full time)	115,000

Estimates of Savings

Savings in teachers	37,000
At salaries double 1959 in 1970, per teacher	$13,000
Economies (37,000 × 13,000)	$481,000,000
Economies at enrollment of 1970 (2.3 × 1956)	$1,106,000,000

These statistics give an exaggerated view of the savings. There will be disproportionate reduction of low-income faculty, and in the large university the faculty does research as well as teaching. Organized research in a recent year accounted for about one-sixth of all general and educational expenditures. For these reasons I would be inclined to estimate these savings at about $800 million; substantial savings are certainly possible.

I do not mean to suggest that we have dealt with all aspects of this problem. For example, organized research is becoming a larger function of institutions of higher learning (IHL). This trend may well continue. The rise has been from $18 million, or 5 per cent of educational and general expenditures in 1929–30, to $375 million, or 16 to 17 per cent in 1953–54, which is an average increase of ½ per cent per year. If the rate of rise from 1929–30 to 1953–54 should continue, by 1970 the percentage will be roughly 25, or more than $2 billion. Indeed the net result will be an increase not of about $800 million, as is suggested by a trebling of all expenditures, but $2 billion, or $1.2 billion additional. (My estimate here is outlays of $2.1 billion.) This is not an unreasonable assumption.

But other assumptions are possible. One is that the research function will increasingly be assumed by government and industry directly. Another is that the growth of research will be at the expense of instruction.

I can envisage other savings, as adumbrated above, resulting from the changing structure of higher education. Low-cost operations tend to become relatively more important. The undergraduate business and education schools, the junior college, and the large urban university grow disproportionately; all of them are low-cost operations. But the high-cost Ivy League, select women's and men's liberal arts colleges, and professional schools of leading universities become less important.

My projections of enrollment are conservative. A rise of enrollment up to 6 million in ten years results from a rise in the ratio of college-age population at college by ½ of 1 per cent per year, as compared to 1 per cent since 1939–40 and 2+ per cent per year from 1951–52 to 1955–56, and the latter despite the reduction of veteran enrollment. The largest rises in this ratio have occurred since 1919, and especially in the last few years. (The ratios to population aged eighteen to twenty-one were 4 per cent in 1900, 12 per cent in 1930, and 35 per cent in 1956. Need I add that a substantial proportion are aged seventeen and in excess of age twenty-one.) [1] In view of the widespread policy of providing IHL within commuting distance of most students, the large growth of the junior college and the strategically located public four-year college; the great expansion of the urban university; the continued relative rise of discretionary expenditures per family; the improved methods of financing students through employment, scholarships, and loans; the almost certain relative gains for women and Negroes, now underrepresented; the rapid expansion of graduate study; the reduction of drop-outs; the increased diversification of IHL—all of these point toward steady gains in the percentage of college-age people at college.

Note especially the tendency of those attached to the labor market and studying part time to increase proportionately. In my estimates I have assumed that they would be part of the 6.4 million. But a large rise in the proportion of part-time students, say from the current 22 to 30 per cent, would mean a rise of part-time students of 1,130,000 and an enrollment probably substantially in excess of 6.4 million.

The trend toward low-cost units needs more elaboration. Thus the rise of enrollment from 1928 to 1956 (my compilation and calculations) was as follows for the high-priced units:

8 Ivy League	41.8
6 other outstanding private universities	29.8
10 outstanding women's colleges	No net change
20 outstanding liberal arts colleges	46.8

Against these increases note a rise of 141.8 per cent in all institutions, an increase from a very small beginning to 452,000 in the junior colleges, a 79.9 per cent increase for forty large urban IHL, and an 87.4 per cent increase for twenty-three large Catholic institutions. The large rise for *all* IHL as compared to the separate categories is explained in part by the tremendous increase in junior colleges and also by large rises in public institutions generally. It is also explained by the fact that the over-all figures include old *and new* institutions, whereas the above table covers only *identical* institutions in both years.

The significance for the future budget lies in part in the continued *relative* losses for the high-cost operations. Increasingly the trend is toward the low-cost institutions: the junior college, the commuting (streetcar) institutions, and the urban colleges. It is likely that the less-favored and the low-cost IHL have large amounts of excess capacity and that the many IHL in small towns have much excess. They especially may gain from the rise of enrollment. At current costs the $500 unit-cost operations are gaining at the expense of the operations costing $1,500 to $2,500.

Let us give one example of the possible trends. The junior college today costs about $600 per student, as compared to an over-all average of about $1,000. From almost nothing in 1929 the junior college has increased its enrollment to 450,000, or 17 per cent of the total, in 1956. A rise to 25 per cent of total enrollment by 1970, in view of the current planning for commuting colleges, is a conservative projection. At a 6-million enrollment, 8 per cent additional is roughly 500,000 additional enrollment beyond what might be expected on the basis of 1956 structures of enrollment. At cost differentials of 1970, the savings might well be about $250 million. This estimate includes an allowance for the larger proportion of part-time students in junior colleges, and note that it is based on the *relative* rise of numbers in these institutions, not on any substantial difference between unit costs in junior colleges and those in the first two years in four-year colleges. In addition, there are the savings related generally to the drift to the four-year commuting college, a drift accentuated by the growth of the metropolitan area.

This shift toward the commuting college involves savings of another type adumbrated above. The proportion of part-time students greatly increases. For example, HEW (Health, Education and Welfare) estimates the proportion of part-time students in 1955–56 in undergraduate instruction at 22 per cent.[1] But in the junior colleges the proportion of part-time students was 40 per cent, or almost twice as great relatively. For the junior college and urban institutions generally, this means reduced costs of hundreds of millions.

Some History

To better understand our present and future problems, we should look back briefly. Here follows a survey of the relation of educational and general expenditures and gross national product (GNP), the latter being the best index of the nation's economic output. The proportion of educational and general income to GNP has steadily risen from 0.23 per cent in 1889–90 to 0.51 per cent in 1929–30 and to 0.70 per cent in 1956–57. I should add that statistics before 1919 or thereabouts are useful only to show very rough trends. Our later estimates will indicate that, in order to obtain the necessary funds by 1970 at current price levels, this proportion of educational outlays to GNP would have to increase by more than 80 per cent. That is to say, we expect a GNP of about $700 billion and educational expenditures for colleges and universities of $9 billion, or 1.28 per cent of the GNP.[2] (Even this is a conservative projection; for I do not allow for the rise of construction outlays, and I assume economies of $800 million.)

What light does history throw on the future? If we study the trends from 1929–30 to 1956–57, we cannot be too hopeful. The ratio of expenditures on higher education to GNP rose by less than 40 per cent in twenty-seven years. Our present goal is an 80 per cent rise of the percentage of GNP in thirteen years, or an average of 6 per cent per year as compared to 1½ per cent per year in the preceding twenty-seven years. Can we do about four times as well in the thirteen years? I believe we can. The earlier period included the Great Depression and a great war and levels of discretionary personal expenditures much lower than currently. What is more, it was a period of costly mistakes in the financing of higher education. Had college administrators, trustees, and legislators not committed a $3 billion mistake, they would have achieved much more. Three billion dollars is the difference between the actual tuition receipts and what they would have been had tuition increased as much as per capita income (the best index of capacity to pay) from 1940 to 1956.

Another indication of what can be accomplished is provided by the history of the 1920s. Then the proportion of income of higher education to GNP rose by 82 per cent, almost exactly our target for the thirteen years under consideration. For the whole period 1889–90 to 1956–57 the rise was disappointing when a comparison is made of an increase of enrollment of about nineteen times to that of population of about three times. The gains per student were not, however, small. But that the college population in the next ten years will rise about five times as much relatively as population, or about 100 per cent, in itself will provide large additional resources *even without* any rise of tuition rates.

Efficiency and Unit Costs

One of the striking features of Table 2 is the large rise of costs per resident student. For example, from 1919–20 to 1956–57 the increase in

Table 2. Higher Education Income in Relation to GNP and Other Variables, 1889–90 to 1956–57

Period	Proportion of general income to GNP, per cent	Consumer prices; 1923 = 100	Resident enrollment, thousands	Education and general income per resident	Value of physical property, millions	Endowment, millions
1889–90	0.23	48	157	$ 137	$ 95	$ 579
1919–20	0.28	108	598	289	741	569
1929–30	0.51	98	1,101	439	1,925	1,512
1939–40	0.58	85	1,494	382	2,753	1,764
1949–50	0.66	142	2,659	689	5,275	2,644
1953–54	0.63	158	2,407	979	8,033	3,313
1956–57	0.70*	163	3,000*	1,000*	10,000*	4,000*

* Estimated.

SOURCE: U.S. Census, *Historical Statistics of the United States, 1789–1845;* Department of Health Education and Welfare, *Statistics of Higher Education: Receipts, Expenditures and Property and Faculty, Students and Degrees,* various issues; and *Economic Report of the President,* Jan. 1, 1959. Estimates and computations are mine.

consumer prices was about 50 per cent, but the increase of educational and general income per resident student was close to 250 per cent. This large relative rise in cost of higher education occurred despite an increase of average enrollment per IHL from 575 in 1919–20 to 1,430 in 1956–57. (In 1889–90 the number was only 157 per institution.) Such large increases in the size of the unit should contribute to reductions of unit costs.

A trend toward higher unit costs in the past, despite the rise in the size of the unit, despite the much greater increase in the low-cost operations (e.g., undergraduate business and education and junior colleges), despite the relative rise in part-time students, points to the likelihood of a continued increase in unit costs. In fact, to some extent we are counting on a continued increase in unit costs. The doubling of faculty salaries and the increase in other costs projected for 1970 largely assumes an improved product which in part matches the rising standard of our economy and to some extent is compensation for the lag in outlays for higher education per student behind the growth in per capita income since 1940. Against this rise we anticipate some economies.

But before we discuss these economies, we should explain the upward trends of the past. The following are the crucial factors that account for higher unit costs:

1. New functions. Our colleges and universities create a *different* product than they did 25, 50, or 100 years ago. They provide more research, health services, employment and counseling aid, intercollegiate athletics, extension services, alumni relations, etc.

2. Better product. The average student receives a better education than in the past. Teachers are better trained; new techniques of teaching are used; equipment and plant are better; according to one expert, the college now as compared with the college of a generation ago yields a five-year product in four years.

3. A more costly product. Each year the cost of services, plant, and supplies rises. The average over the years may be 4 per cent. This increase reflects both inflationary forces and rising productivity. In the economy generally the 4 per cent increased charges are offset by a productivity improvement of about 2 to 3 per cent a year. By this we mean that, for a given input of labor, capital, management, etc., output per man-hour rises 2 to 3 per cent a year. Hence against the increase of prices the businessman can profit from rising productivity. It is then not surprising that, despite substantial gains of wage rates, etc., the price level has risen little more than 1 per cent per year over a period of 120 years.

But in higher education the results are not so satisfactory. The college treasurer has to face the competition of other buyers and sellers, and he therefore also pays, say, 4 per cent more per year, or else exploits his faculty and employees or hires second-rate personnel. Machines do not play the part in higher education that they play in the economy generally. What is more, the internal structure of higher education is such that the exploitation of mechanization and of improvements in teaching methods and use of plant are much below the level that might be achieved if the faculty were employees rather than part of management.

Hence under the pressure of rising costs, the college administrator tends to exploit the faculty through underpayment, lives on capital, deteriorates his product, or seeks additional funds as a substitute for economies. This is, of course, the general picture, with efficiency in many institutions matching that of industry but with that of the vast majority probably inferior.

Unfortunately, we are unable to measure the extent to which the rise of unit costs in higher education reflects an improvement in the product. In so far as it does, then to that extent the rise reflects not inefficiency, but an improved product. Though we have vague notions and measures of rising productivity, they are inadequate. The greatest obstacle is that, as bad as our measure of output is, a measure of input (the quality of the student) is virtually nonexistent.

In regard to the future, I am hopeful that despite the increase of unit costs associated with a rising standard of living—about 30 per cent for ten years—we can introduce economies that will largely offset these rises in costs. Rich opportunities are available to be exploited. First, we can save a great deal by increasing the size of our units. In 1956, there were 378 institutions with enrollments below 200 (20 per cent of the total), 536 with enrollments of 200 to 499 (29 per cent of the total), and 400 with enrollments from 500 to 999 (22 per cent of the total), or 71 per cent of the total with enrollments of less than 1,000. Liberal arts colleges (530), teachers colleges (101), and junior colleges (434) account for most of these low-enrollment units. These institutions should increase their enrollment greatly. There is not much excuse on economic grounds for colleges of less than 1,000. The unit with enrollment of 350 may be acceptable so long as the administrator is aware of the annual cost of having a college so small that church services can be held at one sitting and everyone knows everyone else.

In the professional schools (especially the 90 or so medical schools) the case for units of 1,000 or less is much stronger, and in view of the splits among religious groups and enrollment trends an increase in the size of theological schools will not be easy. But generally, rising enrollments should help bring about units more nearly at an optimum, i.e., sizes that yield low costs.

Second, there is the problem of attrition. Often the parent or student selects the wrong institution, given the quality and objectives of the student. Drop-outs are altogether too numerous, though we should not assume that completion of only one or two years at a four-year college means a complete loss. According to an HEW study, only 39.5 per cent of those who entered a four-year institution in 1950 had graduated within four years. When allowance is made for transfers and graduation after four years, the record is substantially better. The proportion of graduates to entering students may be as high as 60 per cent, ultimately.[3]

The wastes involved would be much reduced if a way could be found to appraise institutions, or even identify them in terms of what their product is. This kind of information is not available. The issue here is not that any such improvements would contribute greatly toward solvency. Rather, what is involved is that for a given outlay the product would improve, and the student and parent would receive larger returns for a given outlay.

Institutions of higher learning can do a better job in reducing costs. The first step is to study costs; great advantages follow. President Hovde of Purdue University has said that the presentation of cost analysis with the budget greatly facilitated the voting of funds by the state legislature.

Indeed, motivation for discovering costs is not so great for colleges as for business. The latter ties costs to pricing; on the whole, IHL are not ordinarily disposed to do so. It is often not easy to discover costs, because the college produces a joint product: undergraduate instruction, graduate instruction, research and other public services. But business estimates costs despite the jointness of costs. Charges are then based on the additional costs involved in producing the joint product, say, cottonseed oil with cotton, and also on capacity to pay. In a similar manner a university may find that undergraduate instruction costs $1,000 and graduate instruction $3,000. This is a fact worth knowing, and it may have some influence on educational policy. For example, the cost to the college of a $2,200 subsidy for each graduate student may result in a policy to limit graduate instruction to x number of able students. A business concern would not sell the product for less than $4,000 if the additional costs are $3,000; the IHL may well, given its "public" functions, sell the product at $800 and incur a "loss" of $3,200. But who would say that it is unwise to try to discover costs?

In the medical schools, where the joint products are many, the best work has been done. In a study of the cost of medical education at Emory University, in Georgia, the following sensible conclusion was drawn:[4]

> Cost analysis, no matter what system is used, is not an exact science but rather—like medicine—an art based upon a science. It is an art in the sense that judgment is an important part of the process. Judgment must be used in such matters as determining how to distribute each overhead cost most equitably and develop the best estimates for the distribution of personnel time, determining where the exceptions to the established rules are justified, or perhaps in considering the relationship of the purpose of an expenditure to the method of distribution. Obviously, these judgments must

be based upon a familiarity with the general philosophy of the enterprise under study. These judgments should be supported by reason, and reason, of course, is frequently debatable.

Running our IHL has become big business. The expenditures now are beginning to approach $4 billion, and in ten or twelve years the total amount may well be $9 billion to $10 billion. Yet surprisingly little concern is had for measuring our costs and finding how the job can be done more efficiently. Indeed the business manager may have complete control, or virtually complete control, over plant operation and maintenance, although this also is limited by scheduling of classes and other items over which the faculty maintains control. Plant operation and maintenance, however, account for only about 10 or 12 per cent of total educational and general expenditures. Indeed in the operation of auxiliary services, which may well account for one-fifth of total current expenditures, the business manager has considerable control as a rule. In this area of operation he can of course suggest a mechanical leaf-raking machine, increased use of IBM machines, the substitution of student care of room as against care by maids with a resultant reduction in room and board, central purchasing, and the like. But he has little control over the educational practices that greatly influence total costs.

This does not mean that the academic authorities take no interest in costs. They, also, have to balance their budgets. In introducing a new program, most good administrators today would, for example, estimate the increased costs involved and suggest the resources that are required to finance it.

One interesting suggestion made by John Dale Russell is that there should be a program of cost accounting as a restraint on introducing new programs. That is, when a new program is to be introduced, the authorities should estimate the minimum amount of money required to run it, irrespective of the number of students. Then costs should be estimated on the basis of varying enrollment under the particular program. A check on the introduction of new programs would then be had.[5]

On the whole, what is disturbing is that the colleges as a rule are not inclined to estimate their unit costs for services already being given. For example, the major universities do not every few years estimate the cost of, say, the freshman curriculum, the cost of running a particular department, or, more important, the cost of turning out a student in one department rather than another. No attempt is generally made to estimate the cost of giving a particular course. These unit costs change greatly from year to year without any inspection by the authorities. It would be helpful, for example, to know how much it would cost to turn out a student in paleontology, say, twenty-five years ago and today, and also to measure against this the value to society and to the student of the output of a paleontology student today as against twenty-five years ago. Similar remarks may be made in regard to other fields as well. What may have been a justifiable expenditure, given educational objectives twenty-five years ago or even ten years ago, is not necessarily a justifiable expenditure today. Therefore, if it is at all possible, it is wise to inspect every few years the costs of a course, of departments, of curricula, etc. It is not easy to transfer resources from one department to another or from one course to another; adjustments can gradually be made, especially through growth.

Undoubtedly the business manager of Northwestern University may have exaggerated when he wrote the following, although his position has some substance:[6]

> Educational administrators have been chosen largely from the field of scholars and they have not been trained in the economic understanding of their assignments. The correlation of the myriad activities in an institution must be doubly watched when a change of educational authority is in process. Scholars rarely approach an administrative appointment in education with an understanding of the intricacies of fund accounting, educational costs, budget control, centralized purchasing, and investment management. As a result, good business management is evident in successful institutions and weak business managements have foredoomed many colleges to extinction. It is a rigorous assignment, for men in these business positions are supposed to be wise enough in education to win the confidence of the educator and sufficiently proficient in executive management to meet the test of trustees who are successful in business management.

Earlier in this paper I suggested the possibility of economies through increases in the student-faculty ratio. Mr. Ruml deserves much credit for having brought this matter to the attention of the country. Indeed, he oversimplifies the problem, and he is too disposed to turn the curriculum over to the trustees. But that a concerted effort by faculty and administration would yield large savings is not open to doubt.

The proliferation of courses is a scandal from the viewpoint of both economics and education. For eleven outstanding institutions I found by actual count a rise of undergraduate courses over fifty-five years from 12,000 to 39,000 and of graduate courses (where available) from 4,500 to 21,700. There are not only too many courses, but too many small classes. Authorities should eliminate many and alternate others. An economics course with three students and a resultant cost of $1,000 per student for this course and $3,000 for the students' other courses may well be justifiable, but it would be even more so if the course were given to six students every other year, and costs reduced correspondingly.

College faculty members seem to want their pay in part in the satisfaction of giving courses for which the only justification is their own interest in the subjects. They often do not understand the relation of these inefficiencies and their own pay. Too many courses; too many small classes; excessive course demands on students; inadequate independent work by students; imposition of tasks on faculty that could be done by assistants paid a dollar or two an hour instead of by professors paid $6 per hour of work; concentration of classes from 10:00 to 12:00 on Monday, Wednesday, and Friday (at pleasure of instructor); and laboratories in the afternoon only—these are among the factors that make higher education so costly.

The Commission on the Financing of Higher Education put the issues of excessive courses very well:[7]

> The greatest extravagance in almost every type of institution from the smallest to the largest lies in the curriculum. This situation usually arises from the absence of even a broad general conception of purpose by which course offerings can be assessed. Partly to meet over-refined needs, partly to attract students, partly to meet competition, real or imagined, institutions have permitted their course offerings to grow more and more numerous, to proliferate far beyond real needs. Too many of our institutions have been victimized by the cult of coverage. Since the complete offering of every conceivable course is impossible, it follows that the selection should be guided by some broad education principles. . . .
>
> . . . and many courses, once started, continue a life of their own until they become gnarled branches of the past, left unpruned while new branches of learning grow all around them. . . . Many faculty members and department heads would do well to remember the aphorism of a distinguished British educator, Sir Richard Livingstone, who said that a great teacher "is known by the number of valuable subjects that he declines to teach."

On the issue of size of class, we have had hundreds of experiments since the famous ones by Hudelson at the University of Minnesota in the 1920s. Almost universally the lesson taught is that the results are at least as good in large classes as in small ones, especially when it is realized that the large class can exploit the first-class teacher. These experiments, moreover, do not test merely the accumulation of knowledge. The famous White physics course on television enrolls 400,000 students, exploits six Nobel Peace Prize winners, gives five lectures a week for a year, and costs $2.50 per student.

In view of the repeated experiments, it is surprising that the folklore of the small class persists. I recall how enthusiastic President Conant used to be about the splendid job being done at the Harvard Law School, where the major courses were large ones and relatively economical to operate as compared to courses in the arts and sciences.

It is surprising to find the data of Table 3 for twenty-five major state universities in 1956–57. The evidence fails to support the case for the small class. Indeed, the tests may not be adequate to measure all the results of the teaching process, but they are reliable enough to suggest that the burden of proof rests on the adherents of the small class.

Table 3. Cumulative Percentages in Classes up to Fifty

Class enrollment	Lower division	Upper division	Graduate division	Total
5 or less..................	4.0%	16.2%	51.9%	13.7 %
10 or less..................	9.6	33.4	74.7	24.9
15 or less..................	19.5	49.0	85.7	36.77
25 or less..................	50.6	72.0	93.4	62.37
35 or less..................	76.6	84.9	96.0	82.03

SOURCE: W. E. Green, University of Mississippi, "A Study in Class Sizes in Major State Universities," in *Summary, Abstracts and Bibliography of Studies of Class Size*, prepared by the Division of Academic Research and Services, Pennsylvania State University, June, 1958, p. 35. (Mimeographed.)

But whatever our views, we are likely to be confronted with a rise of students greatly in excess of the increased supply of teachers at current standards. The only alternatives are a serious deterioration of teaching quality or a more effective use of available talent.

Hence we are likely to have larger classes, greater use of visual aids, reductions in course requirements and hence more independent work, more careful scrutiny of courses and small classes, and a more receptive attitude toward machines both to supplement the teacher and replace him. We can also anticipate that IHL, like industry, will increasingly try to raise productivity by conserving the energies of the teacher, and particularly the most effective teacher, for the most vital tasks. He will lecture to large groups, and he will have increased assistance for secretarial work, preparation of materials, and grading of papers.

Cost cutting can prevail in other fields than the curriculum; in this volume, Mr. Henemen concentrates on many of them. Earlier I discussed briefly the size of the institution. Much wastage results from failure to achieve an economical size. Proliferation of colleges is almost as great an evil as that of courses. In California there are now seventeen public engineering colleges, all trying to be Berkeleys, but what is especially needed are technical schools. In the South there is an excess of law schools with enrollment frequently only at 50 to 60 per cent of capacity. Under political pressure, every city wants a four-year college when the state pays the bill. Location is determined not on the basis of availability of land, facilities, personnel, and proximity to the market as it would be by business, but often by the influence of the politician or the local chamber of commerce.

Is the individualistic development and multiplicity of institutions of higher education justified? A 1938 study by the American Council on Education raised some issues here. Sectional bargaining (politics, etc.) and other influences within the state account in part for the malallocation of universities, the distribution of normal schools, teachers colleges, etc. "These processes and influences have resulted in what under present conditions is an amazingly unintelligent and wasteful distribution of higher educational resources." [8]

Colleges tend to cluster; the question is whether so many institutions are actually needed to perform the higher educational services desirable in their territories. Indeed with the large increases of enrollment since 1938 the excesses and inefficiencies have been whittled down to some extent. Clusters often mean duplication of facilities and courses and malallocation of resources. In some states there is a multiplicity of publicly supported institutions:[8]

> Such multiplication of publicly supported institutions within single states inevitably creates the demand of informed members of the general public and politicians and statesmen who seek public favor through economy and tax reduction campaigns that these conditions be justified or changed.

Often local social and business interests win out over educational intelligence:[8]

> No national government authority has existed and no state government agency has been able or willing to control the demands of local political and economic forces in such a way to secure the development of public and private higher education so articulated as to serve public needs efficiently and economically.

In regard to the professions, it would seem an elementary act of logic to examine the social need for trained men and women in all these professions and to plan educational opportunities for preparation in some relationship to present and probable future demands for those services:[8]

> In the judgment of a very large number of the officers of scholarly and professional organizations and of administrative and faculty members of higher education institutions from whom comments were received, the major obstacle to greater cooperation is narrow institutionalism.

Devotion and loyalty to a single school spring from some causes other than excellence in the performance of educational functions. Another major obstacle is ignorance on the part of controlling boards, administrative officers, faculties, educational organizations, the constituency of these institutions, and the general public.[8]

Another factor making for larger costs is the inadequacy of planning. Never have colleges and universities spent as much time and resources on planning as in the last ten years. Yet one observer who visited forty-two institutions of higher learning, ten of which had enrollments of less than 5,000, found that only one-half had plans. Those with plans considered the possibility of making more efficient use of facilities through study of class schedules, courses offered, student-faculty ratio, teaching loads, and curricular problems generally. A few institutions had underway cost studies to determine the maximum number of students that could be accommodated without increasing the present budget.[9]

I could continue on this subject of economies. Cooperation and coordination among colleges are just beginning. The experiences in the Connecticut Valley; in the Richmond area; in Indiana; the Haverford, Swarthmore, and Bryn Mawr arrangements; the new ten-college program in the Midwest; cooperations among libraries—these are only a beginning. Also, much more could be done to reduce duplication between work at college and school. The gains would be in saving of resources rather than avoidance of bankruptcy.

In short, economies of $1 billion are achievable through improvements in the instructional part of the budget, and much more is possible if we include economies of classroom and other physical facilities and better planning of number, size, and location of units.

Broad Issues of Pricing

Our 1970 budget is likely to be of the order of $9 billion to $10 billion without inflation and $11 billion to $12 billion with a 2 per cent annual inflation. But let us consider the $9-billion to $10-billion budget, always remembering the possibilities of the larger budget. So far I have dealt primarily with economies. It is my hope that of the $6 billion to $7 billion additional needed, an offset could be had through economies *and savings* resulting from movements into lower-cost institutions that might reduce the additional income needed by $1 billion to $2 billion. I am hopeful also that the increase of tuition might yield almost $3 billion additional—less than one-quarter ($800 million) from the gains resulting merely from the rise of enrollment at current rates of tuition, and about $2 billion from rises in tuition. The details are available in Table 12.

Like President Millett, I propose additional funds from all available sources. But he, like the Council for Financial Aid to Education, would obtain about 20 per cent of the $9 billion from tuition and fees, whereas inclusive of current fees and exclusive of additional scholarships, I would depend upon tuition and fees for about $3,900 million, or 40 per cent. Against the council's estimate of 45 per cent from government, I put the government's contribution at about $3,700 million, or 38 per cent from government in all.

These are the major differences between us. Perhaps because I am more impressed by the obstacles to rising contributions by government, as I show later, I depend more on tuition.

It may well be, as several members of a discussion group at Merrill Center contended, that people will insist upon low tuition. The political influence of the students and their families may be decisive. I am sure this will happen in some states. I would, however, distinguish California, where about 30 per cent of the college-age population would be at public IHL, and Massachusetts, where the current percentage is about 4. But if tuition is held at roughly current levels, additional resources will come from government or other sources, or what is more likely, standards will decline.

My position is not that the student should pay full cost; ordinarily that is not necessary. Inclusive of capital, subsidies per student now average $700 to $800. I expect total subsidies will continue to grow. But I also expect that costs per student will rise—though it is possible to reverse the trend of the last hundred years—and more than twice as many students will have to be subsidized. It is possible that I am too much impressed by the obstacles to large rises of public aid, but I do not think so. At any rate, with a doubling of enrollment, subsidies per student will probably decline.

Pricing Further Considered

Institutions of higher learning are nonprofit organizations. To meet their expenses, they depend on tuition and fees charged students, gifts, income on productive funds invested, and government aid. Unlike business, IHL do not charge on the basis of costs. Unlike business, when confronted with deficits, they do not ordinarily react by trying to cut costs or rationalize. They are more likely to respond by seeking additional funds from private or public sources. Even if they are in the red, they will often assume additional responsibilities which may put them further in the red. In the private sector the college president, as former President Conant of Harvard once said, has become a member of the mendicant order; more recently he is pictured as the administrator, popular with his faculty when he is on the tin-cup circuit.

I do not mean to imply that IHL, in setting tuition fees, pay no attention to costs. When endowment is not available and current gifts are relatively unimportant, the college has to charge the equivalent of costs or ultimately disappear. Hundreds of colleges, notably many urban universities and small church-related colleges, inclusive of the Catholic institutions, are frequently in this condition. Even they, however, have accounting systems foreign to business systems. No college, unless the money is borrowed, includes as part of its cost the capital charges. I estimate these capital charges on the basis of a forty-year life and 4 per cent interest at about $400 per student. At Harvard I estimated the capital cost per student at roughly $1,000; yet the treasurer's report does not so much as mention a building.

That costs are not entirely neglected is also suggested by the practice of charging more for medical education than, say, for a business or teachers' program, or by the policy of those land-grant colleges that charge three to four times as much for a nonresident as for a resident of the state, or the tendency to adjust charges to the number of points taken by the student.

In still another respect, the market for college services is peculiar. Alongside the private institutions, which charge fees varying from $0 for tuition (for example, Cooper Union) to $3,000 inclusive of room and board (for example, Bennington), there are public institutions that charge tuition from $0 to as much as $600. *Average* fees, however, recently amounted to about $600 for private institutions and $150 for the public ones. (The fees of public universities tend to be higher than for all public institutions.)

Ordinarily the consumer seeks to buy in the cheapest market, but that is not necessarily true of the buyer of higher education. He is often prepared to pay the high rather than the low prices. Many admission officers have told me that one way for a prestige institution to discourage demand is to reduce its price below that of its rivals. A rational explanation of the concomitance of low public and high private fees, and both low and high private fees, is that the product varies. Each college offers a differentiated product. Indeed, it is difficult, if not impossible, to measure it. But to the student or parent, Manger, say, seems to offer a much better product than Hilton or George, and hence the parent is prepared to pay a differential of, say, $1,000. Snob appeal, sentiment (the college of a parent), genuine values (good faculty, unusual equipment and buildings, vocational gains, for example, the popularity with executives or medical schools of Manger Graduates)—all of these contribute toward the disposition to pay a high price for education at some colleges. Indeed, prestige often carries too much weight, as President Goheen of Princeton told a Congressional Committee in 1958.

Another peculiarity of the market should be noted. Although in the West enrollment in public institutions is several times as great relatively as in the Northeast (80 and 20 per cent, respectively, with extremes of 100 per cent in two Mountain states and 11 per cent in Massachusetts), the ratio of public to private fees is roughly equal in both regions. The dominant seller (that is, the public institution in the West and the private in the East) does not determine the prices charged. What that means is simply this. It might be expected that, since public IHL predominate in the West, where tuition is low, tuition would be correspondingly low in private institutions in the West as compared to similar charges in the East, where the dominant institution is the high-priced private one. But actually, rates in private IHL in the West are as high relative to public institutions as they are in the East.

Competition between the private and public institution is on the increase. Many administrators in private institutions see themselves priced out of the market by the increased differential in tuition between public and private IHL. Indeed, since before World War II, relative increases for public IHL have exceeded those for the private, but absolute differences continue to increase. Evidence of the reduced competitive position of the private IHL is the increase of enrollment by public institutions from 49 to 58 per cent and the enrollment of 85 per cent of the net increase in public IHL in a recent ten-year period. In part this arises from the greater popularity of private institutions when the government financed GI students. The proportion of students entering public institutions exceeds 60 per cent of the total now, and if prices remain relatively stable in public IHL and rise in response to higher costs and standards in private IHL, then the net result might well be an 80:20 ratio of enrollment for public and private IHL within ten to twelve years. In the process many private institutions in a vulnerable financial condition might well be liquidated. Hence the resentment in some quarters against the continued rise of public expenditures for higher education. Here is one estimate of outlays by state government:[10]

	$ Million	Percentage of All Educational Expenditures
1944	175	20
1958	1,086	30

In defense of current trends, the proponents of the public institution insist on the validity of the image of the public institution offering its product to all who can profit and without the deterrent of high fees. In some instances the state constitution actually provides for free education from the nursery to the graduate school. However, under the pressure of taxpayers' resistance and inadequate resources, some such constitutions have been modified, and what is in truth tuition is now designated as fees for services.

Undoubtedly, the public institutions are now under great pressure to increase fees, and not merely to save the private institutions. The real issue is this: Can they continue to charge low prices and increase their subsidies as their proportion of enrollment rises? Where the tradition of free tuition is strongly entrenched, where incomes are high and growing rapidly, and especially where tax systems are not regressive (that is, not with an incidence heavily on the poor), it may be possible to continue to maintain low fees and steadily rising enrollment, absolutely and relatively. California, for example, may be such a state. Despite its unusual public higher education system, with virtually its whole population within commuting distance of a college, California spent a smaller proportion (0.541 per cent) of its personal income on public higher education in 1957 than did Vermont (0.661). Does this not suggest the advantages of high economic status, rapid growth, size (economies of scale), and a strong tradition of public higher education?

In many states the possibilities of growth of public higher education are not nearly so great. Tradition is weak; growth is relatively slow; tax systems are regressive; and independent IHL that have sufficient capacity to absorb a substantial part of additional students and are strong enough to prevent excessive financing of public institutions are dominant. These generalizations apply especially to many states in the Northeast and Middle West and even to some states in the South. Obviously the pressure for appropriation for public higher education will be much greater in California, with 80 per cent of its students in public IHL, than in Massachusetts, where only 11 per cent are in public IHL, although the percentage of college-age population at *all* IHL is roughly equal.

I am not convinced that the present system is the most democratic. Currently the public institutions offer a subsidy inclusive of capital of at least $1,000 per student. But all, poor and rich, receive this subsidy. With average family incomes in excess of $6,000 and with families with students at college receiving an income of $8,000 to $9,000—once allowance is made for the higher average age (and higher income) of parents with children at college and the higher average income generally of families with children at college—the case for indiscriminate subsidies is greatly weakened.

Why not increase tuition by $350 (a policy that by 1970 should yield public institutions $1.5 billion yearly additional) and use $500 million or even more of the additional income to provide adequate subsidies for the poor and able? Then the able poor farm boy or son of the laborer with an income of $2,000 to $4,000 would receive not only a low tuition but also a scholarship to cover a large part of his additional expense. The public IHL would then compete much more strenuously for able students than it currently does, and it would also use its resources much more effectively. (For a contrary view see the paper in this volume by President John Millett.)

Currently, let us note that a comparison of tuition and scholarship money in numerous states yields the following results:

The major state university or land-grant college gives about one-third as many scholarships, relative to enrollment, as its major private competitor gives, and each scholarship yields roughly as much less as the difference of tuition. Wiser *distribution* of subsidies could easily correct this situation!

I am not convinced by some of the arguments presented against the view of a scholarship program such as that offered by the able President of the University of Delaware and former Under Secretary of Education, John Perkins, in his recent provocative book, *Plain Talk from a Campus.* Similar views were expressed at the Merrill Center against my position. President Perkins stresses the practical difficulties of administering a scholarship program based on need, but the College Scholarship Service now operates such a program for about two hundred institutions. The argument of the evils of a vast bureaucracy administering a public scholarship program does not carry conviction; when the stakes are $1 billion to $2 billion, the argument seems to me to be weak. At any rate California, New York, and Illinois are not frightened by these considerations.

Nor am I convinced by an argument used by one of the presidents of an Eastern state university who, at my seminar for college administrators on the economics of higher education, objected to a pricing policy that combined higher fees and more and better scholarships on the ground that we would then be establishing standards.

In recent discussions of tuition trends, many have tended to exaggerate the rises that have occurred. The usual approach is to compare tuition at various types of institutions in, say, the 1930s and 1956. Such studies may reveal a rise of tuition in private institutions of about $300 and in public institutions of less than $100. But there is another approach which seems to me to be at least as relevant. I compare the increase of operating costs per student, of tuition (operating costs divided by number of students),[11] and family income *after taxes* from 1929–30 to 1955–56. What do I find?

Rise of family income	$3,000
Rise of tuition per student minus increase of scholarships per student	100
Rise of operating cost	500
Rise of subsidy, per student	400

AN INCREASING PROPORTION OF
YOUNG PEOPLE ARE GOING TO COLLEGE

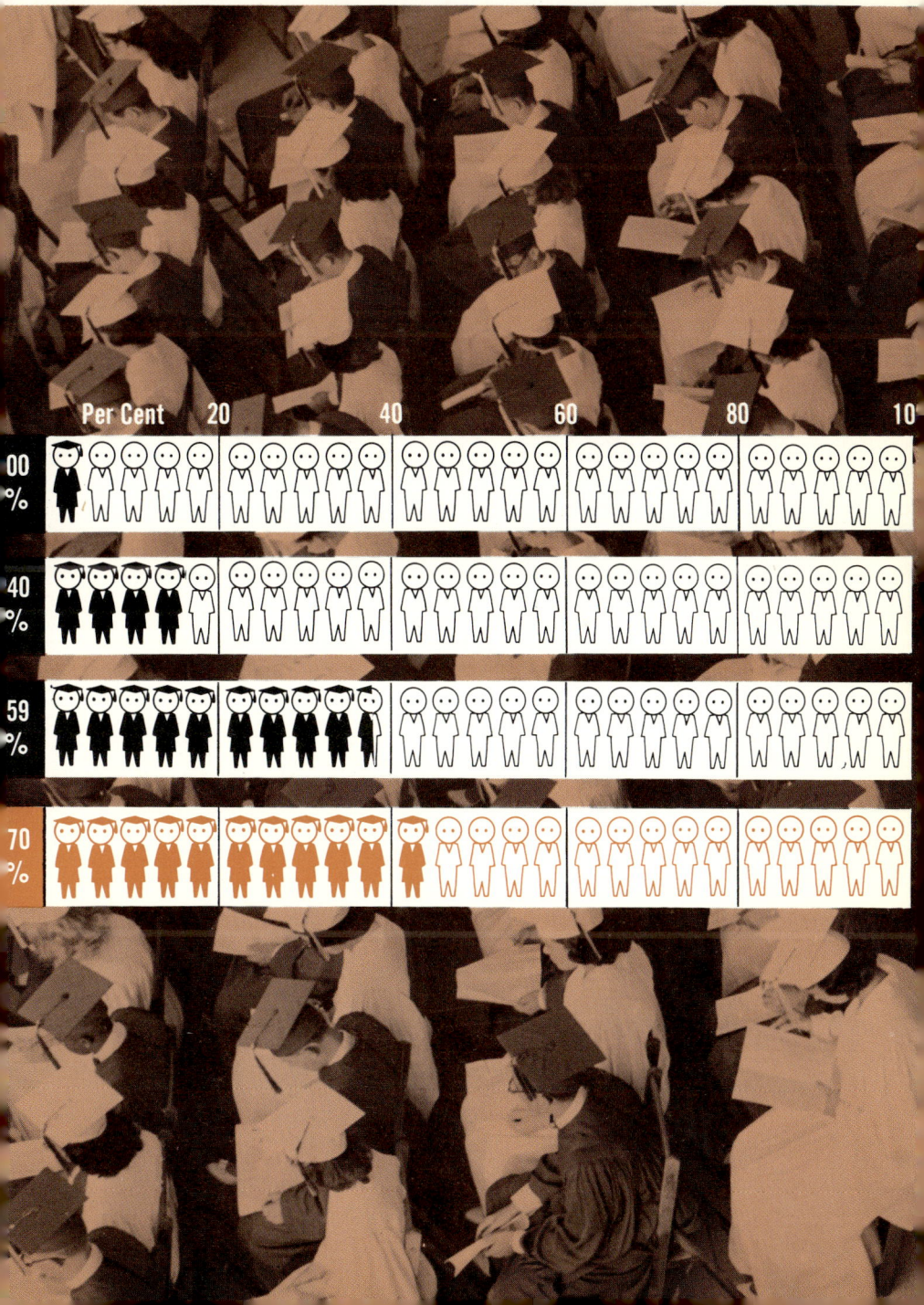

These figures point to a considerable easing of the burden of tuition upon the family finances and a substantial rise of subsidies. One may be surprised at the small rise of tuition shown, namely, about $100 net. The explanation lies largely in the fact that a much larger proportion of students *now* go to IHL where tuition is relatively low. Another factor is that scholarship funds per student have increased by about $30 per student and should be deducted from gross tuition. Consider, for example, the effect of the rise of enrollment of about 300,000 since 1929–30 in junior colleges generally free of any tuition, the growth of urban universities and Catholic institutions, and the reduction of the relative enrollment in the Ivy and other high-tuition groups mentioned above. Consider, for example, the effects on tuition trends of 300,000 additional students at junior colleges who are now paying substantially less than $100 and who otherwise might be paying an average of at least $400. Once we allow for these diversions to low-tuition institutions, the net effect *of this factor* is to reduce rather than increase tuition.

Pricing and Receipts from Students

Above I have suggested that I belong to the high-tuition school, but I hasten to add, not to the *full-cost* school. I support higher tuition because, on grounds of equity, practicability, and need, I see no other solution. That does not mean that we should not seek to obtain as much as is possible and fair from other sources. The sting of higher tuition is likely to be reduced by the increased proportion of students who will, as regular members of the labor market, become part-time students.

From the Civil War until World War II, tuition rose much more than prices and even than per capita income. Yet enrollments steadily rose from 52,000, in 1869–70, to 238,000 in 1899–1900, to 1,101,000 in 1929–30, and to more than three million today. The higher the price the larger the purchases. A rising per capita income and an acceleration of interest in higher education explain this unusual response to pricing of higher education.

College administrators tend to underestimate the strength of the demand for college services. They have kept tuition down because they concentrated too much on price movements rather than on per capita income, the latter a better guide to capacity to pay, and because they failed to relate any increase of tuition to the total costs of going to college. An average rise of tuition of $400 today would mean an increase of tuition costs of about 100 per cent, but in relation to all costs inclusive of income forgone, that is, the income lost while the student studies instead of being a full-time member of the labor market, the rise would be about 10 per cent. A rise in costs of 100 per cent is serious indeed, of 10 per cent much less so.

Administrators of public institutions emphasize especially the relation of pricing to the national gain of higher education, and hence the inference is that tuition should be low because society primarily gains. Here, indeed, is an argument for tuition below costs. But fortunately the student gains, and increasingly so as higher education becomes more and more vocational. Hence on ground of the nation's welfare we can justify low tuition, and on ground of the individual's gain, high tuition. Often the social and individual gains are so commingled that it is next to impossible to measure the relative gains. In medicine, for example, the shortage of doctors points to high social gains and hence low tuition, but the probable lifetime income of a doctor graduating in 1960 at present prices is of the order of $1 million. Is it necessary to subsidize him to the extent of about $15,000 for his higher education? Many adherents to the low-tuition theory contend that those who do well later will repay government through higher taxes, but that seems to me to be an irrelevant point. Tax burdens are determined by income levels. (Actually, in state and local finance the states that provide the major subsidies in higher education do not tax primarily on the basis of income.) The relation of taxes and income is one thing; the subsidies offered for higher education another.

Currently the graduate may look forward to a lifetime income many times the subsidy provided by the college or professional school. To this relative gain, his abilities, environmental factors, and his education contribute. That higher education contributes substantially to income suggests he should be prepared to meet a large part of its cost out of tuition.

But rises in tuition would be unfortunate if they excluded those who might profit from higher education, and hence there is the necessity for improved methods of financing. That the financing of higher education is still primitive contributes toward the deficiences of tuition income and the unfortunate condition of college finance. Before the war about $10 million of scholarship funds was available; today the amount available is more than $100 million. If this sum is put against the more than $6 billion direct costs of higher education to the students and perhaps $15 billion inclusive of income forgone, scholarships yield less than 1 per cent of total student cost. Even this small amount of scholarship money has helped greatly; for since the prewar years, tuition income has increased about ten times as much as scholarships, and without the latter the rise of tuition income would have been substantially less.

I do not agree with the general position that scholarships do not help the institution; they contribute in an important way to making possible more realistic pricing. Opposition to scholarships on the ground of injury done to IHL is not supportable. Occasionally one gets the impression that some spokesmen of public institutions take this position because they fear higher scholarships are a technique that make possible higher tuition; for the public institutions, as tuition rises, experience a loss of competitive position.

Long-term Financing

Perhaps the greatest weakness in the financing of higher education is the failure to exploit long-term financing. Contrast the $3,000 per family of indebtedness available for the purchase of homes, autos, and television sets and the average of about $20 to $30 of loans outstanding per student.

Why should higher education be financed on a cash basis? Education is indeed more than an investment for increasing earning power, but it is nonetheless a very profitable investment for that purpose. Why do mothers who, without any caution, support credit for a house or appliances shudder at the thought of financing their children's education through credit? Here a public relations job is needed above all. I recall borrowing $150 in 1919–20 to complete my education. I felt almost as if I had absconded with the money, and the thought of the burden of the debt overwhelmed me. No one attempted to explain the real extent of the burden in relation to future income.

What is required is financing over the lifetime of the student in so far as resources are not currently available or can be obtained only at the expense of unwise sacrifices. At costs of 1960, the yearly cost of higher education is likely to be about one-third of the average family's income and perhaps one-fourth of the college family's income. Why not spread the costs over a much longer period, even over sixty years, or twenty years of savings before graduation and forty years of credit on the house-mortgage principal.

A combination of saving (implemented by insurance) and credit would greatly facilitate the financing of higher education. The issue of a government saving bond with a 1 to 2 per cent annual premium if cashed for higher education has much to recommend it. The 2 per cent premium might be used also to protect against inflation, though investments in equities may be a preferable approach. But given our attitude toward saving and spending, much more recourse is likely to be had to credit than savings. The latter has one advantage: compound interest works in favor of the project. But the former has two advantages. First, as inflation advances and per capita income grows, the borrower is able to repay under very favorable conditions. This average financing may be achieved with incomes two to four times those at time of borrowing. In fact loans of $1,000 per year would cost only about 1 per cent of probable lifetime income. By exploiting the inflationary and growth process, the borrower would pay back much less, relative to the supply of dollars available, than the real cost of the loan. In this manner the community, generally disposed to shirk its responsibility for education, is forced to contribute more to higher education than would otherwise be forthcoming. Second, in this credit age the service that does not exploit credit loses command of resources in competition with the increasing numbers that do.

Opposition to loan programs stems from lack of interest, poor administration, inadequate public relations, fear of some that a sound program would facilitate higher tuition (as it would), concern that those of low income would hesitate to borrow, and concern that a comprehensive borrowing program would result in excessive choice of professional education leading to high income.

I cannot here answer all the arguments adduced against loan financing, but I can say this: Often the terms are so onerous as to exclude use of loans; administration by the public welfare department (in one state) is obviously a deterrent; and unwise choice of curriculum can be averted by tying repayments to income, for example, 1 per cent of income.

Advances are beginning to be made: the National Defense Education Act, the various state programs, the forced acceptance of aid in part through loans by many outstanding IHL, the increased interest of banks and insurance companies, the possibility of recourse to government guarantees (the most spectacular advances of Federal finance since the war), the famous Massachusetts Institute of Technology plan (now supplemented by a provision for automatic borrowing for tuition in excess of $1,000 from the First National Bank of Boston), and the Harvard Business School programs—these are among the signs of a coming revolution in the financing of higher education.[12]

Above all, we emphasize the points that loan finance puts more responsibility on the student, enables institutions to raise tuition to a necessary level without excessive recourse to scholarships, puts higher education on a competitive basis with other services, forces the community to contribute more to higher education, and helps democratize education by providing finance to all who can profit from education—in the same manner that credit finance has put low-income groups in a position equal to the affluent as potential purchasers of cars and homes.

Government's Contribution

Before discussing government's contributions, I stress the point that tax exemptions are an important advantage for IHL. I estimate the exemption from property taxes at about $500 million (2½ per cent of

$20 billion of property at replacement value), and exemption from income tax at almost $75 million (one-half the income of endowment). We may expect further increases in the contribution of government. Currently state governments provide the largest subsidies. The Federal government's expenditures of about one-half billion dollars are primarily payments for services rendered (for example, research) rather than aid. President Furnas' paper raises some vital questions concerning the adequacy of compensation for research on Federal contracts, and Dr. Calkins has some relevant remarks on research generally vis-a-vis the IHL. How much is made available by state and local governments depends in part upon the income of the nation, the tax structure, and conflicting demands made upon government. For example, that state and local government receive less than 20 per cent of their income from direct taxes and the remainder from highly regressive taxes (as compared with more than 80 per cent by the Federal government from direct taxes on income) increases the difficulties of raising revenue, and especially so for higher education. The beneficiaries of outlays on higher education now or later may be classed as high-income groups.

Again, in the years before 1929, higher education became a favored recipient of state and local expenditures, a trend explained in part by the rising enrollments. But from 1929 to the end of World War II, the Depression and the large demands of the highway program tended to squeeze higher education. In the 1950s higher education again began to improve its relative position; in fact, in 1958 the percentage rise of expenditures on higher education exceeded all other major categories and was twice as great as that for highways.

In the future, getting more state revenue for higher education may become increasingly difficult. Highways, urban redevelopment, and

Table 4. State and Local Expenditures by Categories, 1902, 1922, 1938, 1953, and 1957

	1902	1922	1938	1953	1957
Total expenditures, $ million.........	188	1,397	4,598	16,850	24,234
Distribution of expenditures, per cent:					
Higher education................	7	10	5	8	8
Education: payments to local					
government..................	24	14	14	17	14
Highways.....................	3	27	25	22	25
Public welfare.................	5	3	10	9	11
Hospitals.....................	15	7	5	6	6

SOURCE: U.S. Census: *Historical Statistics of the State and Local Government Finances, 1902-1953*.

especially schools are likely to have high priorities. The usual estimate is that the public school costs (elementary and secondary) are likely to rise from $12 billion to $22 billion in ten years. With the current integration problem confronting the country, it is most unlikely that the Federal government will finance much of the increase. Urban governments are also not likely to be able to contribute much more. Hence state government is likely to have to provide most of the additional funds required for the schools.

In view of the burdens likely to fall upon state and local government in these areas, in view of the rise of their budgets and debts by 300 per cent since the end of World War II, in view of the increased opposition to further expenditures by state and local government, in view of the steady rise by at least 4 per cent in costs per year to meet rising prices of supplies and services without any expansion of activity, in view of all these factors it is not likely that state and local government will be able to expand their contributions by much more than $500 million, or less than 10 per cent of the additional funds required. Actually, $500 million additional annually in ten years reflects the trends as given by the percentage of income taken by these governments in taxes and the percentage of revenue going to higher education. Experience in the last ten years, however, points to the possibilities of a rise substantially more than $500 million, but these projections leave out of account the factors adumbrated above.

In a discussion of state contributions, we should distinguish one state from another. In general, the rich states absorb a smaller part of their income in supporting public institutions, experience smaller relative burdens (that is, smaller percentage of population is of college age), and yet achieve much more (that is, percentage of college-age population at college, or higher educational expenditures per member of college-age population). Unfortunately, many of the states with the largest resources, for example, New York and Connecticut, have no strong public higher education tradition and hence may not expand their public IHL greatly.

In this connection, the reader may be interested in a master table which I prepared for my forthcoming book on higher education and reproduce here as Table 5. The table gives for each of the then forty-eight states variables that throw light upon the following:

1. *Effort:* (a) state expenditures on higher education as a percentage of personal income, (b) total expenditures per student in state IHL (see note), (c) percentage of state tax revenue spent on higher education, (d) index of burden of state taxes, and (e) total state tax revenue per capita. NOTE: The comparisons in columns 7 and 8 of Table 5 are misleading to a small degree in so far as extension outlays vary.

2. *Burden of higher education.* The higher the percentage of college

Table 5. Higher Education and State Finance: Various Indices 1957*

State	(1) Per capita income $	Rank	(2) Current expend. state vs. pers. income Per cent	Rank	(3) Total state tax revenue per capita $	Rank	(4) State tax revenue vs. state pers. income Per cent	Rank	(5) Index of burden of state taxes Index	Rank	(6) Current expend. state IHL vs. state tax revenue Per cent	Rank	(7) Current expend. state IHL per state IHL student $	Rank	(8) Current expend. all IHL per student $	Rank	(9) Total IHL enrollment vs. college-age population Per cent	Rank	(10) Fall enrollment state IHL vs. total IHL enrollment Per cent	Rank	(11) College-age population vs. total population Per cent	Rank
Alabama	1,324	44	0.447	24	72.63	38	5.51	14	4.16	6	8.11	26	613	43	711	28	11.50	44	74.74	10	11.42	4
Arizona	1,750	27	0.488	19	99.28	12	5.38	16	3.07	16	9.07	20	443	48	431	48	25.87	6	97.41	2	10.35	12
Arkansas	1,151	47	0.517	18	70.37	41	6.16	7	5.35	3	8.40	24	728	34	872	7–8	10.07	48	75.92	42	12.13	2
California	2,523	4	0.541	14–15	117.96	5	4.66	27	1.85	36	11.60	1	1,722	1	621	42	35.52	1	32.36	43	12.47	4
Colorado	1,996	16	0.594	10	92.16	15	4.59	29	2.30	29	12.94	9	918	16	814	14	29.91	4	58.00	24	8.00	41
Connecticut	2,821	1	0.164	44	100.31	10	3.58	40	1.27	46	4.57	45	663	40	803	15	24.02	8	30.00	45	7.45	45
Delaware	2,740	2	0.296	36	102.03	9	3.72	37	1.36	45	7.94	27	694	36	606	44	19.68	24	95.93	3	7.14	47
Florida	1,836	24	0.278	38	89.25	18	4.99	21	2.72	21	5.57	43	776	29	653	37	17.64	30	51.97	29	7.20	46
Georgia	1,431	41	0.351	31	83.40	24	5.82	9	4.07	19	6.04	41	642	37	629	39	11.59	43	64.43	17	10.42	11
Idaho	1,630	35	0.401	28	78.63	29	4.86	23	2.98	20	8.24	25	677	37	627	40	15.22	36	63.72	18	10.39	11
Illinois	2,447	6	0.255	39	71.22	40	2.93	46	1.20	40	8.71	22	1,289	3	802	15	21.40	18	28.34	44	8.01	40
Indiana	2,010	15	0.461	22	86.15	22	3.27	42	1.73	40	14.09	4	949	14	774	18	20.26	20	56.83	25	8.72	28
Iowa	1,806	26	0.602	9	99.25	23	4.10	33	2.31	28	14.28	3	1,913	1	777	17	26.37	5	54.00	26	9.15	15
Kansas	1,892	23	0.237	40	89.39	13	4.14	33	3.51	12	13.57	7	584	46	758	22	15.84	43	67.81	14	10.74	16
Kentucky	1,372	43	0.243	43	75.15	34	4.82	24	4.96	4	5.05	44	806	23	619	43	12.07	43	45.36	40	9.98	16
Louisiana	1,566	37	0.530	16	121.63	3	4.76	22	2.71	25	6.83	33	840	23	866	8	15.84	45	67.81	35	9.91	39
Maine	1,663	33	0.301	35	75.15	34	4.50	30	1.86	33	6.68	35	726	26	786	9	11.74	42	57.99	24	8.17	36
Maryland	2,156	10	0.279	37	86.58	22	4.02	35	2.16	33	6.96	26	804	26	833	19	18.89	19	51.16	26	8.09	39
Massachusetts	2,335	8	0.084	48	85.68	23	3.64	39	2.57	41	2.32	48	726	35	872	3	30.04	9	11.70	47	8.50	36
Michigan	2,141	11	0.646	11–12	88.18	11	4.62	28	2.16	33	12.11	15	770	30	822	11	20.99	19	64.83	13	8.83	26
Minnesota	1,850	23	0.577	21	74.11	21	4.76	35	2.57	25	6.18	39	602	44	661	31	23.10	10	68.01	3	11.91	3
Mississippi	958	48	0.474	43	72.80	35	7.67	48	8.01	33	5.83	42	628	42	684	35	10.84	45	60.35	13	8.71	29
Missouri	1,940	18	0.188	41	74.44	44	3.22	44	1.66	25	12.48	26	803	31	635	33	19.75	10	35.20	41	8.49	3
Montana	1,896	21	0.520	17	58.44	17	4.79	39	2.20	39	6.21	42	908	21	732	23	35.20	45	82.11	29	8.56	29
Nebraska	1,896	25	0.439	24	134.61	46	3.12	45	2.23	30–31	2.97	48	882	24	732	5	22.52	31	53.42	23	8.49	23
Nevada	2,423	5	0.338	27	83.05	26	1.99	48	1.68	48	7.47	44	815	22	1,157	1	13.84	33	100.00	1	8.56	48
New Hampshire	1,862	22	0.405	45	49.98	48	6.94	41	0.79	48	12.97	33	925	24	925	2	21.84	35	52.17	28	8.32	31
New Jersey	2,504	3	0.149	47	119.45	19	3.52	48	1.37	44	2.54	47	743	33	641	37	16.78	33	45.10	37	8.58	34
New Mexico	1,686	31	0.885	3	89.20	25	6.24	42	4.12	11	7.18	30	1,005	21	804	34	17.05	34	93.82	42	7.96	6
New York	2,578	45	0.089	31	82.69	27	3.26	43	4.74	13	13.87	6	1,326	2	675	41	24.41	48	9.05	45	11.05	42
North Carolina	1,317	40	0.448	45	80.23	27	3.95	44	3.90	13	9.95	47	924	29	928	29	11.88	41	50.92	6	9.77	17–18
North Dakota	1,435	36	0.777	9	53.51	36	6.39	5	1.45	43	9.45	30	755	23	719	26	18.71	29	90.33	13	9.77	37–38
Ohio	2,255	9	0.201	42	73.51	6	3.53	6	3.95	18	6.16	45	597	45	580	45	19.69	23	24.93	45	10.01	13
Oklahoma	1,619	36	0.610	23	104.44	17	4.22	31	2.99	10	9.95	18	1,177	6	720	12	22.66	12	74.47	43	9.06	22–23
Oregon	1,914	20	0.534	13	111.29	8	3.65	38	1.83	34	9.45	38	597	32	705	31	22.86	22	50.33	25	8.86	25
Pennsylvania	2,190	12	0.230	46	72.35	37	4.22	45	1.58	37	6.31	36	1,096	7	707	39	10.61	3	16.36	46	8.86	4
Rhode Island	1,990	17	0.424	41	73.00	45	3.97	36	2.59	24	6.31	37	1,488	4	701	47	23.26	47	40.36	39	11.11	20
South Carolina	1,180	46	0.682	4	61.56	39	5.61	11	4.06	9	6.79	3	1,472	29	708	27	10.61	21	42.39	27	9.24	7
South Dakota	1,531	39	0.381	30	71.81	39	4.03	34	3.14	30–31	8.49	23	1,040	17	761	20–21	21.54	46	75.16	40	10.95	24
Tennessee	1,383	42	0.342	32	91.36	16	5.32	17	3.35	13	7.65	28	752	32	566	46	14.33	20	53.49	20	8.88	24
Texas	1,791	30	0.939	1	94.37	13	5.58	13	3.02	13	11.84	17	667	46	533	40	20.44	2	36.85	18	9.52	14
Utah	1,694	30	0.661	5	82.53	26	5.01	20	3.35	17	7.65	28	778	28	761	20	34.88	2	62.53	18	8.88	9
Vermont	1,665	32	0.396	29	130.25	2	6.13	8	2.88	20	7.91	20	900	8	900	18	21.20	38	46.26	35	9.52	19
Virginia	1,660	34	0.577	11–12	79.03	28	5.05	19	3.25	17	9.42	19	1,087	20	655	13	13.73	39	64.68	21	9.06	22–23
Washington	2,128	13	0.341	33	79.03	14	4.80	25	2.50	14	6.75	34	543	47	799	46	22.58	13	61.30	16	8.29	35
West Virginia	1,554	38	0.426	25	61.30	28	5.20	18	2.55	27	8.87	22	731	24	731	24	18.68	27	75.00	12	12.28	1
Wisconsin	1,920	19	0.614	7	105.68	7	4.80	18	2.55	26	11.81	15	849	22	761	20–21	18.68	27	62.43	9	8.62	30
Wyoming	2,038	14	0.614	7	105.68	7	5.20	18	2.55	26	11.81	15	1,119	22	761	20–21	17.83	28	68.66	19	9.77	17–18

*Except column 8, which is for 1955–56 and columns 7 and 10 (enrollment) which are for November, 1956. (Columns 2, 3, 4, 5, 6, and item 7 relate to fiscal year 1957.) Description, sources, and other explanations are appended; see p. 78.

age to total population the greater the burden. Compare, for example, Nevada's 6.49 per cent and Mississippi's 11.91 per cent. (This great need and small resources explain in part the large effort and yet the poor results for a state like Mississippi.)

3. *Achievements:* (*a*) percentage of enrollment to total college-age population (ages eighteen to twenty-four) [compare Utah (30.48 per cent) to Maine (8.62 per cent)] and (*b*) *percentage enrollment in public institutions* [compare Nevada (100 per cent) and Massachusetts (11.7 per cent)].

Table 5 throws much light on the situation in 1957. One may ask why, for example, Utah's record is so much better than Nevada's. They are both states with small populations and therefore high-cost operations. Yet though one-third of its students are in private institutions, Utah spends almost 2½ times as large a percentage of its personal income on public higher education and enrolls 2½ times as many students relative to its college-age population as Nevada.

Others may wish to explain the superb record in public higher educa-

Table 6. Comparison of Ten High and Ten Low Per Capita Income States with Regard to Population, Enrollment, Income Payments to Individuals, and IHL Expenditures All Institutions, Twenty States, 1950

Point of comparison	10 high per capita income states	10 low per capita income states
Total population..	45,640,201	27,699,294
Total college-age population............................	2,265,000	1,804,000
Proportion of college-age population to total population, per cent...	4.96	6.51
Total state support of higher education, $ thousand........	154,435	74,633
Total income payments to individuals of the state, $ million	81,054	25,439
Proportion of state support of higher education to total income payments for individuals, per cent................	0.190	0.293
Total resident enrollment..............................	792,473	326,865
Proportion of resident enrollment to college-age population, per cent..	35.0	18.1
Total educational and general expense, $ thousand.........	616,257	207,906
Educational and general expense per member of total population..	$13.50	$7.51
Educational and general expense per member of college-age population..	$272.08	$115.25

SOURCE: All data based on Council of State Governments, *Higher Education in the Forty-Eight States, 1952*, pp. 86–87, 170–72, 191, 194–95, 209–57. (Our computations.)

tion in the West, the average record in the Middle West, vast differences between such states as Oklahoma and Kansas, say, on the one hand, and Missouri and Ohio on the other. And what of the poor record in public higher education in Massachusetts, New York, Connecticut, Pennsylvania, and New Jersey?

Table 6 gives the results for the ten richest and the ten poorest states.

In general, the rich states profit from a lower percentage of college-age population, and though in 1950 they spent only about two-thirds as much for public higher education relative to their personal income, their high incomes nevertheless yielded in dollars twice as much state support. The rich states also had a relative enrollment twice as great, *total* higher educational expenditures three times as great, and total expenditures per member of the population twice as great and per member of the college-age population 2⅓ times as great in each instance as the poor states. Or compare Mississippi and New York.

Table 7. Mississippi and New York; Relevant Variables, 1957, Higher Education

Point of comparison	New York		Mississippi	
	Per cent or $	Rank	Per cent or $	Rank
State expenditures on higher education as percentage of personal income of residents	0.089	47	0.474	20
All expenditures per member of college-age population..........................	$218.99	10	$80.44	48
Proportion of state tax revenue spent on higher education, per cent.............	2.54	47	6.18	39
Proportion of college-age population (18–24) to total population, per cent...........	8.29	40	11.96	2
Proportion of enrollment to total college-age population, per cent...................	23.24	5	9.66	43
Enrollment in public institutions, per cent	35.12	44	78.84	11

SOURCE: Various publications of the Dept. of Health, Education and Welfare and U.S. Census.

Table 7 shows that the poor state has much greater burden (percentage of public expenditures in relation to income and tax receipts, and percentage of state taxes for education) and yet achieves much less (expenditures per member of college-age population and percentage of college population enrolled).

What of the Federal Government? If we succeed in maintaining a healthy economy, our GNP should rise by $150 billion to $250 billion, or by from one-third to more than one-half, by 1970. Federal revenues would then rise at current tax structures by about $40 billion (average) within 10 years. On the assumption that the international situation does not deteriorate ·greatly, the Federal government should be able to contribute more toward financing higher education.

Higher education should have a high priority. The $900 million four-year post-sputnik program under the National Defense Education Act of 1958, only part of which is available for IHL, does not promise too much for the future. One may even question the value judgments of the government: two years earlier, they embarked on a $24-billion road program over thirteen years; two years later, they reappraised the program and found it would cost 40 per cent more.

Surely a contribution of $500 million additional per year for higher education in ten years (exclusive of research) is not unreasonable and one of a billion dollars is not extravagant. Actually I have assumed a rise of $1.3 billion, but it will be noted that about three-fourths is for research and only one-fourth is for increased resources for scholarships, buildings, and the like. (Throughout I assume stable prices and a growth of GNP of 4 per cent per year, as in the years 1948–58.) My proposed nonresearch increase of about $400 million is consistent with some expansion of outlays on defense, housing, social security, development of natural resources, urban redevelopment, area development, and the like; and even with some reduction in taxes.[13]

After much reflection, I have concluded that aid should be in the form of direct grants or loans, not tax remissions. The latter are wasteful; for help is given irrespective of need. Moreover, further erosion of the tax base should not be encouraged. I am even critical of the tax credit program sponsored by the American Council on Education. The non-tax-paying families would get no relief, and from one-third to one-half of the families would receive more relief than is needed. Perhaps the largest contribution that the Federal government can make is through grants-in-aid (on the Hill-Burton hospital parallel) for buildings, as well as credit for buildings and for student loans. Guarantees of student loans for financial agencies, as in housing, would also be helpful. A scholarship program with free choice to students and based on need as well as ability is also on the agenda, although a really successful loan program might greatly reduce the need for scholarships.

Perhaps the toughest problem is the financing of non-revenue-yielding buildings. They are not included in the operations budgets. Unless large economies are achieved in their use, we may be short $500 million yearly. Many public IHL are selling bonds to finance the buildings and propose to use tuition to retire the bonds. The Federal housing program provides loans for dormitories, but a new Federal program to provide grants-in-aid for academic building is sorely needed.

Philanthropy

It is possible that gifts and interest on endowment may provide $600 million annually additional within ten years and thus roughly double the returns from private sources. With the marked improvement in private sources, it is even possible, though unlikely, that the *additional* contribution might rise to $1 billion. But we should not count on that.

In the years since 1929, higher education has experienced a deterioration of its share of the philanthropic dollar. Emergence of demands with a higher priority tied to the Depression and war and the improved methods of raising money by such organizations as Red Cross and Community Funds have reduced the relative funds for higher education. But in the 1950s the growth of alumni drives, appeals to business, development funds, and greatly improved organization are reflected in an improvement, relative and absolute, in the position of higher education. The president of a fine technical school, criticized by his faculty for spending $100,000 for development and the like, could reply that gifts had increased by $1 million yearly.

Possibilities of raising money through private sources are far from completely realized. The drive on corporations yields about $150 million yearly according to the Council for Financial Aid to Education, on or about ⅓ of 1 per cent of corporate profits before taxes, at a cost to the stockholder of less than $45 million. (In general, the expansion of gifts is an excellent method of inducing a government to contribute without danger of interference.) With a maximum allowance of 5 per cent of income, contributions even of 2 per cent would yield almost $1 billion today and $1.5 billion or more ten years from now. With institutions of higher education receiving 25 per cent of the total, their *gains* over current receipts would be $100 million now and about $225 million ten years from now.

Nor has the alumni fund realized its possibilities. At present 1 million alumni of 5 million solicited give $25 million per year. Why could we not expect 20 million college men and women to give an average of $35 each, or a total of $700 million per year, within about ten years? The actual cost to the donor would be about $25. A tight organization like the Community Fund might yield such revenue. In ten years the average college graduate should have an income of at least $10,000, and $25 would be but $\frac{1}{400}$ of it. The women, about one-third of the total, would probably be able to contribute less.

Endowment is concentrated among a limited number of institutions;

fifty IHL account for most of it. Moreover, with the rise of prices, the increased cost of higher education in stable prices, reduced returns per dollar invested, mistakes in management in the 1920s and 1930s, the rise of tax rates, and the increase of enrollment, endowment's relative contribution steadily declines. Since the war, despite the reluctant move to equities, inflation has cost IHL about $1 billion of their prewar endowment, or roughly one-third. Whereas endowment accounted for 25 per cent of income in 1900, by 1929 the total was 10 per cent and by 1956 only 5 per cent. Gifts provided 5 per cent in 1929 and provide about 9 per cent currently.

The day of the great dependence on endowment is at an end. Indeed, a small number of institutions still rely greatly on endowment, but even for most of those, inclusive of those most heavily involved, the income of productive funds steadily becomes less important. In many ways that is unfortunate. Endowment protects institutions against outside pressures, and it also enables them to carry through long-range programs. It should be added, however, that where these advantages might well be most important, that is, for the public IHL, the contribution of endowment is least important. Though these institutions account for 60 per cent of enrollment, their endowment income is less than 10 per cent of the total and their gifts, incidentally, little more than 10 per cent.

We should perhaps add a few comments on gifts and income from productive funds. First, the colleges have been slow to move into common stocks. The case for heavy investments in common stocks is strong indeed when the inflationary trend is considered, and when note is taken of the fact that the corporation is run for the stockholder. Unless bonds yield, say, 2 per cent more than stocks to offset inflationary trends and 3 per cent additional to reflect growth, the case for bonds is weak indeed. Table 8 reveals a reluctance to move into equities. Only by the 1950s were more than 50 per cent of funds in common stock, and even so the rise is explained largely by the increase in the prices of stock, not by aggressive buying of equities.

Second, there is much to be said for accounting procedures that make it possible to make the most effective use of new funds. I assume that the new money is more likely to be tied to current educational needs than restricted endowment funds received, say, twenty-five, fifty, or a hundred years ago. Here I would urge treasurers to enter incoming money at book value in funds where market value exceeds book value. Hence with book values at $20 million and market values at $30 million, the result would be that a new gift of $1 million would earn $\frac{1}{21}$, not $\frac{1}{31}$, of the income. Nuclear physics would gain at the expense of paleontology, and perhaps twenty-five years from now space research would gain at the expense of both nuclear physics and paleontology.

Table 8. Structure of Investment, Colleges and Universities, 1926 to 1957

Source of data	Year	Value, $ million	No. of IHL	Percentage of						
				Bonds	Preferred	Common	Mortgage	Real estate	Plant	Other
Cain[a]	1926	All	8	59.7	9.0	9.2	10.1	5.3	5.5	1.2
	1929	in		62.0	5.4	9.9	12.7	4.6	4.5	0.9
	1933	excess		59.0	5.5	12.7	11.6	7.2	3.2	0.8
	1940	15		42.2	8.2	29.3	4.3	9.7	1.9	4.6
Teachers college[b]	1929	549	45	45.2	5.8	12.6	12.2	18.4	1.4	4.4
	1940	686	45	39.5	9.0	20.6	9.3	16.3	2.0	3.4
Wood, Struthers[c]	1931	537	29	49.8	7.8	10.0	13.5	13.1	...	5.8
Association of American Colleges[d]	1931	614	143 indep. colleges	49.3	5.1	5.1	21.7	10.4	...	6.0
Cain[e]	1940	1,263	120	40.3	10.3	21.8	7.7	15.3	...	4.6
Kirkpatrick[f]	1938	428	12	38.7	10.7	22.5	7.9	15.7	...	4.5
	1947	532	12	42.9	9.2	29.5	4.0	11.4	...	3.0
Scudder, Stevens and Clark[g]	1946	1,300	59	42.0	11.0	30.0	5.5	8.0	cash = 2½	0.5
Cain[h]	1950	1,466	29	45.3	8.0	28.7[i]		16.2	...	1.8
	1951	1,566	29	43.9	7.7	29.5[i]		16.6	...	2.3
Barron's[j]	1952	783	15	39.2	8.5	52.3[k]				
Boston Fund[l]	1956	2,770	56	30.4[m]	4.6	56.5		6.0	1.5	1.0
	1957	2,490	42	32.0[m]	3.3	56.1		8.4		1.2

[a] J. H. Cain, *What Is Happening to College and University Investments and Income?*, American Council on Education Studies, June, 1941, p. 30.
[b] *The Administration of College and University Endowments*, p. 44.
[c] Wood, Struthers & Co.: *Trusteeship of American Endowments*, 1932, Table I.
[d] *Bulletin of the Association of American Colleges*, 1932, p. 74. Totals do not add to 100 per cent.
[e] Cain, *op. cit.*, p. 37.
[f] J. I. Kirkpatrick, *A Study of University Endowment Funds*, 1947, p. 41.
[g] Scudder, Stevens and Clark, *Survey of University and College Endowment Funds*, 1947, p. 17.
[h] J. H. Cain, "College Investment Funds and How They Grow," *College and University Business*, July, 1952, p. 25.
[i] The low level of common stocks is explained by the fact that they are valued at book and hence, by 1950, common stocks are substantially undervalued.
[j] *Barron's*, Mar. 16, 1953.
[k] $143 million, or more than one-third of common stock value, is at book value and hence common stocks are undervalued to this extent. But this breakdown excludes non-security investments. If included, the 52 per cent would be reduced to about 42 per cent. Hence total given is roughly accurate.
[l] *Boston Fund: A Study of College and University Endowment Funds at June 30, 1956*; *Brevits*, by Vance, Sanders & Company, vol. N, no. 21; and *Barron's*, June 17, 1957.
[m] Includes cash.

Third, management of endowment funds should be in the hands of competent men. We have evidence that, when such expertness is not exploited, serious mistakes are made. In this connection we note that the college with small endowment funds cannot afford to manage its own funds. (In the sixty-college study,[14] endowment income varies from 8 to 70 per cent of income.) We need to consider further the issues raised in the 1930s of setting up an organization for handling small endowment funds. Treasurers were fearful of relinquishing their responsibilities by entrusting funds to an institution formed for this purpose. But more recently the same results are being achieved through purchases of shares in investment funds.

Fourth, we are not likely to repeat the egregious mistakes of the 1930s, of relying on formulas which forced treasurers to sell once common stock shares rose beyond a given point and to buy when a given low point was reached.

Fifth, accounting methods as well as investing methods require special consideration. An institution that overdepreciates may cheat its faculty, as at least the administration of one outstanding IHL has been accused of doing. Again, a college that invests heavily in growth stocks for years and does not sell or distribute to offset unrealized gains may be sacrificing its present generation of faculty and students in favor of later generations.

It is possible that the yield of gifts and returns on endowment will rise by $1 billion in ten years. This assumes a sustained drive in the next ten years. Strong pressures in the 1950s were highly successful. Above I suggested a goal of $300 million additional from business and $700 million from alumni gifts within ten years. We certainly should achieve at least half of that sum, or $500 million. In addition, on the basis of the history of the last ten years, we should receive $100 million additional from endowment, or a total rise of $600 million. In this connection we note the estimate of the Council for Financial Aid to Education: a rise of $700 million in nine years ending 1957–58 and in excess of $1,050 million in the twelve years ending 1969–70. A range from $500 million to $1,000 million seems as reasonable a prediction as we can make. If we should achieve the $500 million additional from alumni and business and $100 million from endowment incomes and allow for additional bequests, gifts from foundations, and the like, then the total rise might well exceed $1,000 million by 1970. In part, however, these funds would be available not for our operating budget, but for capital.

Faculty Salaries

Having discussed income, I now turn to the most important cost item, faculty salaries, a central problem in higher education. Here is one of the largest factors bringing about higher costs. Of the total additional bill of $6+ billion, resident instruction, mainly faculty salaries, accounts for more than half. In so far as economies can be introduced, that far the incremental costs of $3.5 billion might be reduced. The proposed increase in pay of 100 per cent over ten years would still not reestablish faculty pay relative to the national pay scale at prewar ratios. The economic status of the college faculty is not by any means what it used to be. In the ninety years since President Eliot introduced a $4,000 salary for full professors, the Harvard average pay for full professors has risen by 300 per cent, prices by 220 per cent, and per capita incomes by 1,300 per cent. Faculty salaries have lagged far behind. From the 1930s to 1956–57 the pay of a full professor in stable dollars at Yale, Columbia, John Hopkins, and Harvard has fallen almost 20 per cent, whereas in the same period that of the average member of the labor market has risen 50 per cent, a relative decline of almost 50 per cent for full professors in outstanding institutions.

But these figures give a somewhat exaggerated picture of the relative decline of income status. First, faculty members now devote a somewhat larger proportion of their time to outside activities for which they receive pay. Second, the proportion of young members of the faculty has greatly increased, as is to be expected in view of the large increase in numbers. Hence to this extent, a given salary for a faculty member in 1960 reflects somewhat higher pay than the same salary in the past. In twenty outstanding liberal arts colleges, in large urban and Catholic institutions, there is evidence of a substantial decline in the proportion of full professors. Finally, fringe benefits have increased to some extent.

Against these factors tending to overstate the decline in economic status are a few that suggest understatement of the loss of economic status. One is the rise of educational achievement of the average faculty member. A second is the increased recourse to part-time faculty, who on the whole, are greatly exploited. Over-all, however, the net results of these factors point to a somewhat smaller loss than is generally estimated.

How much should salaries rise? I have accepted the widely used figure of 100 per cent. Indeed, if increases have already been large, the goal might be more modest; if they have been small, a rise in excess of 100 per cent might be invoked.

What criteria might be used? Previous relationships are one. On that basis, salaries would have to rise more than 100 per cent. The increase that would elicit adequate supplies of teachers of minimum quality is a second measure of need. Since the additional numbers of college faculty needed in the absence of large economies is 100 per cent in ten years, it should be compared with estimated population growth in fifteen years of only about 20 to 25 per cent, of workers by 25 per cent, of white-collar workers by 41 per cent, and of all professional workers by 56 per cent. It is clear that the pay of college faculty must greatly exceed the 30 per cent (in stable prices) to be expected for the whole population. A third measure is the value system in the Soviet Union, which yields an average professional salary that is several times the average worker's salary. On that basis the average college salary now in excess of $6,000 should be at least $25,000 by 1970. However we measure the needed rise, the conclusion is the same: We need a substantial increase in faculty salaries.

It is possible to keep the bill down if we economize on faculty. Since economies are treated elsewhere in this volume, and in full in my forthcoming book, I shall be brief in my observations here. It is possible

Table 9. Current Income of Institutions of Higher Education 1930-70

(In millions of dollars)

Item	1929-30	1939-40	1953-54	1955-56	1957-58	1969-70
Educational and general income:						
Student fees....................	144.1	200.9	554.2	725.9	904.3	3,800*
Federal government:						
For veterans education........	.....	.....	44.4	15.6⎫		
For research................	†	†	282.4	355.6⎬	534.9⎫	
For other purposes...........	20.7	38.9	92.8	122.7⎭		3,700‡
State governments..............	150.8	151.2	751.6	891.6	1,086.1⎭	
Local governments.............	†	24.4	88.2	106.9	130.7⎫	
Endowment earnings...........	68.6	71.3	127.5	145.0	166.6⎬	
Private benefactions...........	26.2	40.5	191.3	245.5	411.0⎭	1,200§
Sales and services..............	†	32.8	165.5	192.4		
Other educational and general....	72.7	11.4	58.6	80.5	346.1	500
Subtotal, educational and general......................	483.1	571.3	2,356.5	2,881.8	3,579.7	9,200
Student aid income..............	†	†	32.9	53.0	70.0	600
Subtotal, education, general, and student aid...........	483.1	571.3	2,389.4	2,934.8	3,649.7	9,800¶
Auxiliary enterprises income.......	60.4	143.9	576.8	694.0	NA	NA
Other current income.............	11.0	†	......	......	NA	NA
Total current income..........	554.5	715.2	2,966.3	3,628.8	NA	NA

NOTE: Figures are rounded and do not necessarily add to totals.
NA: Not available.
* Calculated from 900, current fees + 800, for 90 per cent rise of enrollment + 2,550, tuition rate increase (4 million at 375 = 1,500; 2 million at 525 = 1,050) = $4,250 million. Deduct $450 million for rise of part-time and increased percentage in low-cost units.
† Data not reported separately.
‡ Federal (research) = 1,300; Federal (other) = 500; state = 1,700; local = 200.
§ Endowment = 300; gifts = 900.
¶ Educational and general and student aid, in 1969-70 dollars (assumption, 20 per cent inflation ten years) is $11,760 million.
SOURCE: Office of Education, 1930-56; Council for Financial Aid to Education, 1958; and estimates of the author.

to reduce the number of small classes, alternate more courses, concentrate on lectures supplemented by discussion groups, reduce course requirements for students (and hence save faculty time and stimulate independent study) and provide much more assistance. What businessman of ability would require of his staff who receive $6 per hour for time put in, as do the senior faculties of the better IHL, that they perform such tasks as grading papers, writing letters in longhand, and collecting minutiae for research, tasks which could be performed at a cost of $1–$2 per hour? It is certainly not unreasonable to expect that, through recourse to the suggested measures, the teaching bill might be cut by 25 per cent, or $1 billion in ten years.

We assume here that with the rise of enrollment, competition for faculty will gradually raise salaries to the level here suggested. Obviously, additional resources must flow into college treasuries if these rises are to be forthcoming. Furthermore, we assume that the flow of

Table 10. Current Expenditures of Institutions of Higher Education 1930–70
(In millions of dollars)

Item	1929–30	1939–40	1953–54	1955–56	1957–58	1969–70
Educational and general expenditures:						
Administrative and general expense	42.9	62.8	290.5	358.4	NA	1,000.0
Resident instruction	221.3	280.2	966.8	1,148.5	NA	4,600.0
Organized research	18.0	27.3	374.9	506.1	NA	2,100.0
Extension	25.0	35.3	114.7	141.1⎱	NA	300.0
Libraries	9.6	19.5	73.4	86.1⎰	NA	
Plant operation and maintenance	61.1	69.6	280.0	326.3	NA	700.0
Related activities	*	27.2	188.0	222.3	NA	500.0
Subtotal, educational and general	377.9	522.0	2,288.4	2,788.8	3,700.0	9,200.0
Student aid expenditures	*	*	74.8	96.2	100.0	600.0
Subtotal, education, general, and student aid	377.9	522.0	2,363.2	2,885.0	3,800.0	9,800.0
Auxiliary enterprises expenditures	*	124.2	539.3	639.7	NA	NA
Other current expenditures	129.2	28.5	*	*	NA	NA
Total current expenditures	507.1	674.7	2,902.5	3,524.7		

* Data not reported separately.
NA: Not available.
NOTE: Figures are rounded and do not necessarily add to totals.
SOURCE: Office of Education, 1930–56; Council for Financial Aid to Education, 1958; estimates of the author, 1970.

Table 11. Regular Sessions Enrollments
in Institutions of Higher Education
1900–70

Academic year	Enrollments			Public institutions as percentage of total	Enrollment as percentage of college-age population
	Total	Public institutions	Private institutions		
Actual					
1899–1900	237,592	91,400	146,192	38.5	4.0
1909–10	355,312	166,560	188,655	46.9	5.1
1919–20	597,682	308,570	289,112	51.6	8.1
1929–30	1,100,737	537,001	563,736	48.8	12.4
1939–40	1,494,203	796,531	697,672	53.3	15.7
1941–42	1,403,990	732,111	671,879	52.1	14.7
1943–44	1,155,272	571,406	583,866	49.5	12.7
1945–46	1,676,851	....	....	...	20.8
1947–48	2,616,262	1,326,147	1,290,115	50.7	28.9
1949–50	2,659,021	1,354,902	1,304,119	51.0	29.8
1951–52	2,301,884	1,155,557	1,146,327	50.2	26.8
1953–54	2,514,712	1,356,481	1,158,231	53.9	29.9
1954–55*	2,755,000	1,533,000	1,222,000	55.6	32.1
1955–56*	2,996,000	1,687,000	1,309,000	56.3	35.1
1956–57*	3,244,000	1,849,000	1,395,000	57.0	36.3
1957–58*	3,376,000	1,948,000	1,428,000	57.7	37.3
1958–59*	3,585,000	2,090,000	1,495,000	58.3	38.6
Projections					
1959–60	3,778,000	2,227,000	1,551,000	58.9	39.4
1960–61	3,964,000	2,361,000	1,603,000	59.6	38.9
1961–62	4,212,000	2,533,000	1,679,000	60.1	39.5
1962–63	4,451,000	2,704,000	1,747,000	60.8	40.4
1963–64	4,657,000	2,857,000	1,800,000	61.3	41.5
1964–65	4,860,000	3,011,000	1,849,000	62.0	40.1
1965–66	5,199,000	3,252,000	1,947,000	62.6	40.3
1966–67	5,564,000	3,514,000	2,050,000	63.2	40.6
1967–68	5,926,000	3,776,000	2,150,000	63.7	41.0
1968–69	6,243,000	4,013,000	2,230,000	64.3	43.6
1969–70	6,443,000	4,174,000	2,269,000	64.8	44.4

* Estimates.

SOURCE: Office of Education. 1900–54: *Biennial Survey of Education, 1954–56*, chap. 4, sec. 1, p. 8 and subsidiary tables. 1954–70: Informal estimates contained in statement dated May 18, 1959.

teachers of adequate ability will be forthcoming; a distinct possibility is higher pay for low-quality teachers. In so far as economies in use of manpower are achieved, pay may rise even more than is here assumed, or the required funds for instruction may rise much less than is here assumed. In so far as the rise of enrollment is to be disproportionately in two-year and four-year commuting colleges generally, to that extent a rise of 100 per cent in faculty pay would in fact mean an increase in excess of 100 per cent, and the increase is likely to be disproportionately

Table 12. Explanation of Increase of Tuition Income of $2,900 million

(In millions of dollars)

Increase of enrollment		800
Higher fees:		
Public, 4 million at $375 ($150 to $525)	1,500	
Private, 2 million at $525 ($600 to $1,125)	1,050	
Gross tuition increase		2,550
		3,350
Reduction of $450 million associated with a disproportionate increase of junior college students:		
500,000 with saving of $400	200	
Additional students saving because 40 per cent of junior college students are part time (others are 20 per cent part time) = 100,000 × 300 = ...	30	
Other savings resulting from movement to lower-cost IHL	220	
Net tuition increase		450
		2,900

in young teachers. Again a 100 per cent rise would not be necessary. Possibly where we allow for these factors, the increase in payroll might not have to exceed 75 per cent. The resulting savings may be of the order of $500 million.

Conclusion

I estimate the costs of higher education by 1970 at $9 billion to $10 billion, $11 billion if capital expenditures are included and in excess of $13 billion if we assume reasonably that prices will rise by 20 per cent by 1970 (about 1½ per cent a year).

This is a goal. We may not achieve it, and attainment will be more difficult with inflation than without. By this I mean that it will be more difficult to obtain $13 billion with a 20 per cent inflation than $11 billion without inflation. If faculty and administration should cooperate in eliminating waste, both in the curriculum and elsewhere, without serious effects on the educational product, then financial requirements might be reduced by $1 billion to $2 billion and the probability of reaching our goal would be greatly increased.

The 6+ million students will go to IHL even if income for higher education does not reach the $9, $11, or $13 billion goals suggested above, but they will receive a deteriorated product. Faculty salaries will not double, and the relative deterioration of economic status will continue and might even increase. (A 7 per cent rise per year is required in order to double salaries in ten years; an increase of about 11 to 12 per cent is required in order not only to double as required to recoup past losses and prevent the opening of a new gap.) Failure to obtain required funds would also be reflected in inadequacies of plant.

My best-informed guesses suggest that government, private philanthropy, and economies are not going to close the gap between current outlays of $3+ billion ($4 billion inclusive of capital) and projected outlays of $9+ billion, $11+ billion, and $13+ billion. Hence, rising tuition rates will have to contribute a substantial part of the total budgetary requirements. For private IHL there is no doubt about this; for public IHL the tradition of low rates will slow up the rise. Moreover, conditions vary from state to state. Where traditions of free higher education are strong (and hence political influence of numerous students and alumni of public IHL great), economic growth is rapid, incomes are high, taxes are reasonably progressive, and competing demands for tax money are moderate, tuition may not rise greatly. It is my view, however, that there would have to be and should be substantial rises in many states.

And if primitive methods of financing students are abandoned and adequate recourse is made to long-term loans and scholarships based on need, then not only can our financial problems be solved but equity can be served. That a much larger percentage of students will be at commuting colleges and other IHL within commuting distance and that the proportion of members of the labor market earning regular income and going to college part-time will greatly increase will facilitate student financing. We should also aggressively tap all other sources, and the Federal government should contribute more than currently.

Notes

1. Calculated from Dept. of Health, Education and Welfare, *Statistics of Higher Education, 1955–56, Faculty, Students and Degrees.*

2. The Rockefeller report (*The Challenge to America: Its Economic and Social Aspects,* 1958, p. 72) estimates GNP at $642 billion in 1967 on the assumption of an annual rise of 4 per cent, the gains in the years 1947–57.

3. Department of Health, Education and Welfare, *Retention and Withdrawal of College Students,* 1958, pp. 16, 18.

4. Emory University, *Pilot Study, Analysis of Expenditures, Medical Education Program, 1954–55,* December, 1956, p. 14. (Mimeographed.)

5. See J. D. Russell, "Early Notes on Experience in Coordination of State Higher Education," *Current Issues in Higher Education,* 1952, pp. 83–85.

6. H. L. Wells, *Higher Education Is Serious Business,* 1953, p. 24.

7. *Nature and Needs of Higher Education,* pp. 106–107.

8. American Council on Education, *Cooperation and Coordination in Higher Education,* American Council on Education studies series I, II, no. 5, 1938, pp. 5, 20, 37.

9. T. L. MacMitchell, "Are Institutions Planning Ahead?" *Journal of Higher Education,* November, 1955, p. 465.

10. Council for Financial Aid to Education, *Where's the Money Coming From?,* 1959, pp. 6–7; Dept. of Health, Education and Welfare, *Statistics of Higher Education: Receipts, Expenditures and Property, 1953–54,* pp. 6–7. More significant trends: 1939–40 = $151 million, or 27 per cent; 1953–54 = $752 million, or 32 per cent.

11. A rise in the proportion of part-time students contributes, though not importantly, to the small rise of tuition. (They now are about 20 per cent of the total.)

12. A word about loans for women. They are on the increase, but many young women are fearful of a negative dowry. The answer may lie in special subsidies to women (lower rates and longer period of repayment) and heavier charges on the increasingly large number of women on the labor market.

13. For a further development of this thesis see the essay, "Where Does the Money Come From?" in Adlai Stevenson, *The New America,* 1956, edited by Seymour E. Harris and Arthur M. Schlesinger, Jr.

14. *A Study of Income and Expenditures in Sixty Colleges: A Summary Report,* 1953–54.

Description and Sources of Table 5

SOURCE BY COLUMNS:

1. U.S. Dept. of Commerce, *Survey of Current Business,* August, 1958, table 2, p. 13.

2. Bureau of the Census, *Compendium of State Government Finances in 1957,* p. 27. Expenditures are exclusive of commercial activities and capital outlay. U.S. Dept. of Commerce, *Survey of Current Business,* August, 1958, p. 21.

3. U.S. Dept. of Commerce, *Compendium of State Government Finances in 1957,* p. 11; *ibid.,* 1958, p. 57.

4. U.S. Dept. of Commerce, *Compendium of State Government Finances in 1957,* p. 11; *ibid., Survey of Current Business,* August, 1958, p. 21.

5. Column 4 divided by column 1. For the origin of this measure of "tax burden," see Henry J. Frank, "Measuring State Tax Burdens," *National Tax Journal,* June, 1959. A high index corresponds to a high burden.

6. U.S. Dept. of Commerce, *Compendium of State Government Finances in 1957,* pp. 11 and 27. Expenditures are exclusive of commercial activities and capital outlay.

7. *Ibid.,* p. 27. Expenditures are exclusive of commercial activities and capital outlay. Office of Education, *Opening (Fall) Enrollment in Higher Education, 1957.* Includes all degree-credit students enrolled in state IHL.

8. Office of Education, Prepublication data for *Biennial Survey of Education, 1955–56*, chap. 4, sec. 2. Current expenditures include general administration and general expense, instruction and departmental research, extension and public services, libraries, organized activities related to educational departments. These data are thus comparable in composition to the "Compendium data" used above in state IHL variables. U.S. Dept. of Health, Education and Welfare, *Opening (Fall) Enrollment in Higher Educational Institutions, 1955*, p. 13.

9. *Ibid.*, p. 17; Bureau of the Census, *Current Population Reports*, series P-25, no. 132, p. 7, Feb. 20, 1956. College-age population = 18–24. Figures used are for 1957 and were obtained via a linear interpolation by using the figures given for 1958 and 1963. Migration assumed was that given for 1930–50.

10. U.S. Dept. of Health, Education and Welfare, *Opening (Fall) Enrollment in Higher Educational Institutions, 1956*, pp. 20–45.

11. U.S. Dept. of Commerce, *Current Population Reports*, series P-25, no. 132, p. 7, Feb. 20, 1956. College-age population = 18–24. Figures used are for 1957 and were obtained via a linear interpolation by using the figures given for 1958 and 1963. Migration assumed was that given for 1930–50. *Ibid.*, July 1, 1956; Nov. 13, 1958.

a. The figure for college-age population in California, 1,037,000, obtained through an interpolation, differs from a figure of 1,296,000 furnished by the California State Dept. of Education. Also, the figure for North Carolina, 494,000, differs from that of 483,000 provided by the Institute for Research in Social Science of the Univ. of North Carolina.

Should the state figures be adopted, California would be ranked 4th rather than 1st with regard to Total IHL Enrollment as a per cent of College-age Population, with a ratio of 28.4%. She would be ranked 20th instead of 44th with regard to College-age population as a per cent of Total Population, with a ratio of 9.34%. North Carolina would be ranked 40th (12.14%) instead of 41st in the former column, and 7th (10.80%) instead of 6th in the latter.

b. The New York State Bureau of Statistical Services reports that total state tax revenue in fiscal year 1957 was $1,433,693,000, not $1,440,454,000 as reported in the Dept. of Commerce, *Compendium of State Government Finances in 1957*. If a figure is adopted, New York would be ranked 21st in tax revenue per capita with $88.78, not 19th with $89.20. The difference in columns 4, 5, and 6, involving state tax revenue, would be slight, and would not affect New York's ranking.

c. State Institutions of Higher Education, as used in columns 2, 6, 7, and 10, are defined by the Census Bureau as "Institutions of higher education operated by state governments. Excludes expenditures for hospitals associated with such institutions; for agricultural experiment stations, and for farms and agricultural extension services." Local and regional IHL to which the state government contributes support are thus excluded under this definition.

In such a state as New York, with 66,613 students working for degrees in city or community colleges, as of fall, 1956, this definition results in a somewhat misleading representation of the importance of public higher education. For example, Enrollment in Public IHL as a per cent of Total Enrollment, fall 1956, would have been 31%, rather than 9.05%, which is valid if only the State University of New York is considered.

d. Note that *Current Expenditures of State IHL* do not measure *state expenditures*. Included are expenditures made from tuition, fees, and some other revenues.

4

The Role of Research in the Economics of Universities

C. C. Furnas and Raymond Ewell

Few sociological phenomena can match the rapid growth in the extent and importance of research in the United States during the past twenty years. In 1940 the total amount of research in all organizations and agencies in the country amounted to about $300 million; in 1959 the expenditures for research and development in the nation will be about $10 billion. Taking the inflationary factor into account, this represents an increase in effort over the period of twenty years of about fifteenfold.[1]

In 1940 the Federal Government was spending in the neighborhood of $15 million per year for scientific research and development activities at colleges and universities; in the fiscal year ending June 30, 1958, Federal obligations for this purpose at institutions of higher education or in laboratories managed by them will approximate $440 million. *Possibly as much as two-thirds of the expenditures for all research and development performed by colleges and universities comes today from the Federal Government.*

The most dramatic and visible growth has been in military affairs. In 1939 the total expenditure for research and development in the military field was about $25 million. In 1959 the total expenditures will be about $5.5 billion, an increase of some one-hundredfold, after allowing for inflation.

In the popular mind at least, the results have also been most spectacular in the military field. The atomic bomb, the proximity fuse, workable radar, supersonic aircraft, and guided missiles were all unknown, or even undreamed of, twenty years ago. There have, however, been parallel or similar improvements based on research in a great many other fields, including numerous peaceful pursuits. Many of them have been based on the knowledge gained in the military research program.

Though the national effort has risen some fifteenfold during the last twenty years, there may be those who say that the effective results have not been in that proportion. This is a point which cannot be argued exactly, because there is no universal yardstick to measure value of research results. It certainly is demonstrable, however, that industrial research, if properly carried out and followed up, does pay off severalfold in terms of increases in the gross national product. *Taken all together, it is clear that we have not yet come to the point of diminishing returns in research activities, whether measured in dollars or in terms of national security, public health, or other intangibles.*

Since the end of World War II, a new motivating factor has come in to stimulate the research progress in this country, and that is the competition of the communistic countries, particularly the Soviet Union. This competition is not only in the military field, but also in the industrial area and in contributions to human knowledge. Perhaps most pronounced of all is the factor of international prestige. As nearly as can be foreseen at the present time, this type of competition will be with us for a long time to come.

There is another subtle and creeping motivating factor which is just beginning to be felt, and that is the husbanding of our natural resources. Witness, for instance, the substantial amount of Federal funds which is now being spent on research and development of feasible means of extracting fresh water from salt water. This is in recognition of the impending serious shortages of fresh water in several important parts of the country. Substantial amounts of both industrial and governmental money are also going into the research and development of feasible methods of extracting petroleum products from oil shale, in anticipation of the decreasing supply of liquid crude oil which can be pumped from the ground. Very prominent also is the Federal and industrial support of research and development in the production of nuclear power. At the present time, the primary emphasis is on the fission reaction, but increasing attention to the fusion reaction can be anticipated, particularly if a few scientific break-throughs are forthcoming. Still another area deals with the production of food, which leads primarily to agricultural research, both in this and in other countries. This is in anticipation of the dramatic and explosive increase in population throughout the entire world.

We can also foresee that even in this country, which is reasonably well blessed with mineral resources, there will be an increasing emphasis on research pointed toward the recovery of mineral products from low-grade materials on an economical basis. In general, the problem we are faced with in natural resources is to devise ways and means of getting more and more from less and less.

All this adds up to the observation that major activities in research and development will necessarily be a permanent part of our national pattern. They will increase in cost and in importance.

The Role of Universities[2]

In all of this, whether they like it or not, the universities are in the central and important position. The whole research structure is built around them. If this keystone is weakened, the entire structure will correspondingly deteriorate. If the keystone were removed, the structure would soon collapse.

There are two reasons for the importance of the universities in this complex of activities. First to be mentioned is the actual production of new knowledge and the very significant role which the personnel in universities have in implementing the application, even though they may not be directly involved in the final development and reduction to practice. If one may refer again to examples of World War II, the atomic bomb, the proximity fuse, and practical radar would not have been developed had it not been for a handful of universities and their relatively small number of key scientific personnel. All those projects were closely linked to the universities, and essentially were university-inspired.

Since the end of World War II, university involvement in the national research program looms larger than ever. A great deal of the pertinent and important research work for various Federal agencies, as well as for the Department of Defense, is carried out in the universities. Large programs also go forward in several university-linked organizations. Examples of the latter involvement are the Los Alamos, Livermore, and Radiation Laboratories associated with the University of California; the Argonne National Laboratory associated with the University of Chicago; the Applied Physics Laboratory associated with Johns Hopkins University; the Jet Propulsion Laboratory linked with the California Institute of Technology; and the Servo-mechanisms Laboratory, which is essentially an integral part of the Massachusetts Institute of Technology, as well as the Lincoln Laboratory, which is an adjunct of that same institution.

The sponsored-research programs in universities of the Department of Health, Education and Welfare and the National Science Foundation are large and growing larger.

College and university research is traditionally and usually most effective in the area of basic or fundamental investigation. However, it is impossible to draw any hard and fast line between basic and applied research, and it seems inevitable that the research programs of universities very often become involved in the applied phase. That was not

Table 1. Sources of Funds and Expenditures for Research and Development
in the United States
1958–59

(In billions of dollars)

Sector	Sources of funds	Expenditures
Federal governments	$ 6.5	$ 1.9
State governments	0.2°	0.1†
Private industry	4.0	8.0
Universities	0.16‡	0.83§
Other nonprofit organizations¶	0.10	0.13
Totals	$11.0	$11.0

° Includes appropriations for state agricultural experiment stations, but expenditures by state agricultural experiment stations are included under universities.

† Includes expenditures in state research facilities other than state universities and agricultural experiment stations.

‡ Includes research funds derived from state appropriations, except agricultural experiment stations.

§ See Table 3 for details on this figure. Includes state agricultural experiment stations.

¶ Includes (1) philanthropic foundations, (2) private health agencies such as American Cancer Society and American Heart Association, (3) independent nonprofit research organizations such as Carnegie Institution of Washington, Rockefeller Institute for Medical Research, Woods Hole Oceanographic Institution, Boyce Thompson Institute for Plant Research, Haskins Laboratories, Stanford Research Institute, Mellon Institute for Industrial Research, Armour Research Foundation, Battelle Memorial Institute, Midwest Research Institute, Associated Universities, Inc., Oak Ridge Institute for Nuclear Studies, Inc., and Rand Corporation.

SOURCES: These figures are estimates by R. Ewell, University of Buffalo, based on (1) data for 1953 given in National Science Foundation, *Review of Data on Research and Development*, no. 1, 1956, (2) partial data for 1956 given in *ibid.*, no. 10, 1958, (3) Federal government data for 1958–59 given in National Science Foundation, *Federal Funds for Science, VII*, 1958, (4) private conversations with National Science Foundation staff members. Also, see Table 3 for data on universities.

always true in the past, but in this era, when scientific and technological development flow very rapidly, the close tie-in seems to be inevitable. Despite the fact that many industries are spending an increasing amount on research, with an increasing proportion in the basic areas, and that there are numerous independent research institutes of various types around the country, it seems that in the production of new knowledge and the fostering of its initial application universities will necessarily continue to hold the same key position that they have had during the past half century.

The second aspect of strength of the university program is the traditional activity of instruction. The country is already short of really good research talents, and the condition will probably get worse. It is only from the universities that properly educated and trained young men and women can come to meet the future research demands. Modern scientific developments are such that the instructional process must in itself involve research, particularly at the graduate level. This reservoir of the research talent of the future must be kept properly filled.

For these various reasons, it is of paramount national importance that the college and university research program be amply supported and kept in as healthy a condition as possible. As a nation, are we meeting these conditions? A study of a few data will show that the national pattern at the present time leaves much to be desired.

Table 1 shows the over-all data on the source and place of expenditure of funds for research and development in the United States for 1958–59. While the universities contribute $160 million of their own money toward the nation's research effort, they spend a total of $831 million as a result of grants and contracts from other sectors, principally the Federal government.

Table 2 shows the over-all budget of the 1,871 institutions of higher education in the United States in 1953–54, with comparable totals for 1955–56 and 1957–58. The table shows a total expenditure for higher education of $2.36 billion in 1953–54, $2.89 billion in 1955–56, and an estimated $3.8 billion in 1957–58. Out of $2.36 billion in 1953–54, $375 million was for organized research, or 16 per cent. Actually, the total expenditures for research were much higher than that; including departmental research, the total was probably $483 million (see Table 3), or about 20 per cent of the total budget.

Moreover, Table 2 shows that virtually all of this research activity is concentrated in 184 universities and technological schools whose total budget in 1953–54 was $1.58 billion. Therefore, $483 million represents about 30 per cent of the budget of this group of universities and technological schools. As a matter of fact, these research expenditures are prob-

Table 2. Over-all Budget of United States Universities and Colleges (Not Including Auxiliary Enterprises)

(In millions of dollars)

1953–54 Income	131 universities and 53 technological schools	All institutions of higher education (1,871 institutions)
Student fees	$ 299	$ 554
Federal government:		
Research	272	282
Other purposes	115	137
State governments	502	752
Local governments	33	88
Endowment income	85	128
Gifts and grants	104	191
Sales and services	131	165
Student aid income	21	33
Other income	43	59
Total income	$1,604	$ 2,389

Expenditures

Instruction and departmental research	$ 574	$ 967
Organized research	360	375
Administration and general expense	153	291
Plant operation and maintenance	154	280
Libraries	44	73
Extension and public services	95	115
Student aid expenditures	49	75
Other expenditures	147	188
Total expenditures, 1953–54	$1,577	$ 2,363
Total expenditures, 1955–56	1,900°	2,885
Total expenditures, 1957–58	2,600°	3,800°

°Estimated.

SOURCES: Office of Education, *Biennial Survey of Education in the United States, 1952–54,* chap. 4, sec. 2, 1957 (1953–54 data). Seymour Harris, Dept. of Economics, Harvard University (total expenditure figures for 1955–56 and 1957–58).

ably largely concentrated in about 75 universities and technological schools out of the 184 mentioned, but data for finding the exact percentage are not available.

Table 3 gives further detail on the sources of funds for research in United States universities in 1953–54 and in 1958–59. The two big sources of funds are the Federal government and the universities' own funds, which were $496 million and $160 million, respectively, in 1958–59. All other sources of funds amount to $175 million. All data in Table 3 represent operating funds only and do not include capital construction funds.

The 1953–54 data in Table 3 are taken directly from the reference indicated in the table, except that the $90 million of "universities' own funds" have been rearranged into another breakdown than the one given by the National Science Foundation. However, the total figures are the same. The first subitem of $35 million for "research not sponsored by outside organizations" is "pure" departmental research, research which has no connection with any research project financed partially or wholly by any outside organization. Some readers may feel that this is too low, since it represents only about 6 per cent of the total salaries of the 184 universities and technological schools ($574 million as given in Table 2). Possibly it should be a little higher—maybe $40 million or $50 million— but $35 million was the best estimate that the National Science Foundation could make. Another large part of faculty salaries is included under the remaining two subitems, totaling $55 million, that represent university contributions to the cost of sponsored research. Also, it must be kept in mind that the data in Table 3 include only the natural and social sciences—not the humanities—and the coverage on the social sciences is probably not very complete.

For 1958–59 the item for "research not sponsored by outside organizations" was kept at $35 million. Research has expanded greatly in these five years in the natural and social sciences, but an increasing percentage is being sponsored by outside organizations. Therefore, $35 million for "pure" departmental research in 1958–59 seemed reasonable; if anything, it may be high.

One of the key facts revealed by Table 3 is that the universities are spending $160 million of their own money on research, whereas in 1940 the expenditure was only about $15 million. Out of the $160 million, $95 million is money the universities contribute toward partial support of research projects sponsored by the Federal government and another $30 million is a similar contribution toward the support of research projects sponsored by foundations, health agencies, and industry. There is no doubt that these expenditures represent a great drain on university resources.

The expenditure of $160 million of the universities' own funds represents 6 per cent of the total budget of the 184 universities and technological schools in 1958–59. Even the $95 million contributed toward the support of government-sponsored research projects represents 4 per cent of the total budget of those institutions. The $95 million is divided about 50 per cent for direct costs (largely partial salaries of faculty work-

Table 3. Sources of Funds for Research in United States Universities[*],[†]
(In millions of dollars)

	1953–54	*Estimated* 1958–59
Universities' own funds:		
Research not sponsored by outside organizations	$ 35	$ 35
University contribution to cost of government research and development	35	95
University contribution to cost of other sponsored research and development	20	30
Subtotal, universities' own funds	$ 90	$160
Federal government:[‡]		
Department of Defense	$101	$108
Atomic Energy Commission	17	37
Health, Education and Welfare	19	79
National Science Foundation	1	38
Other agencies	3	4
Subtotal, Federal government	$142	$266
Foundations and health agencies	$ 23	$ 45
Industry	19	25
Miscellaneous gifts and grants	5	5
Total, universities proper	$279	$501
Federal research centers:		
Department of Defense	$ 72	$ 70
Atomic Energy Commission	58	130
Subtotal, research centers	$130	$200
Agricultural experiment stations:		
Federal government	$ 14	$ 30
State governments and miscellaneous sources	60	100
Subtotal, experiment stations	$ 74	$130
Grand total	$483	$831
Total Federal funds	286	496
Total non-Federal funds	197	335
Grand total	$483	$831

ing on the research projects) and 50 per cent for indirect costs which are inadequately compensated by the government.

The Federal research centers ($200 million in 1958–59) and agricultural experiment stations ($130 million in 1958–59) are probably approximately break-even operations for the universities.

Research Budget in a Typical University

Table 4 brings the over-all national research budget picture down to a particular example. This is a hypothetical university which might be either a state university or a private university. It is presumed to have a medical school but no Federal research center or agricultural experiment station.

This university, with a total budget of $20 million in 1958–59, has total research expenditures of $5 million. Most of this money, $2,650,000, comes from the Federal government, but nevertheless the university has to spend $1 million of its own money as a contribution toward support of the research sponsored by the Federal government. The university also receives $750,000 from foundations, health agencies, industry, and miscellaneous sources, but again the university must contribute $250,000 of its own money to be able to accept these outside funds and carry out the research programs associated with them. In addition to these expenditures, the university spends another $350,000 on internal or departmental research which has no connection with any research sponsored by outside organizations.

All this adds up to this particular university spending $1.6 million of its own money on research, and this money obviously has to come from student fees, endowment income, or state appropriations. This situation multiplied many times is the source of the over-all expenditure of $160 million of their own money for research by all the universities of the nation. This represents a great drain on the financial resources of the universities and intensifies their financial problems.

It might be better for the over-all strength of universities if the Federal government, foundations, health agencies, and industry were to support

---

° Data in this table include all research institutes and foundations affiliated with universities, with three exceptions: Armour Research Foundation, Mellon Institute for Industrial Research, and Stanford Research Institute.

† Data in this table include all the natural sciences and social sciences, but do not include the humanities.

‡ Not including Federal research centers (see Table 6) or Federal contribution to state agricultural experiment stations, which are given separately in the table.

Table 4. Research Budget of a Typical Medium-sized University

(This is a hypothetical university with a 1958–59 budget of $20 million, not including auxiliary enterprises.)

Sources of Funds	1953–54	1958–59
Universities' own funds:		
Research not sponsored by outside organizations	$ 350,000	$ 350,000
Contribution to cost of government-sponsored research	350,000	1,000,000
Contribution to cost of other sponsored research	200,000	250,000
Subtotal, universities' own funds	$ 900,000	$ 1,600,000
Federal government	$ 1,400,000	$ 2,650,000
Foundations and health agencies	250,000	450,000
Industry	200,000	250,000
Miscellaneous gifts and grants	50,000	50,000
Total research funds	$ 2,800,000	$ 5,000,000
Expenditures for Research		
Salaries	$ 1,700,000	$ 3,000,000
Supplies, equipment and other direct costs	400,000	700,000
Indirect costs	700,000	1,300,000
Total research expenditures	$ 2,800,000	5,000,000
Total university budget (not including auxiliary enterprises)	$15,000,000	$20,000,000

SOURCE: Prepared by R. Ewell, University of Buffalo.

fewer research projects, but support all of them on a full-cost basis so that the universities would not be weakened financially.

Causes of Deficits in University Research Operations

Table 5 shows more specifically which Federal agencies cause the deficits in the universities' research operations. The two big contributors to these deficits in 1958–59 were the Department of Health, Education and Welfare and the National Science Foundation. The Department of Health, Education and Welfare (principally the National Institutes of Health) gave $79 million to the universities in 1958–59 in the form of research grants, but that required the universities to contribute $40 million more in the form of faculty salaries and indirect costs in order to

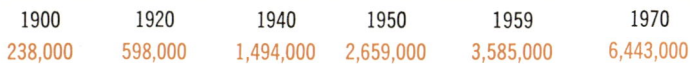

ions						
6						
5						
4						
3						
2						
1						

1900	1920	1940	1950	1959	1970
238,000	598,000	1,494,000	2,659,000	3,585,000	6,443,000

TOTAL NUMBER OF YOUNG PEOPLE GOING TO COLLEGE WILL ALMOST DOUBLE BY 1970

Table 5. Federal Government and University Contributions to Costs
of Federally Sponsored Research in United States Universities

(In millions of dollars)

Agency	1953–54			1958–59 (estimated)		
	Federal contribution	University contribution	Total	Federal contribution	University contribution	Total
Department of Defense........	$159	$15	$174	$179	$17	$196
Atomic Energy Commission....	89	5	94	166	12	178
Health, Education and Welfare	19	13	32	79	40	119
National Science Foundation...	1.4	1	2.4	38	25	63
Other......................	18	1	19	34	1	35
Totals.................	$286	$34	$320	$496	$95	$591

NOTE: Totals may not add precisely, owing to rounding.
SOURCES: Same as Table 1.

carry out the research programs. Likewise, the National Science Foundation gave $38 million to the universities in grants in 1958–59, but again that required the universities to contribute $25 million of their own money. The Department of Defense and the Atomic Energy Commission transfer much larger sums to the universities through research contracts, but they still fail to pay the full cost by $29 million.

The origin of the estimated $65 million shortfall on the grants of the National Institutes of Health and the National Science Foundation may be illustrated by a typical budget for a grant from either of these agencies. Following is the budget for a typical one-year research project computed (A) on the basis of present policies and (B) on a full-cost basis:

	A	B
	Budget under present policies	Budget on full-cost basis
Senior investigator:		
Quarter time during academic year	....	$ 2,500
Full time in summer, 2 months	$ 2,000	2,000
Two research assistants, half time	5,000	5,000
Other direct costs	2,000	2,000
Indirect costs, 15 per cent of direct costs	1,350	....
Indirect costs, 50 per cent of salaries	....	4,750
Totals	$10,350	$16,250

Budget A makes no provision for paying the one-fourth time which the senior investigator (faculty member) spends on this research project: working in the laboratory with the two research assistants, directing their work, and discussing their research results with them. Normally this much research activity requires that the faculty member be relieved of one-fourth of his regular teaching load; additional teaching faculty then have to be hired to make up for it. This is a legitimate charge against a research project, whether sponsored by government, foundation, or industry.

Also, budget A allows only $1,350 for indirect costs, whereas the real indirect cost is $4,750 computed on a 50 per cent overhead basis. Actually, 50 per cent overhead is probably too low to represent an average true cost; 70 or 80 per cent would be closer to reality.

In this example, therefore, the university must supply the additional $5,900 needed to carry out the research project. This example multiplied by several thousand times is the source of the $65 million shortfall incurred by the nation's universities in carrying out research programs sponsored by these two Federal government agencies. *Both the National Institutes of Health and the National Science Foundation should give careful and serious consideration to (1) the concept of paying salaries for the portions of faculty time actually spent on sponsored-research projects and (2) the idea of increasing indirect-cost allowances to something approximating full cost.*

The attitude of universities toward these government research policies varies with the financial well-being of the various institutions. Some of the well-endowed private universities take a rather independent attitude and are not yet particularly concerned over the increasing financial burden caused by these government policies. Also, many of the large state universities, with their access to state appropriations, are not overly concerned about the question. The universities which feel this financial burden most keenly are the not-so-well-endowed private universities, such as New York University, Boston University, University of Southern California, Syracuse University, Temple University, George Washington University, University of Pittsburgh, University of Denver, and University of Buffalo.

There are about seventy-five universities in the United States which produce over twenty-five Ph.D.s per year; this group of schools does virtually all the research done in United States universities. These seventy-five universities can be classified approximately as follows:

Well-endowed private universities (Harvard, Chicago, MIT et al.)   15
Not-so-well-endowed private universities (NYU, Syracuse, Temple et al.)   20
State universities (Penn State, Purdue, California, et al.)   40

This classification indicates that the problem of supplementing government research grants on the basis of present policies is most acute in the middle group of twenty not-so-well-endowed private universities.

Many of the well-endowed private universities have a policy of not permitting faculty salaries to be paid, even in part, from outside research funds, whether from government or private sources. In other words, these universities not only do not ask for payment of faculty salaries on research grants, but would not accept such payment, in many cases, even if it were offered. Such outside salary money is called "soft money" in contrast to salary money from internal university sources, which is called "hard money." Some universities have a fear of having a number of research grants and contracts suddenly terminated at the same time, thereby leaving them with a large number of faculty members on their hands with no budgetary provision for their salaries. This is an illusory fear, since there is little likelihood of this happening under any conceivable future Government policy, particularly if the research grants are administered in a systematic fashion.

While the fifteen or so well-endowed universities can afford to take such an independent attitude toward accepting outside funds for research salaries, the not-so-well-endowed universities simply cannot afford to do so. Government policies which restrict the payment of faculty salaries and adequate overhead have the effect of limiting the research potential of this group of twenty or so universities.

The state universities generally have an intermediate attitude toward this question. Most state universities are willing and anxious to receive all the research funds they can use and are interested in having partial salaries of faculty members paid from research funds. On the other hand, they do not have the extreme financial stringency of the not-so-well-endowed private universities which makes this a matter of urgency for the latter group.

The trend of rising costs, however, will almost certainly lead to shortages of funds in the next decade which will cause the well-endowed private universities and the state universities to change their attitudes toward the necessity of recovering the full costs of research.

Federal Research Centers

Table 6 lists the twenty-eight Federal research centers operated by universities. They are all sponsored by the Department of Defense (twenty centers) or the Atomic Energy Commission (eight centers). The appropriations for these centers have gone up from $135 million in 1954–55 to $200 million in 1958–59. Probably the most interesting observation about this list is that the twenty-eight research centers are located in nineteen institutions, all but one or two of which are among the forty elite institutions in the country. The University of California and Massachusetts Institute of Technology have four research centers each, and the University of Chicago has three.

Table 6. Federal Research Centers Operated by Universities
1958–59

(These twenty-eight Federal research centers received appropriations totaling $135 million in 1954–55 and $200 million in 1958–59.)

Ames Laboratory (Iowa State College)
Applied Physics Laboratory (John Hopkins University)
Applied Physics Laboratory (University of Washington)
Argonne Cancer Research Hospital (University of Chicago)
Argonne National Laboratory (University of Chicago)
Army Mathematics Center (University of Wisconsin)
Atomic Energy Project (University of California at Los Angeles)
Atomic Energy Project (University of Rochester)
Boston University Physical Research Laboratories (Boston University)
Chicago Midway Laboratories (University of Chicago)
Columbia Radiation Laboratory (Columbia University)
Coordinated Science Laboratory (University of Illinois)
Cruft Laboratory (Harvard University)
Electronics Research Laboratory (Stanford University)
Human Resources Research Office (George Washington University)
Jet Propulsion Laboratory (California Institute of Technology)
Laboratory for Insulation Research (Massachusetts Institute of Technology)
Los Alamos Scientific Laboratory (University of California)
Naval Biological Laboratory (University of California)
Operations Evaluation Group (Massachusetts Institute of Technology)
Operations Research Office (John Hopkins University)
Operations Research Group (Massachusetts Institute of Technology)
Ordnance Research Laboratory (Pennsylvania State University)
Project Doan Brook (Case Institute of Technology)
Project Lincoln (Massachusetts Institute of Technology)
Project Michigan (University of Michigan)
Radiation Laboratory (including Livermore Laboratory, University of California)
Radiological Laboratory (University of California)

NOTE: Several other Federal Research Centers are operated by groups of universities and are not included in above list because their funds do not appear in the budgets of the universities involved. These centers include Brookhaven National Laboratory, Oak Ridge Institute of Nuclear Studies, National Astronomical Observatory, and National Radio Astronomy Observatory.

Federal research centers give rise to marked distortions in the budgets of universities. A university without a Federal research center will typically have research expenditures equal to 20 to 30 per cent of the total university budget (exclusive of auxiliary enterprises) whereas a university with a Federal research center may have research expenditures equal to 50 per cent or more of its total budget, the three universities mentioned in the previous paragraph being outstanding examples.

Production of Doctorate Degrees

Table 7 shows the production of doctorate degrees from 1910 to 1958. The production at the present time, 8,000 to 9,000 per year, is about three

Table 7. Production of Doctorate Degrees in United States Universities (Earned Ph.D., Sc.D., and Ed.D. degrees only)

Year*	Sciences	Nonsciences	Total	Percentage in sciences
1910	180	182	362	49.8
1920	323	243	566	57.0
1930	1,072	1,189	2,261	47.4
1932	1,238	1,416	2,654	46.7
1934	1,550	1,280	2,830	54.8
1936	1,547	1,223	2,770	55.9
1938	1,552	1,410	2,932	52.0
1940	1,812	1,478	3,290	55.2
1942	1,833	1,664	3,497	52.4
1944	1,194	1,111	2,305	51.9
1946	956	1,010	1,966	48.8
1948	2,150	2,038	4,188	51.3
1949	2,767	2,526	5,293	52.3
1950	3,591	3,042	6,633	54.1
1951	4,212	3,126	7,338	57.4
1952	4,407	3,276	7,683	57.3
1953	4,721	3,588	8,309	56.8
1954	5,051	3,945	8,996	56.1
1955	5,036	3,804	8,840	57.0
1956	4,787	4,116	8,903	53.8
1957	4,764	3,992	8,756	54.4
1958	4,840	4,102	8,942	54.2

* End of academic year.

NOTE: Sciences includes mathematics, physical sciences, biological sciences, medical sciences, agriculture, engineering, psychology, anthropology, and geography; nonsciences includes everything else.

SOURCE: National Science Foundation, *Scientific Personnel Resources*, 1955, table D-10 (data for 1910–54). Personal communication from National Science Foundation (data for 1955 to 1958).

times the prewar level of 2,700 to 3,000 per year. Production of doctorates has leveled off at 8,000 to 9,000 per year during the past six years. Since research expenditures in universities increased by about 60 per cent during the same period, it must be concluded that a higher proportion of the research in universities is being done by full-time researchers, as compared to graduate students. The nation is certainly going to need more Ph.D.s, which indicates a greater need for support of basic research in the universities, and it must be on a full-cost basis to avoid further weakening of the universities' financial structure.

The Universities' Dilemma

The foregoing material reveals two significant trends. The first is the phenomenal rise in magnitude and importance (actually the necessity) of research, both in the nation as a whole and in colleges and universities. The second important factor is that many of the colleges and universities of the country are now in severe financial straits because they have to pay a substantial part of the cost of the very large sponsored-research programs. This comes at the time of a critical fiscal situation in the institutions of higher learning which bids fair to become desperate in a few years.

In 1939–40 university research amounted to about $42 million all told out of a total national budget for higher education of $520 million, or 8 per cent of the total budget. In 1958–59 university research amounted to $831 million out of a total national budget for higher education of $3,800 million, or 22 per cent of the total budget.

Such a great expansion of research in the universities is all to the good; it is indubitably in the national interest. But at the same time this greatly expanded research program is putting a heavy financial strain on the universities. Government, industry, and foundations are putting more and more money into research in universities, but this has required greater and greater expenditures of the universities' general funds.

In order to hold up their end of the research function, universities are being forced into deficit financing simply because those who are supposed to be supporting research are not paying the full bill. This puts universities in a most serious situation. They *must* carry on substantial research programs in order to fulfill their obligations to the nation. But if the present trend of inadequate payments continues for long, many private universities will be in danger of bankruptcy. The horns of the dilemma are very sharp indeed.

Where does the money come from for these deficits? In effect, it is obtained by diversion of funds that were intended to be used for other purposes. The principal sources that are tapped are student tuition, state appropriations, endowment income, and gifts. There is also the indirect effect of keeping the already low university faculty salaries in a continually depressed state, which is a particularly bad form of subsidy.

In many private institutions in which tuition is the major source of operating income, the research program and the United States government are being largely subsidized by students who, in many cases, are forced to live on a substandard basis. This is a vicious sociological phenomenon, which certainly is not in the public interest.

The general situation is probably best summarized in an article about medical schools which is still apropos even though it is ten years old.[3]

> *No money for overhead*
> But surely with all of these headaches these grants-in-aid must prove a financial bonanza to the medical schools? . . . But certainly the schools should be given enough to cover the operating costs? Not at all. The outmoded custom of twenty years ago still dominates.

The situation may be illustrated still further by another quotation from a recent report on medical schools by the National Institutes of Health:[4]

> The schools expressed the conviction that their finances are already so strained that any further increase in indirect costs not reimbursed by granting agencies would cause serious inroads on their funds for teaching and service. To remedy the situation, the schools in this survey recommend that full costs (direct and indirect) be allowed for research grants and training grants in accordance with some workable accounting system. In a recent meeting the Association of American Medical Colleges adopted unanimously a resolution calling upon Federal granting agencies to allow full costs.

Since the Federal government is the primary sponsor of university research, it is particularly important to analyze its practices. There seems to be a lack of realism in the attitude of the average government agency.

> In June 1955 the National Science Foundation recommended to the Bureau of the Budget that Federal agencies pay essentially all indirect costs of research sponsored by them at educational institutions.[1]

This obviously is a sound policy, but the practice of most of the government agencies is at great variance with the stated principle. The governmental organization which has been most realistic (though not sufficiently so) thus far has been the Office of Naval Research. Immediately after World War II it began sponsoring research at universities on a basis of paying all of the direct costs plus the overhead. It developed a pattern of principles and formulas which became known as the "Blue Book" and has been used for determining the allowable overhead for university grants and contracts. Although this is a step in the right direction, in no case that we know of is the overhead allowable by the Blue Book adequate to cover the actual indirect costs as determined in accordance with sound accounting principles. If we may cite the case of our own institution, the University of Buffalo, our actual indirect costs as determined by a recognized firm of public accountants in a recent year was approximately 82 per cent of direct salaries and wages. The allowable overhead which we obtained under the Blue Book formula was 63 per cent. We think this is typical. In general, the Army and the Air Force have been following the Blue Book formula for university grants and contracts, although they often are more niggardly than the Navy.

Recently a new regulation in the form of *Bureau of the Budget Circular A-21* has been issued; it was presumed that it would correct some of the inequities of the Blue Book. Circular A-21 has been incorporated in the revised *Armed Services Procurement Regulation.* The experience to date indicates, however, that institutions will fare but little, if any, better under the new regulation than under the Blue Book. Further, the accounting is much more complicated. Circular A-21 is not the answer.

Despite the fact that the Armed Forces are, in effect, shortchanging the universities, their performance is far better than other government agencies. The Department of Health, Education and Welfare and the National Science Foundation are the worst offenders. The Department allows a maximum of 15 per cent of total costs—obviously an inadequate figure. To make matters worse, the 15 per cent limitation is at the present time a matter of law. Twice it has been written into the budgetary legislation, and despite valiant efforts on the part of universities and various other organizations, it has not yet been removed.

The National Science Foundation, as was indicated above, gives lip service to paying full indirect costs, but it too is still going along with the pattern of a maximum of 15 per cent.

Further, it is usually difficult, if not impossible, to get either the HEW or the NSF to pay even all of the direct costs. For instance, only rarely will they allow payment to the institutions of a portion of the salary of the principal investigators.

The Atomic Energy Commission has a policy that the educational institution shall pay a substantial proportion of the cost of a project, and Commission negotiators are very skillful in beating down the university in agreements on the proportion which the government shall pay.

These reactions on the part of the government agencies are apparently based on two misconceptions. The first is that universities tend to have a tinge of dishonesty, and hence every conceivable legal effort should be made to be sure that they do not make any money on a research project. In this the government agencies are more than successful, and they nearly always give the excuse that it is necessary and in the public interest.

The rationalizations and excuses for the actions are based on a general policy which has been well expressed by the National Science Foundation:[1]

Goals of Federal Sponsorship

Problems of Government-university relationships in the Federal support of research at colleges and universities should be explicitly and completely dissociated from the budgetary needs and crises of the institutions and from the general issue of Federal aid to higher education. In the consideration and administration of these relationships there should be no implication that Federal sponsorship of research is a convenient subterfuge for Federal financial aid to institutions of higher learning.

This is a realistic policy to which we do not think there is any objection. But it should not be used as a dodge for not paying the legitimate costs of university research.

The second misconception is revealed by statements such as this:

> In supporting research the Government agency is really just helping out on programs that the university would be carrying on anyway; so we are really very good fellows when we are paying only part of the costs.

That general philosophy, which might have had a reasonable rationale forty years ago when university research programs were very small, must now be corrected before we can ever come to any adequate solution of the research problem. The point is that, both in terms of financial realities and in terms of their service to the nation, universities cannot and should not be expected to carry part of the cost of that research which is supported from the outside. To repeat the quotation above, "The outmoded custom of twenty years ago still dominates."

Graduate education is, of course, the most expensive level of education; it is even higher than medical education. In a recent survey the University of Michigan found that the ratio of freshman/sophomore to junior/senior to graduate education was 1:3:8. Purdue University has obtained similar figures. Most people outside universities are not aware of the extremely high cost of graduate education compared to the undergraduate level. The actual cost of graduate education may run from a minimum of about $4,000 per student per year up to as much as $12,000 per year in some institutions.

Although the government is the largest, it is by no means the only, offender. Foundations and health agencies which support research seldom allow any overhead costs at all; even when they do, it is only to an insignificant percentage. Their usual reply to requests for realism is, "If you do not wish to take the grant, there are other institutions that will," a polite form of highwaymanship which is particularly undesirable in the operation of educational institutions. That attitude of foundations will probably continue until the Federal government takes the lead in correcting inequities.

Industry is also guilty to a certain extent. Although when an industry gives a research contract to a university it is usually quite willing to allow payment of senior investigators' salaries and adequate overhead, the same is not true of grants or graduate fellowships. Some industries are now adopting the policy of giving a stipend to the institution along with a graduate fellowship, but it is still only a limited practice. The graduate fellowship, of course, is part of the research pattern, and the tuition payment received therefrom by no means covers the cost of the research and instruction involved. Hence, it would be highly desirable if industry as a whole would recognize that accounting principles that are sound for them must be sound for universities also.

The impact of these unrealistic trends and attitudes can be very serious indeed. At the risk of appearing provincial, we would again like to cite the experience of our own institution, the University of Buffalo. Although our program is small as compared to that of many universities, our research expenditures are roughly $2 million per year, the bulk of it being in the medical sciences. In one recent year, the total expenditure for research was $1,946,000 and the direct salary costs were $1,047,000. If we accept the figure of 82 per cent of salaries as the realistic overhead, we should in that year have collected $860,000 to cover the indirect costs. Actually, our total collection for indirect cost was only $256,000. Thus the bona fide loss on this research program for this one institution was $604,000. This represented about 10 per cent of the operating costs of the instructional and research activities, and it had a very severe impact on the budget. It is an irrational and untenable situation in which year after year the students and faculty have to provide that sort of a subsidy to the United States government and to other organizations.

Incremental versus Proportional Overhead

There is a tendency among organizations making research grants or contracts to universities to think of research as an incremental activity in a university, whence the notion that overhead on research grants or contracts should be computed on an incremental basis. This is an erroneous approach. Research is *not* an incremental, secondary activity in a university; it is an integral, primary activity. In accounting parlance it is a joint product, not a by-product.

It is true that if one considers a university at any given point in time and then adds one more research project to the existing structure, the additional overhead assignable to this one project is quite small. The same might be said of adding one more student or one more course to the curriculum. However, when research expenditures are 25 per cent of the total budget of a university as indicated in Table 4 (and this is typical of many universities), research pays 25 per cent of the salaries in the institute, occupies 25 per cent of the space, is responsible for 25 per cent of the overhead costs; in short, research becomes 25 per cent of the total university. Therefore, it is only reasonable and realistic that all research projects should bear a proportional share of the university's overhead costs and not simply an incremental amount.

There are various approaches to apportioning the total overhead costs of the university among instruction, research, and other activities on the basis of salaries involved, number of persons, space utilized, etc. The Blue Book formula computes overhead as proportional to salaries involved, and this seems a simple and reasonable way of doing it. The new *Bureau of the Budget Circular A-21* uses space utilization as the method of apportionment, a method that is more laborious, less accurate, and no more significant than the salary method. Circular A-21 in its present form at this writing seems likely to increase the universities' burden rather than improve the situation.

A Possible Solution

When one poses a serious problem, he certainly should at least suggest the solution. As we see it, the only solution lies in a slow process of education in the realities of university financing. In order to carry out their function, colleges and universities must carry on a very substantial, and probably increasing, research program. They cannot continue to carry the burden of making up substantial deficits in research. Everyone involved, both the supporters and the supportees, must understand that, which calls for continuing, even though slow, education of congressmen, legislators, government officials, foundations, and industrial officials. If the realities of the situation are placed before enough responsible people often enough, beneficial changes may eventually be forthcoming.

Too Much University Research?

Criticisms are frequently leveled at universities for doing too much research, particularly research that is not directly associated with the teaching process. Such criticisms are most often directed toward the ancillary activities of some of the universities which employ numbers of full-time professional research men. MIT's Project Lincoln and Cal Tech's Jet Propulsion Laboratory are examples of this type of activity.

Whether or not such laboratories and projects are proper for universities depends to a large degree upon the vision of a university's function. Primary justification for the large projects is that they are operated as a public service. Is it appropriate for universities to extend major effort in the area of public service? In our opinion, the realities of life indicate that it is. Certainly, in the middle of the twentieth century the ivory tower is obsolete, and in the case of major projects such as those mentioned it has been amply proved that a university-linked organization is the best place to get objective research of certain kinds accomplished. This is primarily due not only to the stimulation that comes from even minor contact with university faculties, but also to the fact that such organizations are pursuing research per se. There is no vested interest in shaping and guiding the research program to fit in with the production of some eventual product, such as is usually found in even the best industrial research organizations. The academic objectivity has its unique advantages not only for itself and for government, but also for industry.

A well-balanced research program for the nation calls for not only a large number of organizations, but also for great variety. The ancillary activities of the universities, where they are successful, are an essential and a desirable part of the national pattern.

Further, there is a good deal of cross-linkage between such research organizations and the parent university or institute. There are not only graduate students, but also faculty exchanges, which have a great deal of direct benefit even though they are carried out only part time.

There is often the criticism that faculty members become so involved in and imbued with research that they neglect their teaching duties. In individual cases that may be true, but the impact is serious only in a few instances in which conventional undergraduate instruction is involved. Certainly in graduate instruction, with its necessarily large component of research participation, involvement in research of both faculty and student is the *sine qua non* of success. By and large, the research versus instruction pattern is not unbalanced, and there is not very much danger that it will become so.

Balancing the Load

There are many who feel that there is an undesirable imbalance in the distribution of the research activities among the universities of the country. As indicated in Table 2, about 10 per cent of institutions of higher education carry more than 95 per cent of the research program. In general, the research tends to center around those institutions which have strong graduate schools. That is to be expected, of course, because of the close relation between graduate work and research. Although there are almost 1,900 colleges and universities in the country, there are probably about 40 which would be considered as first-rank graduate schools. It would be as dangerous for the authors to name the specific schools as it would to expose themselves to the hazards of picking a beauty queen. However, the figure of 40 is probably a significant one. It does seem that this represents too much of a concentration for a nation the size of the United States, particularly since the outstanding schools have tended to cluster together in a very few regions. Hence it is appropriate to pose the question, "How can the situation be improved?"

There is a good deal of inertia in the system. It is quite natural that contracts and grant support go most easily to the prestige institutions, even though in some departments in some universities the prestige might no longer be justified. There is also a great deal of inertia within the institutions themselves. In many cases, particularly in some of the newer institutions and in those that have not had much emphasis on research in the past, the motivation to seek contracts and grants for sponsored research is lacking. The solution would lie partially in the internal education of the faculties.

Inevitably, however, there is also the fiscal side. It is very expensive, as well as difficult, to build up a strong graduate and research program. If, however, institutions could start such a development with the assurance that their complete costs would be recoverable, we think there would be a fairly rapid change in the attitude of many universities which have been doing relatively little research in the past. There is no desire to make money from the research program, but at least there should be the opportunity to break even.

Probably the organization which can be most effective in spreading the research program is the National Science Foundation. In the first place, it is quite conscious, for political reasons, of spreading its grants on a geographical basis. This indirectly, then, does introduce research programs into some institutions which otherwise would probably not participate to any substantial degree. Also, the NSF program of fellowships and teachers institutes have the general effect of promoting geographical distribution of research interest. But when all is said and done, probably the most effective way of spreading the load in the long run would be for the Federal government to propound, implement, and enforce policies which would allow the institutions to recover the full cost of sponsored research. That would be the best possible stimulus for building up quite a number of universities so that they might move from minor- to major-league status.

Notes

1. National Science Foundation, *Government-University Relationships in Federally Sponsored Scientific Research and Development,* NSF 58–10, April, 1958, pp. 1, 21, and 26.

2. Throughout this paper the word "universities" will be used to mean all

institutions of higher education including universities, colleges, technological institutes, and professional schools.

3. George B. Darling, "Can We Pay for Our Medical Schools?" *The Atlantic Monthly*, June, 1950, p. 38.

4. National Institutes of Health, *A Study of Twenty Medical Schools*, April, 1959, p. 36.

5

Conflict and Cooperation in American Higher Education

Gordon N. Ray

I shall begin by stating two assumptions. The first is that American higher education, although it is an immense and heterogeneous enterprise with weak as well as strong points, fulfills its functions satisfactorily, certainly as satisfactorily as does the higher educational system of any other nation. As President Herman B. Wells of Indiana University has recently said: "American higher education is not a failure. It is not largely misdirected. It is not outclassed. As it stands, it has a promising future. It requires no wrenching, revolutionary reforms." [1]

My second assumption is that the job of planning the future of American education should be left to the professionals in the field. Thus faculty will should be decisive in establishing the broad lines of educational policy, and administrative officers should be relied on to carry out this policy as well as to provide leadership in its formulation. No doubt ultimate control over every institution of higher learning will continue to be exercised by the segment of the public which provides its financial support. But though this constituency should scrutinize closely the aims proposed by faculty and administration, the means used to achieve those aims should be left in their hands.

It is necessary to state these assumptions because a crucial decision faces the nation in planning the financing of higher education. Will it accept the professionals' definition of financial needs and concern itself with determining how resources can be found to meet those needs? Or will it assume an arbitrary limit to resources and concern itself with determining how needs can be diminished?

In my opinion the first approach is demanded, because higher education, like medicine, law, and the operation of our Armed Forces, is only incidentally an "economic activity." Such is its importance to the national welfare that the question of its "solvency" is in a sense irrelevant; funds will always have to be found to meet its necessities. This is the point of view implicit, for example, in the recent report of President Eisenhower's Science Advisory Committee. Noting that the United States spends about $18 billion a year on formal education (about 4 per cent of the gross national product), the Committee asserted: "If we wisely spent twice that much to achieve higher quality, it would be more than worth the cost. Doubling our current annual investment in education is probably a minimal rather than an extravagant goal."

Separate Roles of Faculty and Trustees

An illustration of the pitfalls besetting the second approach is provided by Mr. Beardsley Ruml's *Memo to a College Trustee*. Mr. Ruml regards our present liberal college system as an irrational and inefficient form of economic activity.[2] Hence he proposes a root-and-branch reform of both educational and financial policy calculated in his view to make the system rational and efficient. Anticipating that liberal college faculties will not endorse his proposals to cut sharply the number of courses taught, to increase the ratio of students to instructors, to return to the general employment of large lecture courses, to reduce the number of credit hours required for a degree, to extend the academic year from three quarters or two semesters to four quarters, and so on, he argues that "The Trustees, therefore, must take back from the faculty *as a body* its present authority over the design and administration of the curriculum."[3]

Now it is true that in the United States final authority over a college or university is vested in a body of lay governors rather than in the faculty itself. This arrangement has its historical explanation, but it seems sufficiently anomalous when compared with the system of self-government that prevails in European higher education or with the autonomy enjoyed by American practitioners of such other professions as medicine and law. In practice, of course, members of the typical board of trustees, recognizing their limitations as educational experts, have generally been content to leave effective control of educational policy to their faculties, providing themselves a continuing appraisal of the broad goals of their institution to ensure that they are in the public interest.

Thus it has come to be established, at least in institutions of some academic standing, that a faculty is made up of dedicated professional men and women whose frame of reference is national, not local. As Judge Wyzanski has said, speaking for Harvard's Board of Overseers: "The men who become full members of the faculty are not in substance our employees. They are not our agents. They are not our representatives. They are a fellowship of independent scholars answerable to us only for academic integrity." [4] It follows that a college or university is not a corporation or a government department. Members of its faculty are not employees or civil servants. Academic administrators are not "management" or superior bureaucrats. Instead, faculty and administrators alike belong to a community of scholars with which the decision in all matters of educational policy should rest.

An experiment such as Mr. Ruml proposes is most likely to be tried with faculty sanction by marginal institutions whose existence is in question.[5] In view of the current shortage of qualified college teachers, an attempt to impose such drastic changes on the faculty of a ranking liberal college could easily result in the kind of migration that is said to have occurred from the University of Chicago during President Hutchins' experimental heyday. Nor does the academic profession's only defense lie in faculty mobility. The American Association of University Professors would undoubtedly watch closely such an invasion of faculty rights. Even more substantial opposition might come from groups that have thus far carefully avoided involvement in faculty-trustee relationships: the powerful professional societies representing the several fields of learning.

It is significant that Mr. Arthur Flemming, Secretary of the Department of Health, Education and Welfare, chose as the topic of his recent address to the national meeting of the American Association of University Professors the need for involving faculty members more effectively in the government of their institutions. He saw in their direct participation in decisions concerning budget, personnel, and above all educational policy, the only means by which freedom of teaching and research can be preserved. If Mr. Ruml's proposals gain a sympathetic hearing from the public, the timeliness of Mr. Flemming's warning will be sufficiently demonstrated.

This background is essential to a consideration of the topic of conflict and cooperation as forces affecting the financing of American higher education. The two forces are intimately related, and anything that strengthens the one is likely to weaken the other. A description of our current condition with respect to them will at least serve to underline the grave dangers inherent in conflict and the substantial promise offered by cooperation. It would be too much to hope that conflict can be eliminated, but as its causes are better understood, it can be brought more nearly under control. And cooperation is the chief means for achieving that end.

Conflict between Private and Public Higher Education

By all odds the most dramatic and the most widely publicized of the conflicts which plague higher education is that between private and public institutions. Though it would sometimes seem from the utterances of the participants in the controversy that the two have nothing in common, the distinction between them is in fact anything but clear-cut. Private colleges and universities are beholden to the state in many ways. Their charters and their right to grant degrees are established by the state. They enjoy important subsidies from the state. Their property is exempted from taxation, and since the Federal income tax has become a decisive factor in many individual financial decisions, the tax-deductible status of gifts to private colleges and universities has been a most valuable privilege. They are in receipt of hundreds of millions of dollars annually from the Federal government for contract research, for student-housing loans, and for other purposes. Similarly, public institutions, particularly the major state universities, have come to rely heavily on private support to supplement activities financed chiefly from public funds and to enable them to embark upon other activities for which no public funds are available.

There has always been conflict between private and public higher education, but it is only during the present century that the conflict has become widespread and acute. From the founding of Harvard College in 1636 until the establishment of the University of North Carolina in 1793, all American higher education was private. By 1853 there were only seventeen state universities, none of them as yet of great size or consequence. In the following decades, aided by the Land-Grant Acts of 1862, all but six states came to have state universities supported by substantial recurring appropriations from their legislatures. But until the turn of the century, these institutions hardly threatened the predominance of private higher education.

The last sixty years tell a different story, which can best be presented statistically. Public institutions enrolled 38.5 per cent of the resident students in American institutions of higher learning in 1899–1900, 52.1 per cent in 1941–42. By the latter academic year public institutions were also giving 52.7 per cent of all first-level degrees, 44.9 per cent of all second-level degrees, and 40.1 per cent of all doctor's degrees. During the later years of World War II this trend was for a time reversed. In 1945–46 public institutions enrolled only 46.8 per cent of resident students, and in 1948–49 they gave only 49.3 per cent of first-level degrees, 41.5 per cent of second-level degrees, and 39.5 per cent of doctor's degrees. But in the last decade the pendulum has swung back with a vengeance. In 1958–

Table 1. Number of Earned Degrees Granted by Institutions of Higher Learning in the United States

Year	First-level degrees				Second-level degrees				Doctor's degrees			
	Public institutions	Private institutions	All institutions	Per cent public inst.	Public institutions	Private institutions	All institutions	Per cent public inst.	Public institutions	Private institutions	All institutions	Per cent public inst.
1957–58	198,731	167,017	365,748	54.3	37,954	27,660	65,614	57.8	4,614	4,328	8,942	51.6
1956–57	181,030	159,317	340,347	53.2	35,161	26,794	61,955	56.8	4,484	4,272	8,756	51.2
1955–56	162,237	149,061	311,298	52.1	33,095	26,199	59,294	55.8	4,583	4,320	8,903	51.5
1954–55	147,404	139,997	287,401	51.3	32,291	25,913	58,204	55.5	4,560	4,280	8,840	51.6
1953–54	148,330	144,550	292,880	50.6	30,701	26,122	56,823	54.0	4,656	4,340	8,996	51.8
1952–53	155,609	149,248	304,857	51.0	31,113	29,910	61,023	51.0	4,127	4,182	8,309	49.7
1951–52	163,856	168,068	331,924	49.4	31,527	32,060	63,587	49.6	3,469	4,214	7,683	45.2
1950–51	193,845	190,507	384,352	50.4	31,472	33,660	65,132	48.3	3,043	4,295	7,338	41.5
1949–50	217,389	216,345	433,734	50.1	26,192	32,027	58,219	45.0	2,668	3,965	6,633	40.2
1948–49	180,828	185,870	366,698	49.3	21,056	29,707	50,763	41.5	1,996	3,054	5,050	39.5
1947–48	136,180	136,131	272,311	50.0	17,696	24,753	42,449	41.7	1,580	2,409	3,989	39.6
1941–42	97,707	87,639	185,346	52.7	11,063	13,585	24,648	44.9	1,401	2,096	3,497	40.1
1939–40	96,652	89,848	186,500	51.8	12,157	14,574	26,731	45.5	1,367	1,923	3,290	41.6
1937–38	82,442	82,501	164,943	50.0	9,590	12,038	21,628	44.3	1,142	1,790	2,932	38.9
1935–36	69,369	73,756	143,125	48.5	7,245	10,998	18,243	39.7	1,026	1,742	2,768	37.1
1933–34	63,452	72,704	136,156	46.6	7,198	11,066	18,264	39.4	996	1,819	2,815	35.4
1931–32	62,875	75,188	138,063	45.5	7,747	11,592	19,339	40.1	962	1,938	2,900	33.2

SOURCE: *Biennial Surveys of Education in the United States*, Office of Education bulletins for the years involved. The data are not available for private and public institutions separately, prior to 1931–32.

59 public institutions enrolled 58.3 per cent of resident students and gave
54.3 per cent of first-level degrees, 57.8 per cent of second-level degrees,
and 51.6 per cent of doctor's degrees[6] (see Table 1).

The financial accompaniments of this shift from private to public predominance are less readily documented on a national scale.[7] Perhaps they
can be best illustrated by comparing the incomes of a major private and
a major public institution of higher learning. In 1911–12 Harvard University had an income of $2,487,470, the University of Illinois an income
of $1,624,651. Harvard remained well in advance of Illinois until 1945–46,
when the respective totals showed the narrow margin of $19,931,450 to
$18,415,202. In the next decade Illinois moved increasingly ahead, until
by 1955–56 its income was $63,016,808 as compared to Harvard's $45,-
358,240. (See Tables 2 and 3.) The gap has continued to widen.

Table 2. Harvard University Income by Sources

Year	Endowment	Gifts for current use and receipts for special purposes	Tuition and other student income	Contract reimbursement and other receipts	Total
1911–12	$ 1,198,940	$ 328,490	$ 863,100	$ 96,940	$ 2,487,470
1915–16	1,413,860	374,090	1,049,750	97,710	2,935,410
1920–21	2,443,860	934,920	1,439,340	918,240	5,736,360
1925–26	3,972,130	1,359,110	3,190,060	963,190	9,484,490
1930–31	5,833,020	2,196,710	5,592,277	1,424,933	15,046,940
1935–36	4,670,460	1,424,620	5,497,670	939,540	12,532,290
1940–41	5,409,080	1,825,510	5,899,690	619,520	13,753,800
1945–46	5,656,550	1,681,690	5,795,300	6,797,910	19,931,450
1950–51	7,823,610	5,647,370	12,480,660	6,381,540	32,333,180
1955–56	11,528,750	10,338,970	15,567,440	7,923,080	45,358,240

In these figures, I suggest, lies the basic cause of the conflict between
private and public higher education. The historian Richard Hofstadter
noted in 1952 that "with the decline of the great individual fortunes, the
business community has, at least for the moment, lost its will or capacity
to sustain education in the style to which education feels it has a right to
be accustomed."[8] Since that time such institutions as Harvard and Yale,
Chicago and Princeton, have successfully conducted major fund-raising
campaigns, but less prominent schools have not attracted comparable
benefactions. And meanwhile all private education has observed the
seeming inevitability with which increased income accrues to public colleges and universities, at least in our wealthier states. It is not surprising
that its spokesmen have expressed a certain envy of this segment of the

Table 3. University of Illinois Income by Source

Year	Institution's income	State	Federal	Private (endowments, gifts, and grants)	Total
1911–12	$ 316,849.08	$ 1,192,400.00	$ 112,402.00	$ 3,000.00	$ 1,624,651.08
1915–16	449,772.34	2,016,870.95	148,732.54	. . . . .	2,615,375.83
1920–21	900,873.06	2,426,753.54	337,465.84	5,953.93	3,671,046.37
1925–26	1,164,531.11	4,260,898.05	375,553.31	14,720.00	5,815,702.47
1930–31	1,314,875.11	4,644,254.21	461,715.41	231,553.62	6,652,398.35
1935–36	1,474,965.49	4,381,650.08	632,497.62	154,946.57	6,644,059.76
1940–41	2,302,272.81	5,432,500.00	983,307.77	501,940.59	9,220,021.17
1945–46	4,486,444.98	9,978,321.82	3,389,334.65	561,101.49	18,415,202.94
1950–51	9,980,511.65	27,139,367.14	4,232,950.57	1,723,657.54	43,076,486.90
1955–56	12,698,448.39	38,798,752.52	8,675,596.57	2,844,010.91	63,016,808.39

American institutional structure, which apparently, like T. S. Eliot's True Church,

> need never stir
> To gather in its dividends.

Undeniably some public institutions have profited greatly from this prosperity. Their rising salary scales, their expanding facilities, and their open-ended programs have given them substantial advantages in attracting able faculty members. Their comparatively low tuition charges have assured them of a steady flow of students. But meagerly supported public institutions remain, and in any event even the most favored have not had everything their own way. The combination of traditional prestige and continuing excellence of program in leading private institutions exerts an irresistible appeal to many of the nation's outstanding scholars and teachers and to a majority of the nation's outstanding students. As a result there has developed vigorous rivalry between the two groups.

In the past, American higher education has profited greatly from the salutary emulation of public and private institutions, but in recent years the competition has sometimes assumed a form most damaging to their joint cause. One can understand the exasperation of the president of a small private college which is struggling for survival as he observes the handsome plant, the generous salaries, and the burgeoning enrollment that tax money makes possible in a nearby public university. But one cannot therefore excuse his misleading assurances, usually to audiences uninformed about such matters, that private institutions alone uphold religion, free enterprise, academic freedom, attention to the individual student, and the tradition of liberal education, all the while exercising exemplary frugality in expending their resources. Spokesmen for public higher education have less incentive for attack, but in defending their institutions, they too have been led into intemperate and misleading statements about their private rivals. The result of these debates has been to undermine the public's faith in higher education generally.

At the 1958 meeting of the American Council on Education, Chancellor Kimpton of the University of Chicago called attention to this "growing schism between our public and our private institutions." As a consequence early this year the Council issued an important statement entitled "The Need to Close Ranks in Higher Education." It reads, in part:[9]

> A great and unique strength of American higher education stems from the historic coexistence of strong private institutions and strong public institutions. American society benefits from the maintenance of both types, each at its best. Rivalry among institutions, and between groups of institutions, is healthy when conducted in an atmosphere of mutual respect. But generalizations which attribute qualitative characteristics to institutions simply because they are public or private go beyond the facts. There are strong institutions and weak ones in both groups. Differences among the members within a group are much greater than are differences between the two categories. The strength and value of a college flow from *what it is*, not from the category to which it belongs. It is as shortsighted as it is false to promote one segment of higher education at the expense of another.

The analysis is judicious, and the counsel is wise. But since causes of conflict remain, the conflict itself will not easily be suppressed. At least educational leaders should be alert to its dangers.

Intrastate Dissensions Among Public Institutions

Conflict in American higher education is not limited to the relationships between private and public institutions. It is even more in evidence in the relationships among public institutions. It should be noted, however, that whereas debate between public and private institutions has been carried on chiefly at the national level, dissension among public institutions has been most virulent within state boundaries. Colleges and universities of like characteristics in the several states may be athletic rivals, but having like interests, they are apt to be academic allies. The real conflict occurs among institutions, often with very different aims and standards, that look for financial support to the same state legislature, and the fact that it is thus intrastate means that such organizations as the American Association of Land-Grant Colleges and State Universities, the State Universities Association, and their Joint Office of Institutional Research can be of little assistance in appeasing it. This conflict has intensified over the last thirty years as the Federal government has preempted an increasing proportion of tax funds, leaving the many agencies dependent on state support to compete for the smaller proportion of tax funds that remain.

From North Carolina to California and from Texas to Michigan the same pattern has developed. Within each state the several public colleges and universities, representing different regional interests and responsible to different governing boards, pursue their individual programs. In time growing disharmony leads them to attempt coordination through voluntary association. But though exchange of information is thus facilitated and joint action sometimes proves possible in noncontroversial areas, these institutions inevitably shy away from hard decisions on vital questions. It is too much, after all, to expect an institution voluntarily to acquiesce in actions hostile to its own interests. Thomas Carlyle tells a barnyard fable current at the time of the French Revolution which is applicable here. A farmer asks a chicken with what sauce it would like to be eaten. The chicken responds that it doesn't want to be eaten at all. Whereupon the farmer replies, "You are wandering from the point."

Faced with the necessity of reconciling or controlling institutional rivalries, these voluntary organizations are apt to deteriorate into theaters for invective in which a premium, in terms of results achieved, seems to be placed on unprofessional behavior. The Illinois Joint Council on Higher Education is by no means the most turbulent of these groups, yet from two years of personal observation of that body I could provide examples of each of the Shakespearean degrees of quarreling—from the retort courteous and the quip modest, through the reply churlish, the reproof valiant, and the countercheck quarrelsome, to the lie with circumstance and the lie direct. It is unnecessary to point out with what glee these exchanges are described by irreverent reporters on the front pages of their newspapers ("Prexies Clash at Meeting!") and how damaging they are to the cause of higher education.

Confronted by this unedifying picture, disillusioned citizens and harried legislators are impelled to call for a controlling agency legally empowered to deal with questions which by their nature cannot be resolved by decisions within institutions, to review conflicting interests and render firm judgments after thorough and impartial study, and to develop for each of the several state-supported institutions an appropriate role in a coherent system that will best serve the higher educational needs of the state. The next step is typically the establishment of a pattern of voluntary coordination of budget requests and other activities (as in Indiana, Ohio, and, most recently, Michigan), or even the legal creation of a coordinating agency (as in Iowa, Wisconsin, and North Carolina). But since the same special interests remain, the result of such a move may be merely to shift the conflict from one arena to another.

Conflict exists as well, of course, among private institutions, where competition for financial support, faculty, and able students is wide-spread. But there is little to report about such conflict, since in the nature of the case it rarely becomes part of the printed record. Certainly it has not attracted the public attention devoted to the nationwide debate between public and private education or to the intrastate disagreements of the public colleges and universities.

Unifying Forces

Thus far I have dealt with the divisive forces operating in American higher education. Springing as they do from deep-seated conflicts of interest, they constitute a persisting threat to the national welfare. Fortunately there are also powerful unifying forces at work. Much might be said, for example, of the attempts to mitigate conflict between private and public institutions made by such national organizations as the American Council on Education and the Association of American Universities. Particularly encouraging in this connection is the way in which the Council for Financial Aid to Education has developed. This organization, which originally spoke only for private colleges and universities, now has three representatives from public institutions on its board, and emphasis has correspondingly shifted in its program. The work of these national organizations in circulating information and evolving responsible statements of policy has been invaluable in maintaining before the great public the united front so necessary to the health of American higher education.

Still more significant in promise, if not yet in accomplishment, is another kind of cooperation: the efforts of the colleges and universities themselves to improve services and effect economies through joint studies and programs. There is a vast network of such cooperative relationships in American higher education, which it is both enlightening and encouraging to survey.

Most far-reaching and productive are the regional cooperative arrangements evolved by the public institutions. On Frederic Jackson Turner's principle that "we are in reality a federation of sections rather than of states," three major regions of the United States have established higher educational compacts. These ventures have had the support of the Council of State Governments, a joint governmental agency of all the states, and two of the three compacts have been confirmed by Congress. They are financed by annual grants from participating states, and they have enjoyed generous aid from the foundations.

The pioneer organization is the Southern Regional Education Board, which since 1949 has operated under a compact signed by sixteen states: Alabama, Arkansas, Delaware, Florida, Georgia, Kentucky, Louisiana,

Maryland, Mississippi, North Carolina, Oklahoma, South Carolina, Tennessee, Texas, West Virginia, and Virginia. By means of "contracts for services" and "student aid contracts" the SREB enables states not offering work in medicine, dentistry, veterinary medicine, or social work to send its students for training to states in which such work is offered, thus at the same time providing funds and qualified students to strengthen existing programs (in private as well as public institutions) and avoiding the establishment of expensive and unnecessary new programs. During the academic year 1958–59, 847 such students were accommodated. The SREB also conducts programs for training and research in mental health, forestry, city planning, nursing, petroleum sciences, and other fields, and serves as a clearing house for information and as a general planning agency for the states which it serves.

The Western Interstate Commission for Higher Education, which includes thirteen states (Alaska, Arizona, California, Colorado, Hawaii, Idaho, Montana, Nevada, New Mexico, Oregon, Utah, Washington, and Wyoming), was established in 1953 on the pattern of the SREB. The WICHE too has developed student exchange programs in medicine, dentistry, veterinary medicine, mental health, nursing, graduate training in the arts and sciences, and in other areas. It also acts as a fact-finding and planning agency for regional educational programs.

The smallest of these regional organizations is the New England Higher Educational Compact, which since 1955 has served Connecticut, Maine, Massachusetts, New Hampshire, Rhode Island, and Vermont. Thus far its activities have been chiefly in the field of medical and dental training, in which a student exchange program is in operation. But its general mission is to provide information and planning as needed and, particularly, to avoid unnecessary duplication of facilities.

It will be noted that, apart from New York, New Jersey, and Pennsylvania, all states except the twelve Midwestern states are represented in these compacts. This gap may be attributed to the fact that higher education in the Middle West is dominated by a unique group of large, complex, and relatively self-sufficient universities. All of the Council of Ten institutions, for example, appear in Dr. Raymond Walters' list of the twenty largest schools in the United States, and all are likewise complex institutions whose broad and well-balanced programs are designed to satisfy the general higher educational needs of their states.

It is for this reason, presumably, that exploration by the Council of State Governments into the possibility of a Midwestern interstate compact have come to nothing. In the meantime, another kind of regional organization has been formed. With the aid of grants from the Carnegie Corporation of New York there was organized last year a Committee on Institutional Cooperation of the Council of Ten Universities and the University of Chicago. This differs from the three regional compacts in two ways. It is voluntary rather than legal. And instead of including all the public institutions in the seven states over which it extends, it is made up of nine major public institutions (University of Illinois, Indiana University, State University of Iowa, University of Michigan, Michigan State University, University of Minnesota, Ohio State University, Purdue University, and University of Wisconsin) and two major private institutions (University of Chicago and Northwestern University). The committee is presently engaged in a joint study of common needs, which it hopes will lead to cooperative action.

Though not so inclusive as among public colleges and universities, large-scale experiments in cooperation among private institutions are not lacking. Early this year, for example, ten private Midwestern colleges (Beloit, Carleton, Coe, Cornell, Grinnell, Knox, Lawrence, Monmouth, Ripon, and St. Olaf), which together enroll about ten thousand students, joined together as the Associated Colleges of the Midwest. With the aid of a Ford Foundation grant they have launched a joint attack on their educational and financial problems through the cooperative exploration of such areas as fund raising, purchasing, faculty recruitment, and research.

Similarly there are many instances of group programs which include both public and private institutions. The activities of the Richmond Area University Center, which includes sixteen institutions as affiliates, are well known. Four New England schools in close geographical proximity, Amherst, Mount Holyoke, Smith, and the University of Massachusetts, share resources and make joint faculty appointments. The Midwest Inter-Library Center in Chicago stores the little-used books and periodicals of nineteen universities, thus increasing the reservoir of scholarly materials available to each institution while effecting real savings. The physics departments of fifteen leading universities have joined in support of the Midwest Universities Research Association (MURA), which conducts a cooperative program at Madison, Wisconsin. A "research triangle" has been created in North Carolina to serve the common needs of Duke University, the University of North Carolina, and North Carolina State University.

Cooperation between individual institutions, both public and private, is of course a commonplace throughout the nation. The Universities of Chicago and Texas have a joint program in astronomy, and the University of California and Stanford University are cooperating in several areas of graduate work. This type of arrangement is perhaps best illustrated, however, among the major midwestern institutions. The latest inventory, that compiled by the Committee on Institutional Cooperation during the present year, devotes four pages to listing by key title programs ranging from Adult Education to Scandinavian Studies.

Higher Education: Our Long-range Defense

In 1947 President Truman's Commission on Higher Education maintained that:[10]

> American colleges and universities must envision a much larger role for education in the national life. They can no longer consider themselves merely the instrument for producing an intellectual elite; they must become the means by which every citizen, youth, and adult is enabled and encouraged to carry his education, formal and informal, as far as his native capacities permit.

As the nation's postwar mood of generosity has faded, and as the enormous cost of such a program has become evident, there has been a retreat on the part of some educational leaders from this sweeping position. A tendency can be noted among spokesmen for the private sector of higher education to claim that this position is unwise as well as impracticable. Their case is forcefully presented, for example, by Professor Douglas Bush of Harvard University in an article for the *New York Times Magazine* significantly entitled "Education for All is Education for None." [11]

Such spokesmen sometimes look to British and continental higher education for illustrations of the benefits to be derived from drastically restricting admissions. Reading their arguments, I am reminded of a letter which Thomas Jefferson, America's great early apologist for higher education, wrote to a friend after first crossing the Atlantic in 1785:[12]

> Behold me at length on the vaunted scene of Europe! . . . You are perhaps curious to know how this new scene has struck a savage of the mountains of America. Not advantageously, I assure you. I find the general fate of humanity here most deplorable. The truth of Voltaire's observation offers itself perpetually, that every man here must be either the hammer or the anvil. It is a true picture of that country to which they say we shall pass hereafter, and where we are to see God and his angels in splendor, and crowds of the damned trampled under their feet.

It was to avoid duplicating such a state of society that our early statesmen made the United States, in Lincoln's classic phrase, a nation "conceived in liberty, and dedicated to the proposition that all men are created equal." Ever since, education has been the instrument by which such equality has been rendered workable. As the nation has grown in strength and prosperity, the unique American conception of an obligation to provide universal educational opportunity has been extended to increasingly higher levels, and Prof. J. K. Galbraith can accordingly assert that in the United States "investment in education, assessed qualitatively as well as quantitatively, becomes very close to being the basic index of social progress." [13]

We have seen how conflict in American higher education today stems chiefly from competition, direct or indirect, for financial support. Similarly, the most powerful motives thus far impelling colleges and universities toward cooperation have been to economize on existing programs and avoid embarking on new ones. American higher education can entertain little hope either of building a foundation for permanent harmony or of comprehensively exploring the possibilities of cooperative arrangements as long as its representatives are committed to trying to make do with anything like their current level of support. Instead they should unite in proposing that "The basic choice for the people of our country is between expenditures for higher education and expenditures for other things." [14] The Armed Forces are our short-range defense. In a very real sense education, and particularly higher education, constitutes our long-range defense. With regard to both, the nation can "afford" what it has to have.

Notes

1. "Investment in Survival," *Business Horizons*, p. 49, Spring, 1959.

2. In his foreword Mr. Ruml grants: "It would have been possible to proceed from the point of view that the economic and financial needs of the college arise from a duty to protect a curriculum and methods of instruction of unquestioned merit and revealed value." *Memo to a College Trustee*, McGraw-Hill Book Company, Inc., New York, 1959, p. xi.

3. *Memo to a College Trustee*, p. 13.

4. See *Harvard Alumni Bulletin*, vol. 56, pp. 316–317, Jan. 23, 1954.

5. Mr. Ruml's collaborator, the late Donald Morrison, in effect admits this (pp. 75–76): "No one can predict where leadership [in putting Mr. Ruml's proposals to the test] will arise. The colleges which are now regarded as the strongest may not in fact be the source of this leadership. An institution under stress is likely to see its problems more clearly and be more resourceful and determined in seeking solutions than an institution confident of survival without extraordinary efforts on its part."

6. The percentages for enrollment in public institutions would be substantially lower if only degree-granting institutions were included. Nearly three-quarters of American junior colleges enrollment is in public institutions. Since statistics are not available for regular-session resident enrollments in 1945–46, the percentage cited for this year is based on fall-term resident enrollments.

7. See, however, Table 14 of *Higher Education in the Forty-eight States*,

which provides comparative data between 1918 and 1950.

8. Richard Hofstadter and C. de Witt Hardy, *The Development and Scope of Higher Education in the United States*, New York, 1952, p. 105.

9. Washington, 1959, p. 1.

10. *Higher Education for American Democracy*, New York, 1947, vol. 1, 101.

11. January 9, 1955, pp. 13, 30, 32.

12. Julian P. Boyd (ed.), *The Papers of Thomas Jefferson*, vol. 8, Princeton, N.J., 1953, 568.

13. *The Affluent Society*, Boston, 1958, p. 345.

14. *The Need to Close Ranks in Higher Education*, p. 3.

6

Opportunities for Improved Management in Higher Education

H. J. Heneman

As seen in the preceding papers, although estimates vary widely, the projected additional capital and operating expenditures for higher education in 1970 will be considerably greater than they are today. Also in the preceding papers an attempt has been made to determine from what sources the money needed to meet these added costs will come. It was pointed out by Mr. Harris, in his thought-provoking contribution, that a part of the total cost could be met by an estimated $1 billion or more annually to be obtained through economies and sounder management of colleges and universities.

It is difficult to determine with accuracy how much money may become available as a result of better management practices, because suitable data upon which to base firm projections are unavailable. It is true, however, that sounder management can produce substantial savings and that these should not be overlooked. It is significant that a growing number of governing boards, presidents, and faculties are showing an interest in making economies in nonessential internal operations. Among corporate donors, legislatures, alumni, and the public there is a growing belief that institutions of higher education have an obligation to improve the effectiveness with which they use their resources if they expect to get wholehearted support for their requests for tremendously larger amounts of money.

Fortunately, experience has shown that it is possible to effect economies both in capital and operating expenditures without impairing the quality of education and research. In fact, by avoiding unnecessary expenditures through better management, many institutions have found that funds become available for use where they are needed, as in better salaries for the faculty. It should be clear that money unnecessarily spent on administration, teaching, and the wide range of supporting services found in a modern university is money diverted from the essential job to be done.

Although economies in internal operations can be a significant source of funds, it would be a mistake to equate sound management exclusively with economies. Sometimes sounder management dictates that more money be spent. Some colleges and universities, especially the smaller ones, are undermanaged and are not spending enough for good administration.

The fact that better management for some institutions means the opportunity to effect economies and for others may mean additional expenditures underscores the importance of examining the subject of management in higher education on the basis of individual institutional situations rather than on a basis of broad generalizations.

The information contained in this paper has come from more than one hundred actual studies of management in educational organizations. The colleges and universities referred to anonymously later in this chapter include Ivy League institutions, men's colleges, women's colleges, land-grant universities, and statewide university systems. They vary in size from fewer than five hundred students to many thousands. In addition to including all types of colleges and universities, they range geographically from Massachusetts to California and from Minnesota to Texas. It probably can be said that their operations represent a fair cross section of present practices and that the opportunities they have presented for improved management and economies are typical, if this generalization will be permitted.

It is not the purpose of this paper to substantiate any estimates of income from internal economies made elsewhere in this book. Rather, the purpose of the paper is to show where and how sounder management of colleges and universities may be obtained and what some of the benefits of improved management and administration may be. In the pages which follow there are discussed, first, certain principles, practices, or other factors which contribute to more effective administration, since economies cannot easily be obtained without a sound system of management, and, second, some of the tangible and intangible results which come through more effective management. Observations are made concerning the following subjects: the scope of college management, attitudes toward sound management, governing boards and chief executive officers, planning and controls, the importance of sound organization, the use of people, the use of money, the use of plant, instructional costs, areas and methods of economies, and interinstitutional cooperation. There also are summarized a number of economies actually effected which are illustrative of what colleges and universities can do.

The Scope of College Management

In September, 1957, and in October, 1958, *Fortune* magazine published articles which dealt with the problems of the "educational industry." The reference to education as an industry will, of course, be displeasing to some. Yet, in terms of the thousands of persons employed, the millions of dollars spent annually, and the hundreds of millions in which physical property is valued, education is a tremendous enterprise. As shown by Mr. Harris in an earlier paper, the annual expenditures on higher education operations in a few years may be about $10 to $12 billion. Capital expenditures would be in addition.

The percentage of the total annual operating expenditures of a college or university which goes for instruction and research varies widely. In large and diversified universities, the percentages of total expenditures for educational purposes (instruction, research, libraries, other educational operations, and faculty annuity payments) are reported to range from 50 to approximately 75 per cent. However, a study made a few years ago showed that in sixty colleges the average percentage of annual expenditures for educational purposes was only about 41 per cent.

For illustrative purposes, let us assume that a university's annual expenditures are divided on a 60:40 basis, the 60 per cent going principally to the instructional units for the items listed in the paragraph above and the remaining 40 per cent for the salaries of nonteaching personnel and for materials, supplies, and services in a wide variety of activities that include buildings and grounds maintenance, food service, housing, business office, intercollegiate athletics, intramural athletic program, a radio station, a motor pool, a printing and publications department, a heating plant, a student center, and an infirmary.

The president is held responsible for the administration of all of the affairs represented in both sides of the budget. That so much of his time and energy must be devoted to activities which are of a nonacademic nature is one of the factors which causes some presidents to become disenchanted with their jobs. Yet the management responsibility is there and cannot be avoided. The problem is how best to organize, plan, and direct this wide range of activities.

Three observations may be made concerning the twofold split in the

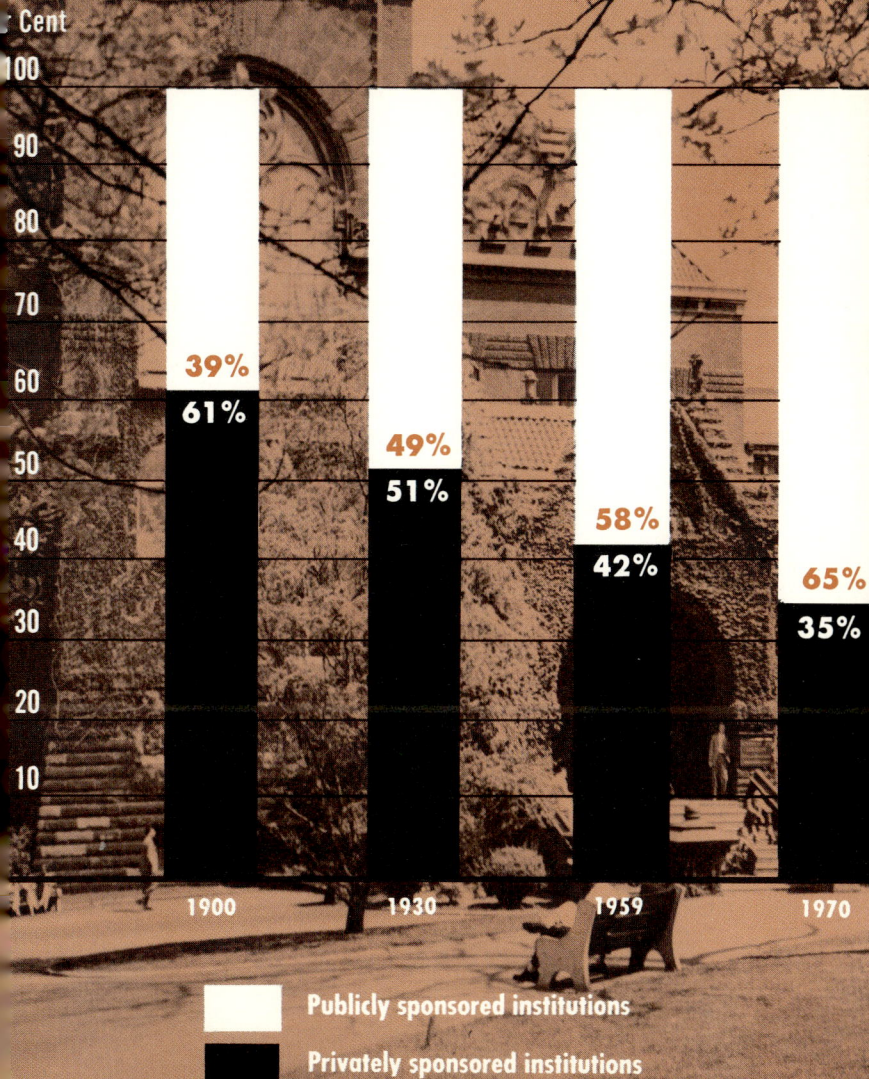

TREND IS FOR
STUDENTS
TO GO TO
PUBLICLY
SPONSORED
INSTITUTIONS

Per Cent

100
90
80
70
60
50
40
30
20
10

1900 — 39% / 61%
1930 — 49% / 51%
1959 — 58% / 42%
1970 — 65% / 35%

☐ Publicly sponsored institutions
■ Privately sponsored institutions

budget of the university referred to above. The first is that the share of annual expenditures which goes for the main purposes for which the university exists, that is, instruction and research, is possibly not as large as many think. The second observation is that many persons often fail to remember that the supporting and auxiliary services and other activities represented in the noninstructional side of the budget are as extensive as indicated. The third observation is that every dollar unnecessarily spent on supporting services and activities is diverted from salaries and supplies for persons engaged in instruction and research.

Attitudes toward Sound Management

The job of managing a college or university is more difficult and complex than the task of running a business of comparable size. Notwithstanding his responsibility, the university president usually is not as well paid as his business counterpart; he often will not have the staff aides to assist him in discharging his duties; and his attitude toward the significance of sound management often is underdeveloped as compared with the attitude of his business opposite. The benefits of effective administration in higher education will be obtained when those responsible for the direction of our colleges and universities have a better understanding of the significance of better management.

The compelling factors of cost, price, and competition are frequent reminders to the business executive that he must use his resources wisely and economically. Not so with the university president. He often does not know whether the money, the people, and the plant entrusted to his care are being fully and effectively used. In cases of deficit operations, it has been traditional to think only of where to turn for additional funds. Requests are made of alumni, corporate and general foundations, and other donors. State legislatures are asked for larger appropriations. There is an increased willingness to accept larger sums from the Federal government. Tuition charges may be increased. Many university presidents have tended to turn to new sources of income rather than react to deficit operations by including in their thinking how it might be possible to reduce deficits by upgrading the administration of their institutions.

This difference in attitude toward the importance of sound management is understandable. The objectives of a college or university are quite different from those of a profit-making business enterprise. It is more important to have as the head of a university a person who can further the educational objectives of the institution than one who is management-minded but unaware of the importance of the primary objectives. The chief executive officers of many universities traditionally have come from the ranks of scholars. There has been little in their experience to give them administrative responsibilities or expose them to the importance of good management. In short, unlike their business counterparts, college and university presidents customarily are not chosen for their managerial skill, and they frequently are out of their depths where administrative management is concerned. This is an almost unique situation in the various fields of organized human effort, since the head of a university may be selected without having demonstrated the qualities necessary for successful leadership. It is almost accidental if a large number of the selections turn out well.

The Carnegie Corporation, in its annual report for 1958, pointed out that the transition of the scholar to administrator creates problems and that the scholar who has not had administrative experience may be incapable of dealing with the responsibilities which face him. Although he may learn on the job, he does so with great cost to himself and to others, including the institution which he serves.

It is to be hoped that there will be concerted effort, perhaps by a foundation, to establish a program that would give persons destined for responsible executive positions in universities the kind of composite training that would help them discharge their responsibilities. The training should involve much more than merely exposure to their own colleagues on a conference or workshop basis. College administrators should have the benefits of what has been learned about executive leadership in many fields.

Some colleges and universities have recognized that a combination of talents is required for their sound and effective management: When the president is a strong academic leader, he has on his staff one or more persons whose major contribution to the institution is in the field of management; when the president himself is endowed with management skills, his staff includes as second in command one whose strength is in academic leadership.

It is an inescapable fact, however, whether or not it is a palatable one, that a university today is a complex enterprise. Although a college or university cannot be operated like a business, it is possible to apply the principles of sound management, and there is ample room for business-like methods in directing the affairs of institutions of higher education. It also is true that the competition for tax and gift dollars already is keen and will become even greater. In this competitive situation there may be the element which forces a greater recognition of the importance of effective management. Developments will depend in large measure upon the wisdom with which the governing boards and the presidents of our colleges and universities discharge their responsibilities.

Governing Boards and Chief Executive Officers

One of the major problem areas in the operation of a college or university is at the level of the governing board and in the relationships of the board and the chief executive, whether he be called a president or chancellor or have some other title. Governing boards often do not assume and do not know how to discharge their responsibilities. Boards usually are composed of sincere and well-intentioned persons who often are successful in business or professional life but are unfamiliar with the operations of a university and are somewhat overawed by educational problems. They may even be effective board members in a business enterprise, but in a college or university they sometimes do not know how to establish control over policy and often experience a sense of futility.

There are figurehead boards whose members contribute little or nothing to the management of the college or university, and there are meddling or interfering boards whose members seek to demonstrate their strength and ability by getting into the details of administration and who circumvent the president to deal directly with his subordinates or with members of the faculty.

For their part, presidents often neglect to use their boards as a source of strength. Some presidents dread meetings with their governing boards and look upon the members with suspicion and as a group with which they are in conflict. Some seek to withhold information from the board and to keep the board at arm's length.

Much needs to be done to define and improve the role of governing boards and the relationships of presidents to their boards in order to strengthen college management. A board, to be effective, requires strong leadership and staff support from the administration under it, and it is the responsibility of the president to see that they are provided. A president should welcome the advice and counsel which a strong board can give him; a wise board should hold the president responsible and should not circumvent or undercut him.

The president should see that his board deals with major matters and not with trivia. Governing boards should seek to establish objectives and policies and to insist upon the selection of good people. They should ask for assistance from the president and his chief administrative and educational officers in defining educational objectives; developing a plan of organization for administration; establishing requirements for plant, money, and people; and planning for the longer periods of time. Once objectives and policies have been systematically defined and approved by it, the governing board should permit the administration to conduct its affairs within the framework of those policies.

Many boards and presidents fall into the error of thinking that the governing board is exercising controls over administration when it approves each purchase order or passes upon the hiring of a new stenographer in the business office. When the board has reviewed the justification in support of the expenditures proposed in the annual budget, that should be ample to control all purchases, since they should all be included in the budget. Similarly, if the administration has prepared a table of personnel strengths for the university by major organizational unit and the table has been approved by the board, that is all that is required at the board level, and stenographers or any other employees should be hired within the limits of the personnel policies established. The detailed kind of control followed by so many boards tends to get boards involved in the minutiae of administration and diverts their time from matters of genuine importance.

Boards need to exercise controls to make sure that established policies are being followed, which means that they should be furnished with systematic reports on a regular basis. The reports may be monthly income and expenditure reports by organizational unit and function that compare actual operating results with the budget; they may be reports on personnel strengths, fund-raising progress, or other matters. Any plans of the administration to amend or depart from established policies should, of course, be reported promptly to the board for consideration.

Governing boards vary greatly in size. There is no magic number as to size, although large boards usually are dominated by a smaller group, such as an executive committee. Among our client colleges and universities have been boards as small as seven and as large as one hundred. The average size seems to run about fifteen to eighteen members. It might be noted here that self-perpetuating boards should fight the tendency toward inbreeding and becoming overaged.

Usually, boards operate through committees. The committee structure of some boards is a bewildering maze of outmoded and outdated bodies which provide little support to the board as a whole in dealing with the major problems of institutional management and may complicate internal administration. However, the basic committees which normally are found to be most useful include the following: educational policies, budget and finance, buildings and grounds, student affairs, development and planning, and executive. It is surprising how many boards fragment these committees and create bodies which either confuse basic areas of management or fall into disuse.

It is very important that there be sound staff work in support of the governing board. That means that agenda should be prepared well in advance of meeting dates, so that all items may be studied by board members prior to meetings. There should be supporting materials for all major items on the agenda which set forth the policy question or issue involved, background information of a factual character which bears upon the problem, and recommended action. All too often boards are put in the position of taking hasty action because a matter is "sprung" on them by the administration. Boards should immediately discourage any president who seeks to follow this practice.

The president should use his chief administrative and educational officers as his staff in preparing materials for board meetings. Some person should be designated as a secretary to the board to see that minutes and records are properly maintained, that decisions are communicated to persons affected, and that reports on action taken are transmitted back to the board. In a small college this might be a part-time function, whereas in a larger university it frequently is a full-time job.

Many presidents have found the combination of talents present in a strong board as well as a wise board chairman to be sources of strength. Strong presidents use the counsel of their boards through their committees in the various phases of internal management. They know how to profit from the contacts which individual board members have and which are valuable in public, legislative, and foundation relations or in fund raising. Strong presidents have found advantages in having a board chairman who can serve as spokesman for the university or college on certain matters. These presidents also have found advantages in having a chairman who can be an informal channel of communication and with whom the president can consult rather than take all matters to the board formally.

Members of boards and college and university presidents should keep in mind that the responsibility for the affairs of the college or university has been vested in the governing board. The board should not shrink from exercising its authority intelligently. The president should not fail to provide the leadership, guidance, and information which boards need so that they may discharge their responsibilities effectively. The keystone of good management is to be found in sound relationships at the board-president level.

Planning and Controls

A wisely managed business enterprise knows that nothing is more important to it than its own future. A good deal of thought and effort will be devoted exclusively to planning the future development of the business.

In our colleges and universities the planning function often is neglected. Unfortunately, the lack of forward planning contributes to unsound management practices and to costly and inefficient administration and instruction.

In all of the discussion of increasing enrollments, the basic question of who should attend college (that is, who should enroll at the approximately 1,800 institutions commonly listed by the United States Office of Education) has not been dealt with. It must be assumed, therefore, that present admissions policies generally will continue.

An individual college, however, should define what it wants to be, what it plans to teach, what its educational standards are, what clientele it will serve, what kind of faculty it must have to do the educational job defined, what its enrollment objectives are, what physical plant is necessary, what funds will be required, and other matters relating to the objectives of the college. It is surprising how many colleges and universities have not taken a five-year, or ten-year or longer, look at themselves by projections into the future. What may seem like elementary questions, such as the items summarized above, go unanswered. As a result, growth is apt to be unplanned. New degree programs and their necessay crourses of instruction are spawned with little control. Staff and funds are diverted to courses or to other activities which are on the periphery of the basic educational objectives of the institution. Unnecessary buildings sometimes are constructed. Funds are drained into nonessential activities.

We have seen facilities built for a professional school which were larger than needed because no analysis of enrollment had been made. The added upkeep cost represents an unnecessary drain on annual income. In another instance, the kind of student records to be kept and the procedures for keeping them were determined without knowing what the policy of the college with regard to the expansion of enrollment would be. Investment was made in mechanized equipment which now will be inadequate. Or take the case of a liberal arts college which had not determined its educational objectives and thought that an indication of greatness was a multiplicity of degree programs. With its limited resources, this resulted in an overworked and underpaid faculty. It is not necessary to add to these illustrations, but it is worth noting that these things occur even in our "better" universities.

To get planning under way, a president should obtain from each of his principal administrative and educational officers a definition of policies and objectives in his own area of responsibility, whether it be curriculum, admissions standards and student affairs, business and finance, management, plant, or alumni relations. These specific plans should be reviewed and coordinated into an over-all plan and submitted to the governing board for consideration and approval. Projections of requirements for resources based upon this over-all plan should be made for a five- or ten-year period. The annual budget and the supporting justifications for funds submitted with the budget should be in terms of this longer-range plan. Annual reprojections should be made in the light of experience so that the intermediate or longer-range plan may be adjusted to experience. The board should request regular reports on actual developments in order to evaluate the soundness of planning and determine the need for revisions in projections.

It is not intended to be implied here that all aspects of the affairs of a college or a university can be laid out in detail after the manner of a Russian five-year plan. However, it is pertinent to note that there could be very much more planning than there now is and that college management would benefit from the introduction of planning practices. Inadequate salaries could be increased in many institutions if the staff, including the faculty, did not have to help pay for activities and commitments which are not pertinent to the attainment of a sound educational program. The attempt of one college to introduce an element of longer-range planning is shown in the interesting and informative paper by Mr. Tickton.

Importance of Sound Organization

It is impossible to have effective and efficient internal management of a university's affairs without a sound organization for administration. This means that related functions should be grouped together under a single managerial head, that responsibilities should be clearly fixed, and that reporting relationships should be clearly understood. There should be no doubt who is accountable for what and to whom. These arrangements should be made clear at the level of management immediately below the president and on down into the departmental level.

The president should recognize that he cannot do everything, and he should organize and staff his institution so that he may utilize his strengths effectively and have assistance in the areas in which he is less strong. Although the president alone is responsible for the internal management of the university, he should define responsibilities and delegate them to his subordinate officers in the principal areas of administration: academic programs, business and finance, plant and grounds, student affairs, planning and development, and possibly others. Even in a small college parts of the total responsibility can be divided and delegated to persons who serve in an administrative capacity on a part-time basis.

Unless a president has a sound internal organization and adequate staff assistance, he will not have the time to provide leadership and to think. He may find that he is busy being his own superintendent of buildings and grounds, his own registrar, his own personnel officer, or his own

food-service director and that presidential functions are not being discharged at all.

The president of an Eastern men's university which recently revised its
organization for administration and placed it on a sound basis has said
that he now is as busy as ever, but with important subjects.

In arranging responsibility for functions in his plan of organization,
the president should make every effort to assign primary responsibility
for every major aspect of the university's affairs to some administrative
officer. To be sure, it very often is the case that more than one part of the
organization of the university is involved in a given matter and should be
consulted or should participate in decision making. However, that is true
in almost any organization; the fact is not a reason for diffusing responsibility by placing parts of it in all persons who are involved. It should
be possible to fix primary responsibility in one administrative officer, who
then also has the responsibility to consult with the others concerned.
The president should not have to look to several persons for an answer
on most questions. He should look only to one person.

The unwillingness or failure to fix administrative responsibility is
largely responsible for one of the greatest defects in college administration, and that is the plethora of committees. It is because primary responsibility has not been fixed in a single administrative officer that it is necessary in many institutions to conduct administration by the town-meeting
process, a notoriously time-consuming and ineffective way to get things
done. In one well-known university, we found at the president's level
twenty standing and forty-three *ad hoc* committees involved in administration. These committees were exclusive of those involved in academic
matters. Some committees, of course, will continue to be necessary, but
the number of committees should be limited in size rather than multiplied. Committees are not a substitute for sound organization.

The Use of People

Each department, office, or functional unit of the organization should
be staffed with the persons needed to discharge the organization's responsibilities. Staffing should be in terms of the purposes or objectives
to be carried out and of the workload involved. The positions, by type
and classification, required for each unit of the organization should be
prepared in a systematic form by the administration and approved by the
board.

A major problem in the personnel field is that colleges and universities
often find it difficult to get the caliber of persons needed to do specific
jobs because of the generally low ceilings on salaries. As a result, many
institutions will hire greater numbers of persons at low salaries, thereby

substituting quantity for quality. Actually, they would be better off in many cases to pay higher salaries to fewer persons. A recent study showed that the median salary of the principal business officers in a group of large colleges and universities was about $10,000. Many had salary levels lower than that figure. Yet these officers were responsible for operations running into the millions, and in other fields persons on their level of responsibility would be more highly compensated in order to attract highly competent talent.

The importance of good leadership and direction should be recognized and paid for, and hopefully the time will come when salaries for administrators as well as faculty will be at a level to attract superior persons in the required numbers. It is virtually impossible to obtain sound planning, direction, and control over expenditures with mediocre talent. Effective and economical administration begins with competence at the top at each level of management.

As in industry, the job of management has become more difficult and complex in colleges and universities. But unlike industry, educational institutions have been slow to take steps to develop and train administrative talent. Executive-training programs are gradually making their appearance, but, as noted earlier, much needs to be done through organized efforts to identify and develop management talent. It is not unusual to find a college or university with important administrative positions to be filled and without qualified persons to fill them. As in many other not-for-profit fields, the universities have a greater need for more affirmative action and positive programs in the field of personnel administration.

The Use of Money

Colleges often get into financial difficulty by planning expenditures without careful regard to available income. Further, unplanned expenditures or expenditures outside the budget also are responsible for financial problems. Some institutions have a tendency to live beyond their means.

A budget is an annual financial plan established to carry on the activities necessary to achieve the college's or university's objectives. It should include all income and expenditures. Budgeting is not something that happens once each year; rather, it is a year-round operation and provides one of the most effective means of obtaining economies.

Each level of management from departments on up should be asked to determine, on an annual basis, the job it is to do and what it will take by way of people, supplies, materials, equipment, services, and facilities to it. This should then be translated into dollar requirements. All estimates of expenditure prepared in this manner then should be consolidated into an over-all budget consistent with the university's income position. If a deficit is consciously planned the reason for the deficit should be known and the amount of the differential to be made up by fund-raising solicitations or other means should be established in advance.

Budgeting should be an instrument for planning and for making persons with administrative responsibility management-conscious, and this includes deans. The president and his finance or budget officer should require all estimates of expenditures to be justified in terms of workload or the job to be done, such as square feet of classroom to be painted, acres of campus to be maintained, the number of meals to be served at a certain cost per meal, the volumes to be purchased for the library, the number of trips for faculty members to attend professional meetings, student credit hours taught, and class size. This provides a basis on which to determine needs and offers an opportunity to transfer or direct money and people to the areas of highest priority or importance. This system of building up estimates of expenditure provides standards and yardsticks against which performance can be measured.

Unfortunately, many colleges and universities do not require such supporting data for proposed expenditures but instead make comparisons only with amounts spent in the preceding year or years. It is not unusual to find an administrative officer appearing before the finance committee of a university's governing board and justifying a request for funds on the basis that it is the same as last year, or only five per cent more than last year and stating that this is not an unreasonable increase. Of course, it is not known whether the funds spent the preceding year were too great or too small, and it is difficult, if not impossible, for the finance committee to determine what workload was involved, whether objectives were accomplished, and what standards of performance were followed. Requirements for services may change from year to year, and in many cases standards of performance should be improved. These will have an effect on both the number of people and the amount of dollars required to carry on a particular function.

Once the expenditures have been approved, each level of management should be informed of the funds available for his office, department, or function for the coming year. On a regular basis, preferably monthly, each level of management, including the governing board, should be given a statement showing the status of actual income and expenditures compared to budgeted estimates. Financial reports of this type will enable the university's administration to become aware of any expenditure or income problems on a current basis. The administration is thus provided the opportunity to deal with fiscal problems during the year rather than let them accumulate and become even more severe by having to be dealt with at the end of the year. Financial controls can be simple and yet effective.

The Use of Plant

Much concern has been expressed about the tremendous cost of the additional instructional facilities which it is believed will be needed to take care of the greatly expanded college enrollment anticipated by 1970. As already noted, the estimates of projected costs for facilities vary widely. This variation in range is not surprising when it is considered how little really is known about the extent to which classrooms are now used. If instructional facilities were to be used no more intensively in the future than they are now, the additional expenditures would be great indeed.

Some have pointed out that, if our colleges and universities operated on a year-around basis, automatically large additional numbers of students could be taken care of without any expansion of physical plant. Whether or not institutions of higher education will operate full-scale the year around as during World War II, or on some other basis, is a question which has not been faced.

Under present practices, it is not unusual to find classrooms and laboratories used no more than 40 to 60 per cent of the available hours during the week. The student-station utilization is even lower. Typically, classes often are scheduled for the morning and laboratory sessions for the afternoon, a practice which automatically limits utilization of some facilities to 50 per cent. There ought to be classroom utilization of 80 per cent before construction of new facilities is undertaken.

Not long ago, when a Midwestern university was making plans for a fund-raising campaign to pay for a new classroom building, an analysis was requested of the extent to which the present facilities were used. The results showed that classroom utilization was at about the level of 55 per cent and student-station utilization at about 35 per cent. An analysis of room size and class size showed that there were too many classrooms with capacities of 75 to 150, and that classes with 25 to 35 students were held in such rooms. Fortunately, the partitioning of some of the larger classrooms solved the immediate need for additional instructional facilities without the large capital expenditure which would have been required for a new building. Further, in this particular instance, a rescheduling of the times when laboratories were used enabled needs to be met without constructing new laboratory facilities.

This illustration could be multiplied, with variations, many times over. The conclusion to be drawn is that there are great opportunities for better planning and control over the assignment and use of classrooms and laboratories. Better management would reduce anticipated capital expenditures by an undetermined but substantial amount, as will be seen later in this chapter.

Not only may unnecessary capital expenditures result from poor utilization of existing space, but large sums also are spent for buildings for which there is little or no need, or for facilities for which there is not as great a demand as for others. A Southern college recently spent several million dollars for a new building for a professional school in which there had been declining enrollment and interest for several years. Certain policies pursued by that particular state are changing the economy of the region in a way which almost guarantees a continued decline in need for that facility. On that same campus there was an obvious and demonstrated need for new facilities to meet the demands in various fields of science. Those requirements could not be met, however, because the college had committed its funds for new construction for some years to come for a building which should have been very low on the priority list, if included at all.

The high cost of modern construction places a premium upon full utilization of existing facilities and on scientific planning with respect to determining the needs and priorities for new physical facilities.

Instructional Costs

At the outset it should be understood that better planning of curricular offerings, controls over class size and student credit hours taught, restrictions on new course offerings, and the application of some measure of cost accounting to instructional expenditures need not interfere with the traditions of academic freedom. The careful and effective use of resources, a function of management, and academic freedom are quite different things.

Further, it is not suggested that a college faculty should be regimented or subjected to a tightly knit form of organization such as might be effective in other lines of endeavor. On the contrary, freedom and relaxation for academic departments may contribute to the development of thought and to new frontiers in learning.

However, the economies possible in the instructional side of the budget no longer should be overlooked. Many persons have expressed concern over the proliferation of courses and the fragmentation of subject matter which has gone on almost unchecked in many colleges and universities. Majors have been multiplied, and the courses to be taken in these majors have expanded college catalogs tremendously. Peripheral courses, no matter how interesting to the instructors, may be luxuries which the college cannot afford if they mean diverting dollars or expanding teaching load and thereby adversely affecting the instruction required for the college's primary educational mission.

The ideas of proper class size and student-faculty ratios that are held by many should be subjected to objective, scientific analysis and no doubt drastically revised.

Beardsley Ruml and the late Donald Morrison, in their *Memo to a College Trustee*, have called attention to some of the opportunities to improve academic practices and salaries, and to the benefits to be derived from a revision in present thinking regarding the college calendar, course management, and instructional methods in liberal arts colleges. According to the thesis advanced in that volume, present financial resources are adequate to accomplish marked improvements in faculty salaries and in the essential instruction job to be done.

The Fund for the Advancement of Education, in its publication, *Better Utilization of College Teaching Resources,* summarizes some of the attempts to use in instruction such new methods and techniques as television, films, and faculty aides, all designed to make resources go farther and maintain or improve standards of teaching.

Thus far there has been insufficient experience with the new, experimental programs of various kinds to determine all of the implications for instructional costs. However, the dean of faculties in one well-known college has estimated that curriculum reorganization and even a limited use of mechanical aids and equipment could save 10 per cent of instruction costs and at the same time improve the quality of teaching.

Areas and Methods of Economies

The previous sections of this paper have dealt with principles or practices which, if applied, would make for more effective use of available financial, physical, and human resources and for economies in operating and capital expenditures. Some or all of these principles or practices can be applied in every aspect of a university's operations, including the academic area, and such supporting services as business office procedures, purchasing, buildings and grounds maintenance, and auxiliary enterprises.

It may be pertinent here to consider two questions: First, what are some of the indicators which suggest that study and analysis of operations may be necessary; second, what are some of the methods which have been successful in bringing about economies in operations? These will be discussed, briefly, in order.

Among the indicators or warning signals are the following:

- Rapid and unplanned growth in enrollment, staff, and plant
- Operating deficits

- A declining percentage of the total expenditures allotted to instruction and research
- An increasing percentage of total expenditures for maintenance, administration, salaries of nonacademic personnel, or other supporting expenditures
- Auxiliary enterprises which do not pay for themselves
- Increasing unit costs, where they are measurable
- Expansion in course offerings
- Growing number of small classes
- High rate of personnel turnover
- Poor staff morale
- Increasing questioning or interference by competent members of the governing board

The methods or practices which have successfully produced economies in a wide variety of colleges and universities cover a wide range and include many which are prosaic and undramatic. Yet even the small economies in seemingly insignificant operations can amount to substantial totals in given situations. Some of the methods of achieving economies which have been successful are as follows:

- Defining the objectives of the institution
- Defining responsibilities and clarifying the organization for administration
- Establishing sound budget procedures and improved financial reports
- Analysis of unit costs
- Scheduling maintenance and repairs on a planned basis
- Adoption of a work-order and job-cost system in repairs and maintenance
- Mechanization of accounting, student records, etc. (if the size of the workload justifies)
- Introduction of labor-saving equipment (automatic dishwashers, laundry machines, leaf rakers, fork-lift trucks, power tools, business machines, etc.)
- Staggering payrolling and bills payments to avoid peaks and valleys in business office workload
- Establishing a secretarial pool
- Eliminating or reducing maid service in dormitories
- Controls over use of automobiles in the motor pool
- Use of multileaf forms in the registrar's and business office
- Centralized purchasing for quantity discounts
- Inventory controls
- Reviewing insurance coverage
- Control over utilities and telephones

- Standardization of supplies and equipment
- Portion control of food served
- Control over new courses and majors
- Control over class size
- Training supervisory persons

Knowledge that these, or other, methods or practices can produce economies is not enough. A further requirement is the presence of management-minded administrators and persons at various levels of supervision who will initiate action to control expense.

For purposes of emphasis, the reader is reminded that the soundest way to control expenditures and to make certain that funds are used where they are needed most is effective budgeting. That is basic. As already noted, sound budgeting procedures should be accompanied by analysis of functions, workloads, and methods.

It is also true that sound management means not only control over expenditures, but also that income-producing activities such as food service, dormitories, and bookstores should pay for themselves. Further, a number of institutions have found that their fund-raising efforts have been more successful as a result of sound management planning. They have raised more money because they have a plan of where they wish to go and a more scientific basis of determining their needs.

Interinstitutional Cooperation

Within the limitations of available space little can be said on the subject of interinstitutional cooperation. However, it is to be hoped that colleges will make the most of possibilities to cooperate with each other when that is practicable, not only for the sake of economies, but also to improve academic programs.

As noted in the paper by Gordon N. Ray, regional groups are developing certain forms of cooperation, and in centers where colleges are physically near each other, as in the Philadelphia area and the Connecticut Valley, there is some pooling of resources. Generally speaking, however, colleges are almost fiercely competitive and duplicate the programs and services of their neighbors even if it means an inferior product because of the strain on individual resources.

Opportunities for cooperation among colleges situated near each other are present in both the nonacademic and the academic areas, as the following listing may suggest:

- Common purchasing
- Common storage
- A centralized business machine center
- Common use of maintenance personnel and equipment

- Specialized library resources for joint use
- Sharing faculty personnel in short supply, as in certain fields of science
- Common courses or degree programs

The opportunities are great, but the surface has hardly been scratched. It is not possible to estimate the economies and improvements in quality which may be possible through programs of full-scale cooperation, but they are large.

Demonstrated Economies

The foregoing sections of this paper have reviewed certain basic principles and practices which make for better operations. Progress, improvement, and economies depend upon the recognition and application of these principles. The concluding section of this paper directs attention to some of the tangible and intangible results of improved management. A few of the tangible accomplishments resulting from the application of the principles of sound management in individual colleges and universities are given in the summary below.

- A large Eastern university consolidated its business machine units and established controls over its printing and publications program to effect economies in annual operating expenses of approximately $60,000.
- An Eastern men's university revised some of the practices in its business operations and in its student housing and food services to achieve annual economies of more than $400,000. This was about 6 per cent of the nonacademic expenditure.
- Another well-known Eastern university revised its scheduling methods and staffing for plant and grounds maintenance and repair, improved its purchasing procedures, and improved business operations generally to achieve economies of over $1 million. This was approximately 9 per cent of the annual expenditures for nonacademic affairs.
- A Midwestern women's college improved its organization for administration, established fiscal controls, installed labor-saving equipment and machines, eliminated surplus personnel, revised its insurance program, reduced utilities costs, and improved income from auxiliary enterprises to attain economies of almost $460,000 annually. This was about 15 per cent of total expenditures.
- A Southern college revised its class size upward, introduced management controls over course offerings, and eliminated surplus personnel to achieve economies equivalent to a salary increase of slightly more than $1,000 for every member of the faculty. These savings amounted to about 5 per cent of the expenditures for instruction purposes, including extension work.

• A commission for higher education in an eastern state was given a proposed program for new classroom facilities to cost a little over $100 million. An analysis of the utilization of space already available, and use of the enrollment data prepared by the educators, showed that no new space would be required for classroom purposes.

The above are only a few illustrations of the opportunities which many colleges and universities have to reduce or eliminate expenditures and find funds internally to help finance operations. It is unsound to generalize on the basis of the actual results achieved in a limited number of institutions, but it is safe to say that the application of sound management principles and techniques can substantially reduce the projected expenditures for higher education and that internal economies should be looked to as a source of funds.

In addition to the tangible results which come from improved management there are intangible benefits which cannot be assessed in terms of dollars but which may be no less important. These intangibles include the following:

• A greater sense of purpose
• Focusing attention on objectives
• Better understanding of responsibilities
• Strengthened organization for administration
• Greater awareness of the techniques of good administration
• Improved employee morale

In conclusion, it should be clear that economies in operating expense are possible in all areas, including the academic. It also is apparent that unnecessary capital expenditures can be avoided. These things can be done without impairing the standards of service or the quality of education.

This is a time for open-mindedness, inventiveness, and progressive thinking to meet the problems presented by expanding enrollments and the need for more money. It is a time for colleges and universities to determine priorities and then allocate their resources to the priorities established.

7

The Long-term Budget Projection: A New Management Tool for College and Universities

Sidney G. Tickton

For many years, industrial firms, merchandising organizations, and government agencies have made long-range projections of income and expenditures on which to base their policy decisions on production planning, sales programs, new plant construction, new debt commitments, etc. The merchandising of a new product for nationwide consumption, for example, may span a decade from the time the laboratory research has been completed until the sales promotion has placed the product in millions of homes. Commitments of time, money, and resources can be allocated by responsible corporate officials to a long-term program only after the detailed plans have been worked out, plans that take into account all factors likely to be relevant. Sometimes two or more assumptions are used to allow for possible variations in timing, prices, costs, the extent of the market, the availability of finances, and the like.

The building of a new highway, bridge, airport, or public utility is likewise preceded by a detailed projection into the future of the operating accounts, giving full effect to possible changes in economic, social, and environmental factors that may impinge on the outlook for receipts and expenditures. If the financing involves the issuance of securities, particularly revenue bonds, the projections are the work of appropriate specialists, are heavily documented, and may cover a time period of twenty to thirty years. They frequently become the entire basis upon which the project is organized, financed, and carried forth.

A less complicated example involving long-range projections of receipts and expenditures can be observed any day in the real estate field. Apartment houses, shopping centers, and office buildings are bought and sold on the basis of a probable income and expenditures analysis running from a few years to half a century ahead.

Although colleges and universities have long-range-planning problems similar to those of industry and trade, it is unusual for them to engage in long-range fiscal planning. Recently, a few small liberal arts colleges decided to work out a long-range-analysis technique built around their budgets. Their objective was to gain some financial perspective for the decade ahead, taking into account all their long-range commitments such as tenure, automatic-increase salary schedules, fringe-benefit arrangements with escalator clauses, and current maintenance on buildings to be constructed from funds provided by special gifts, campaigns, or borrowing, as well as rising prices and nationwide increases in the levels of faculty salaries.

These colleges recognized that institutions of higher education are not strictly business activities but that, on the financial side, their operations are certainly subject to business-type analysis. With the perspective provided by the projections, they were able to arrive at some new policy decisions on size of student body, faculty, building program and gift program, educational objectives of the college, and details of the curriculum, with the knowledge of what each individual decision meant to the operation of the college as a whole.

The purpose of this paper is to describe the process followed by one of these colleges, to indicate the types of data needed and the basis of the projections made, and to describe the results obtained. By using a technique similar to the one described, other colleges and universities can work out their own future pictures (in greater or lesser detail as their situations warrant) and can use organized data as a basis for new decisions on their future activities.

Another purpose of this paper is to indicate that the analysis process, although not difficult, requires considerable discipline; that is, the effect of every management decision on the budget, this year, next year, or for the entire period ahead, must be taken into account. One decision may involve a number of additional decisions; for example, a projection of the size of the student body requires related projections on the size of the faculty, the size of classes, number of courses, and space requirements. Precision of projection is not as essential as is the reasonableness of the estimates and the following through of the process at all points where there are budgetary consequences.

As indicated elsewhere in this book, the management problems of colleges and universities will grow tremendously, both in size and in complexity, during the next few years. To meet these problems, top officials will need to sharpen old management tools and fashion new ones. The long-term budget projection is just such a new management tool.

We hasten to add, however, that the particular procedure described in this paper is only an example of an administrative technique which is in the early stages of development. Officials who prepare long-range projections for colleges and universities could be expected to improve the technique during the next few years and to incorporate for each college some amendments to reflect the needs of that particular institution. At some colleges and universities it might be necessary to set down a series of alternative assumptions and to run through the entire projection process a number of times before arriving at a series of figures which are both practical and desirable.

Description of the College

For the purposes of this case study, we shall call the institution that we are describing Ashford College. It is a four-year liberal arts college located on a 60-acre campus, in a town of 30,000 in the Midwest. Originally started in the 1830s and originally related to both Congregational and Presbyterian churches, the college is now a privately controlled institution accredited to the North Central Association. It offers B.A., B.Mus., and B.Mus.Ed. degrees.

There are 800 students, 64 per cent of whom are men. Ten per cent of the students are married. Of the students, 556 live on campus in college-owned properties, 150 live on campus in fraternity houses, and 94 are commuters and live at home. Seventy per cent of the students come from a radius of 300 miles, nearly all from middle- and upper-middle income families. Half of the students who enter Ashford do not stay for the entire four years. Drop-outs include many women who marry and some men who transfer to five-year programs in engineering and business administration, as well as some students who transfer to the state university for preprofessional courses.

Ashford's campus is surrounded by the town and has been protected in recent years by the purchase of adjoining properties, some of which have been demolished and others of which have been turned into college offices and residences. It will be necessary to buy additional adjoining property in future years. The college plant consists of three classroom and office buildings, two gymnasiums, a music building, a library with 85,000 volumes, observatory, infirmary, chapel, athletic field and dormitories. Laboratories, libraries, and classrooms are equipped primarily for the benefit of the student rather than for research.

Although a few of the buildings are relatively old, the plant is in first-class shape, and extraordinary maintenance is not a problem. The campus needs some new landscaping, and a new fine arts building is planned for 1962. Dormitories, dining halls, and student union facilities are used to capacity. An expansion of the college will require additional living quarters and recreation and eating facilities.

Classes meet five days a week, primarily between 9 A.M. and 4 P.M., and on Saturday morning. The school year runs from September 20 to June 5. Although there is no summer program, the college acts as host to a number of conferences during July and August, which permits it to employ its dormitory and dining hall staff on a year-round basis.

The college engages in intercollegiate athletics with neighboring institutions. There is a comprehensive intramural program; there is also an ROTC unit to which most of the men students belong.

The First Step: Background Data

As the first step toward the preparation of a long-term budget, Ashford's president asked the business manager to assemble some data on the operations and activities of the college for the past ten years. The information submitted is shown in Table 1.

The business manager found that nearly all the information requested was readily available from the books and records of the college. In setting down the student and faculty figures, he used the full-time equivalents averaged for the year. Faculty included those on leave with pay, excluded those on leave without pay. Physical education instructors were included, but ROTC officers were excluded, inasmuch as their salaries are not paid by the college. Fringe benefits included the college's contribution to its pension plan, social security, major medical insurance, and group life and health insurance.

The Second Step: Assumptions for the Future
(United States as a Whole)

As a second step toward the preparation of a long-term budget for his college, Ashford's president, with the head of his economics department, worked out a number of basic assumptions about the character of the United States economy as a whole during the next ten years. Within this framework, he worked out with his dean some assumptions on the outlook for higher education. The objective was to improve the reliability of the calculations by allowing for changes likely to occur in the environment

Table 1. Historical Data on Ashford College
1949–59

Item	1948–49	1952–53	1957–58	1958–59
Data on Students and Faculty				
Number of students.............	834	775	759	800
Number of faculty..............	70	67	63	65
Student-faculty ratio............	11.9:1	11.6:1	12:1	12.3:1
Average tuition per student......	$ 470	$ 593	$ 806	$ 817
Total compensation of faculty:				
Salary......................	$ 262,374	$ 285,733	$ 355,111	$ 389,790
Fringe benefits..............	9,736	18,572	23,270	30,770
Average compensation of faculty:				
Salary......................	$ 3,748	$ 4,265	$ 5,637	$ 5,997
Fringe benefits..............	139	277	369	473
Data on endowment and gifts				
Amount of endowment				
(book value)..............	$2,914,300	$4,103,600	$4,472,800	$4,600,000
Total income from endowment...	177,862	184,019	201,889	221,830
Rate of return (on book value)....	6.10%	4.48%	4.51%	4.82%
Amount of gifts received:				
For endowment..............	$ 143,400	$ 57,200	$ 100,414	$ 100,000
For plant...................	....	....	30,000	40,000
For other uses..............	39,000	100,000	210,874	326,091
Data on educational plant and				
equipment				
Book value...................	$2,282,000	$3,295,000	$4,633,000	$4,650,000
Replacement value.............	....	....	....	4,150,000
Data on Budget Income				
Educational and general:				
Student fees................	$ 390,790	$ 417,418	$ 611,678	$ 653,870
Endowment income..........	137,920	147,868	161,676	150,525
Gifts......................	31,057	58,643	120,667	197,652
Organized activities..........	19,928	21,121	23,430	27,559
Other items.................	4,437	4,730	25,873	56,040
Subtotal, educational, and				
general.................	$ 584,132	$ 649,780	$ 943,324	$1,085,646
Auxiliary enterprises:				
Residences..................	$ 71,370	$ 92,766	$ 170,349	$ 192,000
Dining halls.................	175,942	175,658	173,361	225,000
Student union...............	....	21,019	32,082	36,000
Other......................	....	35,957	58,965	56,000
Subtotal, auxiliary enterprises	$ 247,312	$ 325,400	$ 434,757	$ 509,000

in which the college would operate. The assumptions for the years 1959–70 were as follows:

1. The United States will be blessed with a high-employment economy without a war or other national disaster.

Historical Data on Ashford College (continued)

Item	1948–49	1952–53	1957–58	1958–59
Student aid:				
Gifts and endowment.........	$ 23,174	$ 31,850	$ 122,420	$ 162,244
Other allocations to student aid	4,300	20,300	54,803	68,756
Subtotal, student aid........	$ 27,474	$ 52,150	$ 177,223	$ 231,000
Total income............	$ 858,918	$1,027,330	$1,555,304	$1,825,646
Data on budget expenditure				
Educational and general:				
General administration........	$ 53,549	$ 63,487	$ 86,437	$ 91,557
Student services..............	41,771	73,210	81,199	92,121
Public services...............	29,574	37,031	74,040	70,980
General institutional expense...	10,456	29,028	56,107	94,674
Instructional expense..........	271,988	322,731	440,826	520,364
Organized activities...........	37,443	30,652	31,239	35,991
Library......................	31,358	33,305	43,917	44,587
Plant operation and maintenance	115,289	136,777	163,682	190,631
Subtotal, educational and general.................	$ 591,428	$ 726,221	$ 977,447	$1,140,905
Auxiliary enterprises:				
Residences...................	$ 59,583	$ 95,767	$ 170,349	$ 192,000
Dining halls.................	148,968	151,302	173,361	225,000
Student union...............	1,786	21,017	32,082	36,000
Other.......................	....	35,957	58,965	56,000
Subtotal, auxiliary enterprises	$ 210,337	$ 304,043	$ 434,757	$ 509,000
Student aid:				
Scholarships.................	$ 26,875	$ 53,743	$ 173,421	$ 228,533
Fellowships and prizes........	440	759	3,802	2,467
Subtotal, student aid........	$ 27,315	$ 54,502	$ 177,223	$ 231,000
Total expenditure.........	$ 829,080	$1,084,766	$1,589,427	$1,880,905

2. Prices can be expected to increase during the period, say, about 1 per cent each year on the average.

3. The number of students going to colleges and universities can be expected to double by the end of the period.

4. State universities, city colleges, and community and junior colleges will provide for a large share of the increased college enrollment.

5. There will be a substantially larger number of applicants for admission to private liberal arts colleges. These colleges will be able to select students of better than average academic ability. Parents of the students (except scholarship students) will be able and willing to pay an increasing tuition charge.

6. The large number of applicants to private liberal arts colleges and their willingness to pay increasing tuition will be made possible by the high-employment condition of our national economy and by the feeling on the part of a sufficient number of parents that private liberal arts colleges will provide a superior education for their children.

7. Salaries of college faculty members will double, on the average, nationwide, during the next five to ten years as recommended by the President's Committee on Education Beyond the High School.

8. Although there will be a growing number of Federal and state scholarships for college students, they will constitute a minor percentage of the total number of scholarships necessary for higher education. Continued solicitation by all private colleges and universities of private gifts for scholarship purposes will be necessary throughout the period.

9. Long-term loans to private colleges will be available from the Federal government, state governments, or commercial sources for the construction of dormitories, dining halls, student unions, and other revenue-producing facilities. Private gifts will be required, however, to provide funds for the construction of classrooms, laboratories, libraries and other facilities from which direct revenue is not ordinarily obtained.

The Third Step: Assumptions for the Future (the College Itself)

As the third step toward the preparation of a long-term budget, Ashford's president, dean, and business manager worked out a number of basic assumptions that would be involved in a projection for ten years ahead. They were the following:

1. The purposes and objectives of the college will remain unchanged, that is, the college will continue to provide high-quality undergraduate education in the liberal arts for young men and women of better than average academic ability.

2. Teaching methods will remain essentially unchanged except for a greater emphasis on independent study and a larger number of student teaching assistants.

3. The college calendar will remain essentially unchanged.

4. Services to students will remain essentially unchanged.

5. The college will continue to be essentially residential in character. Increases in students over the present number will have to be accompanied by an expansion of dormitory or other living quarters.

6. Enrollment will grow approximately as follows:

1957–58	759	1960–61	975
1958–59	800	1961–62	1,100
1959–60	875	1962–63 and after	1,250

7. Enrollment by 1962–63 will consist of 60 per cent men, 40 per cent women, to be arrived at as follows:

	Men, per cent	Women, per cent
1958–59	64.3	35.7
1959–60	63.0	37.0
1960–61	62.0	38.0
1961–62	61.0	39.0
1962–63 and after	60.0	40.0

8. Upperclassmen (juniors and seniors) will comprise a growing proportion of the student body, increasing from 36.8 per cent in 1958–59 to 45.0 per cent by 1962–63. This will permit the filling up of the upperclass courses which are now underpopulated. It will be achieved when necessary by working with a number of junior and community colleges, expanding scholarship grants to students at such colleges, etc.

9. The ROTC program will continue at the college, enrolling the same proportionate share of men students as heretofore.

10. The teaching faculty will grow approximately as follows:

1958–59	65	1961–62	78
1959–60	67	1962–63 and after	84
1960–61	73		

This growth takes into account the filling up of the upper classes, a trend away from small sections, and the expansion of independent study for average and above-average students. (The honors students already carry on a substantial volume of independent study but at high faculty-student cost ratio.)

11. Faculty salaries will double, on the average, between 1958 and 1968. The averages arrived at for each year (after some adjusting of the scale to make the totals balance out) were as follows:

1957–58	$ 5,637	1963–64	$ 9,190
1958–59	5,997	1964–65	9,650
1959–60	6,900	1965–66	10,133
1960–61	7,390	1966–67	10,640
1961–62	8,055	1967–68	11,172
1962–63	8,753		

12. Fringe benefits for the faculty (which at Ashford include TIAA pension program, group life and health insurance, major medical insurance, and social security) will grow from 6.5 per cent of salaries in 1957–58 to 15¾ per cent of salaries by 1963–64 and will continue at that level.

13. Sabbatical leaves will be provided to the extent of 1½ per cent of the faculty salary budget in 1960–61; 1¾ per cent in 1961–62; 2 per cent

in 1962–63; 2¼ per cent in 1963–64, and 2½ per cent in 1964–65 and thereafter.

14. In the future the budget for the college will be divided into four parts as follows: (a) educational and general, (b) auxiliary enterprises, (c) scholarship, and (d) plant.

Educational and General Budget

15. The educational and general budget will be balanced each year, without gifts, starting in 1962–63. It will include the following items: (a) general administration, (b) student services, (c) public service and information, (d) general institutional expense, (e) instruction, (f) organized activities related to educational departments, (g) library, (h) operation and maintenance of physical plant, (i) depreciation reserve on educational plant and (j) contingency reserve.

16. The projection of general administration expense includes allowances for the addition of one secretary in the school year 1960 and one clerk in 1961. Student services include allowances for the addition of a full-time doctor in 1961, a dean of men in 1962, and one secretary in each of the years 1961, 1962, and 1963. Public service and information includes an additional person in each of the years 1960 and 1961. Library expenditures include the addition of one professional staff member in 1961.

17. The item for depreciation of educational plant will be based on estimated replacement value of buildings as listed in Table 2. These

Table 2.

Year	Estimated replacement value	Amount for depreciation	Rate, per cent
1959–60	$4,200,000	$ 22,500	0.535
1960–61	4,250,000	34,500	0.811
1961–62	4,300,000	43,000	1.00
1962–63	5,600,000	70,000	1.25
1963–64	5,650,000	84,000	1.49
1964–65	5,700,000	98,000	1.72
1965–66	5,800,000	140,000	2.41
1966–67	5,800,000	140,000	2.41
1967–68	5,800,000	140,000	2.41

amounts will be transferred to a special fund to be used for repairs and remodeling of the plant and to repay the endowment funds for amounts invested in the plant.

18. The item for contingencies in the educational and general budget will amount to 3 per cent of expenditures for the fiscal year 1960–61 and 5 per cent of such expenditures thereafter.

19. The educational and general budget will be financed from the following sources of income: (a) tuition and fees, (b) endowment income (unrestricted), (c) income from organized activities, (d) miscellaneous income, (e) income from administration of auxiliary enterprises, and (f) gifts and grants as follows:

165,000 in 1959–60;
$100,000 in 1960–61;
50,000 in 1961–62.

No gift money will be allocated to this budget in 1962–63 and thereafter.

20. Starting in 1962–63, the tuition will be computed by (a) estimating the total educational and general budget; (b) subtracting from this total the estimated unrestricted income from endowment, organized activities, and the miscellaneous sources shown above; and (c) dividing the remainder by the average number of students expected for the year.

Auxiliary Enterprises Budget

21. The auxiliary enterprises budget will cover income and expenditure of residence halls, dining halls, student union, and book store. It will be balanced in all years after: (a) transferring book store and student union profits to scholarship fund (NOTE: The book store and student union will aim to make a 5 per cent net profit on operations after payment of all costs); (b) including an administrative charge amounting to 5 per cent of total operating income to cover the supervisory time of the business manager and the record-keeping function of his office; and (c) including a charge for amortization of borrowed funds, interest, repairs, and remodeling amounting to:

5 per cent of estimated replacement value in 1959–60
6 per cent of estimated replacement value in 1960–61
7 per cent of estimated replacement value in 1961–62
7½ per cent of estimated replacement value in 1962–63 and thereafter

NOTE: An amount equivalent to this charge will be transferred each year to the Auxiliary Enterprises Reserve Fund, from which costs of amortization and other expenses will be paid in whatever year they occur. This procedure will serve to smooth out the financial effect of repairs and remodeling operations over the years.

22. Auxiliary-enterprise services will be essentially the same in the future as in 1957–58. Student living quarters will be operated as a single unit, and uniform charges will be made for all rooms. Charges will be estimated on the basis of 95 per cent occupancy.

23. Student living quarters will be expanded only as enrollment actually increases. When dormitories are financed by borrowing (either from

endowment funds, government sources, or the commercial market), they will be amortized over fifty years with interest on the unpaid balance.

Scholarship Budget

24. The college's objective will be to provide a total of scholarships and wages paid to students for on-campus employment equal to 25 to 30 per cent of the college's annual income from student tuition and fees in order to assure the desired composition of the student body.

25. The scholarship budget will include amounts allowed by the college for tuition, room, and board. It will exclude compensation for student employment. This will be paid to the student out of funds appropriated to the function he performs. It will also exclude loan funds (which are created at Ashford in the first instance from gifts or from government sources). Loans are expected to be recovered ultimately by the college and to be used again on a revolving-fund basis.

26. The scholarship budget will be self-balancing. It will be financed by current gifts and endowment income specifically earmarked for scholarships, state or Federal scholarship funds, if any, and profits from the operation of the book store and student union. Inasmuch as the scholarship budget will not be financed from other sources, special efforts will be made to build up scholarship funds. Loan funds will be built up, also. An extended payment plan financed by bank credit will be worked out as soon as possible.

Plant Budget

27. The plant budget will consist of expenditures for land, buildings, and major equipment. Minor equipment will be included in the educational and general budget.

28. The plant budget will be financed entirely from endowment income earmarked for plant, current gifts for plant, special campaign gifts for plant, and long-term loans for plant, if any are desirable and available.

29. The college will raise $1,300,000 for a fine arts building and construct it in 1962. This building will permit the college to expand art, music, and drama facilities which are now inadequate. There will be no other classroom buildings constructed between 1959 and 1969.

30. Better utilization of space will make it possible to expand Ashford's enrollment from 800 to 1,250 without increasing the educational plant beyond the addition of the fine arts building. It may be necessary, however, to schedule more classes in the late afternoon and some in the evening and to put classes regularly on a forty-four- instead of a thirty-eight-hour week. (NOTE: in this connection: Five evening classes were in

operation in 1958–59 for the convenience of students who preferred more daytime hours for extracurricular activities and sports.)

Endowment Funds

31. Gifts and bequests to build up endowment funds will amount to $100,000 a year. The return on endowment investments will amount to approximately 4.8 per cent of book value per year throughout the period of the projection.

32. Four per cent interest will be paid on endowment funds invested in the educational plant.

The Fourth Step: Making the Ten-year Projection

In light of:
* The historical data about the college
* The assumptions for the future of the United States economy
* The assumptions for the future of higher education, generally
* The assumptions for the future of the college

which were now on hand, Ashford's president, dean, and business manager worked out the projection of the college budget for the decade ahead. At this point, the working time required for the preliminary calculations and discussion was just about two days.

The group found that the process involved making a number of initial guesses, following the trends indicated by historical figures, and then adjusting the projections subsequently in order to arrive at a proper balancing of the figures. The projections were worked out on both the income and expense side on four accounting work sheet schedules as follows:

A. Educational and general budget
B. Scholarship budget
C. Auxiliary enterprises budget
D. Plant budget

In some cases the details were not filled in; the broad picture was enough to work with. In other cases subsidiary tables were needed to assemble subtotals or additional working data. The four accounting work sheet schedules and two illustrative subsidiary tables are reproduced as an appendix to this paper. Table 3 picks up the main figures for 1959, 1963, and 1968 from the work sheets and emphasizes the four parts of the budget, each of which is balanced within itself.

A budget is a financial plan in which all the factors involved are interrelated to the extent that they involve money. Ashford's president found,

Table 3. Ten-year Budget Summary for Ashford College
(In thousands of dollars)

Expense items	1958–59	1962–63	1967–68	Income items	1958–59	1962–63	1967–68
Educational and General				*Educational and General*			
General administration....	$ 92	$ 149	$ 168	Tuition and fees........	$ 654	$1,813	$2,301
Student services........	92	159	192	Endowment income.....	151	190	205
Public services.........	71	118	135	Gifts and grants	198	0	0
General institutional				Organized activities.....	28	34	35
expense.............	95	102	112	Miscellaneous income...	56	29	32
Instructional expense....	520	966	1,232	Administration of auxil-			
Organized activities......	36	45	48	iary enterprises.......	0	45	60
Library...............	45	67	80	Operations deficit*......	55	0	0
Operation and mainte-							
nance of educational							
plant...............	191	334	402				
Depreciation of reserve,							
educational plant......	0	70	140				
Contingency...........	0	101	125				
Total, educational				Total, educational			
and general.......	$1,141	$2,111	$2,633	and general....	$1,141	$2,111	$2,633
Scholarships				*Scholarships*			
				Income earmarked for			
				scholarships:			
				Book store and student			
				union profits.......	$ 1	$ 9	$ 17
				Endowment..........	34	39	53
				Gifts.................	129	375	470
				Operating deficit*.......	67	0	0
Total, scholarships...	$ 231	$ 423	$ 540	Total, scholarships..	$ 231	$ 423	$ 540
Auxiliary Enterprises				*Auxiliary Enterprises*			
Residences and dining halls	$ 417	$ 743	$ 981	Room and board charges	$ 417	$ 743	$ 981
Book store and student				Book store and student			
union...............	92	152	184	union...............	92	152	184
Total, auxiliary				Total, auxiliary			
enterprises........	$ 509	$ 895	$1,165	enterprises.......	$ 509	$ 895	$1,165
Plant				*Plant*			
Fine arts building.......	$ 0	$1,300	$ 0	Income earmarked for			
Other buildings and				plant construction:			
grounds.............	50	10	50	Gifts..................	$ 40	$1,300	$ 40
				Endowment..........	10	10	10
Total, plant				Total, plant			
construction......	$ 50	$1,310	$ 50	construction....	$ 50	$1,310	$ 50

* Covered by transfers from college's reserve funds.

in recapitulating the results, that changes in some of the critical factors in his college's future worked out as follows:

Student-Faculty Ratio

1958–59	12:1	1962–63	15:1
1960–61	13:1	1967–68	15:1

Tuition and Room and Board Charge per Student

	Tuition	Room and board	Total
1958–59	$ 817	$ 755	$1,572
1960–61	1,208	825	2,033
1962–63	1,450	875	2,325
1967–68	1,841	1,032	2,873

Faculty Compensation

	Average salary	Including fringe benefits
1958–59	$ 5,997	$ 6,470
1960–61	7,390	8,143
1962–63	8,753	10,038
1967–68	11,172	12,932

Utilization of Space

	Per cent used	Basis, hours per week
1958–59	40	38
1967–68	65	44

Percentage Changes 1959–1968

Average tuition per student . . . .   +125%

Average compensation per faculty member, including benefits . . . . . .   +100%

Endowment income per student allocated to educational and general budget . . . .   − 13%

Gifts per student allocated to educational and general budget . . . . . .   −100%

Given these changes in critical factors, the necessary fund raising would be as shown in Table 4.

Table 4. Fund Raising Required
(In thousands of dollars)

Year	Educational and general budget	Scholar- ships	Endow- ments	Plant	Total
1958–59	$198	$128	$100	$ 40	$ 466
1960–61	100	285	100	40	525
1961–62	50	305	100	40	495
1962–63	0	375	100	1,300	1,775
1963–64	0	400	100	40	540
1967–68	0	470	100	40	610

Ashford's president found that the ten-year budget gave him a coordinated timetable. There was a detailed noting of actions to be taken for each segment of the college's life in each of a series of time periods. For example, the plan provided that for the school year 1962–63 as compared to 1961–62:

- The student body would increase by 150.
- The faculty would increase by six.
- The tuition and room and board would go up by $106, to $2,325.
- Faculty salary would go up by $698 to reach an average level of $8,753.
- Top faculty pay would go to $18,000.
- Fringe benefits would go up 2 per cent of pay to reach 14.7 per cent.

This meant that every decision or action taken by the board, the administration, or the faculty in 1959, and in subsequent years too, would have to be weighed against the objectives of the long-range plan. Did it fit into the plan, did it amend the plan, was it premature, or was it out of line?

The Fifth Step: What They Did about It

The ten-year budget projection set forth in summary fashion a preliminary and tentative plan for operating the college during the decade 1959–68. Although the possibilities of miscalculation were obvious, Ashford's president felt that he had, for the first time, a coordinated set of assumptions. From them he drew the following critical conclusions about the future of the college:

1. Ashford could balance its educational budget each year in the decade ahead.

2. Balancing the budget would mean that tuition would go up, but within the realm of possibility.

3. Budget balancing meant that the size of the college would grow, but not so large as to change the character of the college.

4. Budget balancing allowed for the doubling of faculty salaries, on the average, between 1958 and 1968.

5. Within this framework, Ashford could look forward to a top faculty salary of $18,000 to $20,000 within a few years, compared to $10,000 now.

6. The financial objectives could be achieved while maintaining first-class education objectives.

7. The student-teacher ratio would need to go no higher than 15:1.

8. If greater independent study were encouraged and some large lectures were introduced, the 15:1 ratio would allow adequate opportunity for all the necessary seminars and small discussion groups desired by the faculty, with a teaching load of no more than the present twelve hours per week.

In the light of these conclusions, Ashford's president submitted the

of Dollars

9.2 Billion
up 149%

1958 – 70

Endowment
and Gifts
up 100%

Other
Sources
up 67%

Government
up 106%

3.7 Billion

2.3 Billion

Student
Fees
up 322%

.5 Billion

| 1940 | 1954 | 1958 | 1970 |

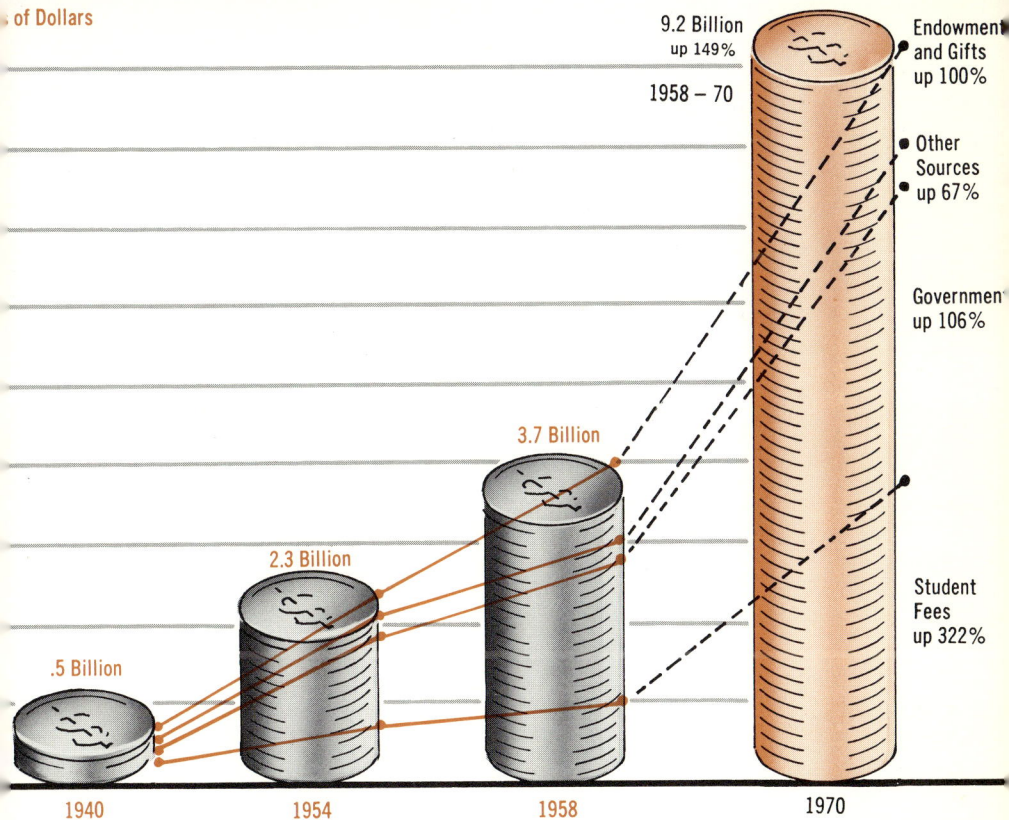

COST OF RUNNING COLLEGES AND UNIVERSITIES*
AND SOURCES OF FUNDS

ational and general budget only.

ten-year budget to his trustees for discussion and study. At the succeeding annual meeting, the document was adopted as the basis of a program for action. It was clear to all, however, that the planning document would never be looked upon as a fixed, unchangeable blueprint for the next decade; it was, rather, a thoughtfully developed set of guide lines to be used in charting the course of the college's future.

One other point emerged from the meeting. The president and the trustees agreed that through the preparation and study of the long-range budget they had begun to realize for the first time how their college was really put together. They observed as they never had before:

. . . how a decision on one aspect of the college's activities controlled important decisions on another;

. . . how short-term commitments and expediency frequently determined the course of the college's long-run future;

. . . how the failure to consider long-range implications of today's decisions (because projections of the distant future were thought to be too speculative) could, in itself, subject the college to a host of substantial but unintended risks;

. . . how the mere postponing, for the time being, of a decision on a critical item could be of great and direct influence on future operating results.

They concluded that this dynamic technique could be of greatest use as a management tool only if the assumptions and figures were examined and constantly revised in the light of the social and economic changes occurring on the campus and in the country at large. They concluded also that long-range planning is a continuing job. The president put it this way:

As our long-term objectives and our projections move toward us with time, they must be reassessed, readjusted, and reevaluated. Meantime, of course, we must also be ready to push our projections further into the future in order to keep the guideposts visible ten or fifteen years away.

General Footnote on the Technique Described

For colleges other than the one described, it might be necessary to run through the procedure described above a number of times with alternative assumptions in order to arrive at a series of figures which would be practical and desirable at all points of the projection. A small college in the East with 300 students, for example, found that projections built around a prospective growth of 400 to 500 students by 1970 left it with either a large deficit or a salary scale that was too low. Successive projections involving 600 and then 700 students, with appropriate changes in assumptions, were necessary before the figures could be brought into balance.

Accounting Worksheet A: Educational and General Budget 1958–68, Ashford College

Item	1957–58	1958–59	1959–60	1960–61	1961–62	1962–63	1963–64	1964–65	1965–66	1966–67	1967–68
Expense											
General administration	$ 86,437	$ 91,557	$ 116,054	$ 126,738	$ 139,960	$ 149,000	$ 153,185	$ 156,890	$ 160,575	$ 164,280	$ 167,975
Student services	81,199	92,121	97,319	121,311	145,556	159,166	165,556	172,000	178,595	185,110	191,525
Public service and information	74,040	70,980	86,443	99,750	109,460	118,175	121,500	124,800	128,200	131,550	134,900
General institutional expense	56,107	94,674	59,919	69,575	85,200	101,900	103,660	105,570	108,030	109,940	112,350
Instruction	440,826	520,364	605,598	696,828	811,960	966,056	1,021,685	1,071,862	1,122,384	1,174,655	1,231,745
Organized activity related to educational departments	31,239	35,991	39,120	41,000	42,000	45,000	45,500	46,000	46,500	47,000	47,500
Library	43,917	44,587	46,107	54,785	58,785	66,935	69,615	71,995	74,375	76,755	79,885
Operation and maintenance of physical plant	163,682	190,631	238,608	266,550	293,735	333,770	344,500	352,500	376,000	387,500	402,000
Educational plant rehabilitation and depreciation fund	0	0	22,500	34,500	43,000	70,000	84,000	98,000	140,000	140,000	140,000
Subtotal	$977,447	$1,140,905	$1,311,668	$1,511,037	$1,729,666	$2,010,002	$2,109,201	$2,199,617	$2,334,659	$2,416,790	$2,507,880
Contingency (1960–61, 3%; thereafter 5%)	0	0	29,396	45,331	86,483	100,500	105,460	109,981	116,733	120,840	125,394
Total expense	$977,447	$1,140,905	$1,341,064	$1,556,368	$1,816,149	$2,110,502	$2,214,661	$2,309,598	$2,451,392	$2,537,630	$2,633,274
Income											
Student fees	$611,678	$ 653,870	$ 910,050	$1,177,368	$1,478,149	$1,812,502	$1,905,661	$1,997,098	$2,130,392	$2,214,130	$2,301,274
Endowment income	161,676	150,525	180,737	185,000	187,000	190,000	195,000	195,000	200,000	200,000	205,000
Gifts and grants	120,667	197,652	165,000	100,000	50,000	0	0	0	0	0	0
Organized activities	23,430	27,559	27,910	30,000	32,000	34,000	34,000	35,000	35,000	35,000	35,000
Other sources	25,873	56,040	28,420	29,000	29,000	29,000	30,000	30,000	31,000	31,000	32,000
Administration of auxiliary enterprises	0	0	28,957	35,000	40,000	45,000	50,000	52,500	55,000	57,500	60,000
Total income	$943,324	$1,085,646	$1,341,064	$1,556,368	$1,816,149	$2,110,502	$2,214,661	$2,309,598	$2,451,392	$2,537,630	$2,633,274

Subschedule A-1: Budget for Instruction in Detail, 1958–68, Ashford College

Item	1958–59	1959–60	1960–61	1961–62	1962–63	1963–64	1964–65	1965–66	1966–67	1967–68
Salaries and benefits:										
Faculty salaries	$389,790	$462,357	$539,523	$628,273	$735,273	$772,039	$810,641	$851,173	$893,732	$938,418
Sabbatical leaves	7,694	10,000	8,093	10,995	14,705	17,371	20,266	21,279	22,143	23,460
Student assistants	30,770	37,400	14,000	16,000	20,000	21,000	22,000	23,000	24,000	25,000
Faculty benefits			54,952	78,032	107,978	121,475	127,555	133,932	139,780	147,867
Total	$428,254	$509,757	$616,568	$733,300	$877,956	$931,885	$980,462	$1,029,384	$1,079,655	$1,134,745
Departmental instructional allocation:										
Total	$30,266	$37,000	$45,000	$48,000	$50,000	$51,000	$52,000	$53,000	$54,000	$55,000
Other instructional expenses:										
Faculty candidates expense	$1,200	$2,000	$2,000	$3,000	$4,000					
Faculty research grants and publications	511	3,000	3,000	4,000	6,000					
Faculty traveling fund	1,000	1,500	1,500	2,500	4,000					
Faculty per diem travel expense	230	500	500	1,000	1,000					
Faculty seminar	10,000	0	0	0	0	Breakdown not estimated				
Miscellaneous instruction expense	1,000	1,000	1,000	1,200	1,500					
Faculty moving expense	2,700	8,000	7,000	8,000	9,000					
Faculty entertainment for students	100	150	150	200	300					
Chapel service expense	735	750	750	850	1,000					
Rental of Congregational church	910	910	910	910	1,000					
Adult education classes expense	0	0	0	0	0					
Duplicating	5,030	5,551	5,700	6,000	7,000					
Special grant 1	10,000	10,000	10,000	0	0					
Special grant 2	16,000	13,000	0	0	0					
Special grant 3	10,000	0	0	0	0					
Total	$59,416	$56,361	$32,510	$27,660	$34,800	$35,200	$35,600	$36,000	$36,500	$37,000
Summary:										
Salaries and benefits	$428,254	$509,757	$616,568	$733,300	$877,956	$931,885	$980,462	$1,029,384	$1,079,655	$1,134,745
Departmental instructional allocation	30,266	37,000	45,000	48,000	50,000	51,000	52,000	53,000	54,000	55,000
Other instructional expense	59,416	56,361	32,510	27,660	34,800	35,200	35,600	36,000	36,500	37,000
College examiner's office	2,428	2,481	2,750	3,000	3,300	3,600	3,800	4,000	4,500	5,000
Total	$520,364	$605,599	$696,828	$811,960	$966,056	$1,021,685	$1,071,862	$1,122,384	$1,174,655	$1,231,745

Subschedule A-2: Budget for Operation and Maintenance of Plant, in Detail, 1958–68, Ashford College

Item	1958-59	1959-60	1960-61	1961-62	1962-63	1963-64	1964-65	1965-66	1966-67	1967-68
Administration of buildings and grounds:										
Salaries..................	$ 10,215	$ 10,424	$ 11,400	$ 12,200	$ 13,000	Breakdown not estimated				
General expense...........	1,500	500	550	650	750					
Transportation and equipment........	0	350	400	425	450					
Total..................	$ 11,715	$ 11,274	$ 12,350	$ 13,275	$ 14,200	$ 15,000	$ 15,750	$ 16,500	$ 17,250	$ 18,000
Custodians:										
Salaries..................	$ 59,621	$ 66,186	$ 72,500	$ 78,000	$ 92,000	Breakdown not estimated				
Student help..............	0	825	900	1,000	1,100					
Custodial supplies.........	4,500	4,000	4,400	4,700	5,000					
Laundry and cleaning......	350	325	350	375	450					
Rodent and pest control...	460	425	450	475	500					
Equipment and tools.......	0	1,100	2,000	2,100	2,200					
Campus police............	750	2,200	2,500	2,600	2,700					
Total..................	$ 65,681	$ 75,061	$ 83,100	$ 89,250	$103,950	$106,000	$107,000	$120,000	$123,000	$127,000
Utilities and maintenance:										
Salaries..................	$ 11,865	$ 8,490	$ 9,300	$ 10,200	$ 11,200	Breakdown not estimated				
General utilities maintenance	4,000	2,750	3,000	4,000	5,000					
Water....................	1,500	1,400	1,600	1,800	2,000					
Electricity...............	17,600	17,300	18,000	20,000	22,000					
Equipment and tools.......	300	300	500	600	700					
Total..................	$ 34,965	$ 30,240	$ 32,400	$ 36,600	$ 40,900	$ 42,000	$ 43,000	$ 46,000	$ 48,000	$ 50,000
Heating and air conditioning:										
Salaries..................		$ 14,665	$ 16,000	$ 17,600	$ 18,300	Breakdown not estimated				
General maintenance expense		10,700	12,000	14,000	16,000					
Fuel for main plant........	$ 19,000	22,000	23,000	24,000	25,000					
Fuel for other instructional buildings (gas).	600	1,600	1,800	2,000	2,200					
Water treatment...........	0	550	1,000	1,100	1,200					
Equipment and tools.......	0	150	300	400	500					
(Charge to Auxiliary Enterprises)	(13,800)	(13,800)	(13,800)	(13,800)	(13,800)					
Total..................	$ 5,800	$ 35,865	$ 40,300	$ 45,300	$ 49,400	$ 51,000	$ 52,500	$ 55,000	$ 56,500	$ 58,000
Campus maintenance:										
Salaries..................	$ 8,605	$ 6,515	$ 7,200	$ 8,000	$ 8,800	Breakdown not estimated				
Student help..............	750	750	800	1,000	1,200					
General expense and maintenance	3,450	3,400	4,000	4,500	5,000					
Arborists.................	2,100	2,100	2,300	2,400	2,500					
Equipment and maintenance.	0	250	500	600	700					

Trees and shrubbery:										
Planting	0	200	1,000	2,000	3,000					
Spraying	0	700	1,000	1,250	1,500					
Gas and oil	0	300	500	600	700					
Equipment and tools	0	650	2,000	3,500	5,000					
Total	$ 14,905	$ 14,865	$ 19,300	$ 23,850	$ 28,400	$ 30,000	$ 31,000	$ 32,000	$ 33,000	$ 35,000
Building maintenance:										
Salaries	$ 27,870	$ 23,330	$ 26,000	$ 28,500	$ 36,000					
General building maintenance	16,015	0	0	0	0					
Science hall remodeling	0	2,000	0	0	0	Breakdown not estimated				
Furniture and fixtures; new, repairs, and renewals	3,780	5,800	10,000	12,500	15,000					
Surplus property	100	500	1,000	1,000	1,000					
Elevator maintenance contract	0	188	200	210	220					
Equipment and tools	0	460	1,000	1,500	2,000					
Total	$ 47,765	$ 32,278	$ 38,200	$ 43,710	$ 54,220	$ 57,500	$ 60,000	$ 63,000	$ 66,000	$ 70,000
General service and trucking:										
Maintenance of equipment	$ 0	$ 1,250	$ 1,400	$ 1,450	$ 1,500					
Insurance on institutional plant	5,800	6,000	6,500	7,000	7,500	Breakdown not estimated				
General trucking	4,000	2,250	2,500	2,700	3,000					
Equipment and tools	0	200	500	600	700					
Total	$ 9,800	$ 9,700	$ 10,900	$ 11,750	$ 12,700	$ 13,000	$ 13,250	$ 13,500	$ 13,750	$ 14,000
Interest on endowment at 4%	0	29,325	30,000	30,000	30,000	30,000	30,000	30,000	30,000	30,000
Total operation and maintenance of physical plant	$190,631	$238,608	$266,550	$293,735	$333,770	$344,500	$352,500	$376,000	$387,500	$402,000

Accounting Worksheet B: Scholarship Budget, 1958–68, Ashford College

Item	1957–58	1958–59	1959–60	1960–61	1961–62	1962–63	1963–64	1964–65	1965–66	1966–67	1967–68
Income for scholarships:											
Endowment	$ 32,213	$ 33,805	$ 34,000	$ 34,000	$ 37,000	$ 39,000	$ 41,000	$ 44,000	$ 47,000	$ 50,000	$ 53,000
Gifts	90,207	128,439	274,000	285,000	305,000	375,000	400,000	430,000	450,000	460,000	470,000
Book store and student union	300	1,390	3,000	5,000	8,000	9,000	9,000	11,000	13,000	15,000	17,000
General college funds	54,503	67,366	0	0	0	0	0	0	0	0	0
Total	$177,223	$231,000	$311,000	$324,000	$350,000	$423,000	$450,000	$485,000	$510,000	$525,000	$540,000
Expenditures for scholarships	$177,223	$231,000	$311,000	$324,000	$350,000	$423,000	$450,000	$485,000	$510,000	$525,000	$540,000
Expenditures for student employment on campus	$ 37,317	$ 40,566	$ 45,000	$ 50,000	$ 55,000	$ 62,000	$ 65,000	$ 65,000	$ 70,000	$ 75,000	$ 80,000
Scholarship expenditures and student employment expenditures together:											
Amount	$214,540	$271,566	$356,000	$374,000	$405,000	$485,000	$515,000	$550,000	$580,000	$600,000	$620,000
Portion of tuition income, per cent	35	42	39	33	27	26	27	27	27	27	27

Accounting Worksheet C: Auxiliary Enterprises Budget, 1958–68, Ashford College

Item	1957–58	1958–59	1959–60	1960–61	1961–62	1962–63	1963–64	1964–65	1965–66	1966–67	1967–68
Factors entering into auxiliary enterprises budget											
Enrollment:											
Total	759	800	875	975	1,100	1,250	1,250	1,250	1,250	1,250	1,250
To house in dormitories	558	556	650	730	730	756	790	790	868	903	950
To feed in dining halls	433	550	630	680	780	920	950	950	950	950	950
Room charge	$ 305	$ 345	$ 350	$ 365	$ 400	$ 400	$ 400	$ 450	$ 470	$ 485	$ 492
Board charge	400	410	430	460	475	475	500	525	530	535	540
Total	$ 705	$ 755	$ 780	$ 825	$ 875	$ 875	$ 900	$ 975	$ 1,000	$ 1,020	$ 1,032
Income from auxiliaries											
Room and board	$343,710	$417,000	$498,500	$580,000	$661,500	$743,000	$799,333	$855,666	$912,000	$946,500	$981,000
Other	91,047	92,000	107,000	122,000	137,000	152,000	158,000	164,000	170,000	177,000	184,000
Total income	$434,757	$509,000	$605,500	$702,000	$798,500	$895,000	$957,333	$1,019,666	$1,082,000	$1,123,500	$1,165,000
*Expenditures for auxiliaries**											
Residence halls	$170,349	$192,000	$227,500	$267,000	$292,000	$305,000	$320,000	$355,666	$408,000	$438,500	$468,000
Dining halls	173,361	225,000	271,000	313,000	369,500	438,000	479,333	500,000	504,000	508,000	513,000
Other	91,047	92,000	107,000	122,000	137,000	152,000	158,000	164,000	170,000	177,000	184,000
Total expenditures	$434,757	$509,000	$605,500	$702,000	$798,500	$895,000	$957,333	$1,019,666	$1,082,000	$1,123,500	$1,165,000

* Includes charge for amortization of borrowed funds, interest, repairs and remodeling, an amount equivalent to which is transferred each year to the Auxiliary Enterprises Reserve Fund; includes also administrative charge equal to 5 per cent of operating income; includes also charge equal to book-store and student union profits, which are transferred to scholarship funds.

Accounting Worksheet D: Plant Budget, 1958–68, Ashford College

Item	1957–58	1958–59	1959–60	1960–61	1961–62	1962–63	1963–64	1964–65	1965–66	1966–67	1967–68
Source of Funds											
Gifts:											
Regular	$30,000	$40,000	$40,000	$40,000	$40,000	0	$40,000	$40,000	$40,000	$40,000	$40,000
Special campaign		0	0	0	0	$1,300,000					
Endowment income	8,000	10,000	10,000	10,000	10,000	10,000	10,000	10,000	10,000	10,000	10,000
Total income	$38,000	$50,000	$50,000	$50,000	$50,000	$1,310,000	$50,000	$50,000	$50,000	$50,000	$50,000
Expenditures											
Fine arts building	0	0	0	0	0	$1,300,000					
Other land and buildings	$38,000	$50,000	$50,000	$50,000	$50,000	10,000	$50,000	$50,000	$50,000	$50,000	$50,000
Total expenditures	$38,000	$50,000	$50,000	$50,000	$50,000	$1,310,000	$50,000	$50,000	$50,000	$50,000	$50,000

NOTE: Fund raising or construction could be shifted from one year to another if necessary.

For colleges other than the one described, it might also be necessary to develop detailed space-utilization projections to 1970, with estimates of number of class meetings correlated with the number of classrooms available. This would be essential, for example, at some of the city colleges where classroom space is already used from 8:00 A.M. to 10:00 P.M. five days a week and a half day on Saturday. Additional enrollments, in such cases, would require new space immediately.

There is one other point: To be most useful to college trustees (who examine college accounts and budgets rather infrequently), a long-range plan should be followed by a series of regularly scheduled progress reports. These should pick up the main figures (say, of the 1959 projection) and compare them with accomplishments in 1960 and 1961, as well as with the revised plans proposed for subsequent years. Reports of this type could well be attached to the annual budget as an appendix.

8

The Role of Student Charges

John D. Millett

No other aspect of financing higher education is fraught with more emotional bias or with more collateral complexities than the matter of student charges. It is impossible to consider the question of student fees as a source of educational and general income for our colleges and universities without becoming entangled in far-ranging issues of educational philosophy and practice.

There are only two facts about student tuition fees which are incontrovertible. One is that these charges have already become an important source of financing for both privately and publicly sponsored institutions of higher education. The other is that in absolute terms student charges have increased substantially in the past twenty years. Few persons believe that the increases are at an end. It is when one begins to debate how much the increases ought to be that the shouting starts.

For the academic year ending June 30, 1958, it has been estimated that 25 per cent of all educational and general income was derived from tuition and fees paid by students.[1] For 1,025 privately sponsored colleges and universities, it is estimated that student charges provided 46 per cent of educational income. For 364 publicly sponsored colleges and universities the proportion of income for educational purposes obtained from student charges has been estimated at 8 per cent.

Actually these data are distorted by the large sums of money received from Federal government agencies for research. Today, formally organized research activities financed in whole or in part by government grants and corporation and foundation gifts have become a major undertaking of higher education, especially of most universities. The extent and the financing of these research endeavors have become a major concern for educational operation and management, as discussed elsewhere in this volume. The point here is simply that research income and expense have added a new element in the fiscal analysis of higher education.

It is reasonable to estimate that well over half a billion dollars in the academic year 1958 were spent by institutions of higher education for specific research projects. Probably most of this outlay was obtained from Federal government contracts and grants. If allowance is made for income for this specific purpose, and for certain public service activities of public institutions, I believe we will find that privately sponsored colleges and universities obtain from 60 to 70 per cent of their educational and general income for current operating purposes from student charges, while publicly sponsored institutions obtain from 20 to 30 per cent of their income from this source.

In so far as actual amounts are concerned, the study of the Council for Financial Aid to Education shows that student fee income for higher education rose from some $154 million in 1943–44 to over $904 million in 1957–58.[1] This was an increase of almost six times. When one examines the increases made at individual colleges and universities, the actual change is more vividly revealed. Twenty-five years ago the tuition charge at many private colleges and universities of high prestige along the eastern seaboard amounted to $400 a year; as of 1959–60 this charge had risen to as high as $1,450. At many good liberal arts colleges in the Middle West the tuition charge in the 1930s often amounted to about $250 a year; today the same charge is about $1,000. At many of the older state universities of the Middle West, the amount contributed by the student to current enducational income has risen from about $50 an academic year to about $200.

Actually, the system of student charges at publicly sponsored universities is more complicated than the foregoing figures might indicate. Another $100 or more is collected from students on a compulsory basis for the support of a student health service, student activities, and building funds. To some extent these same or similar purposes may obtain income from an all-inclusive fee at private colleges and universities. Moreover, state universities charge a much larger fee than that indicated above to the student who enrolls from outside the state in which the particular institution is located.

The Basic Issue and the Complications of Meeting it

We are generally agreed that higher education must have more income in the years ahead. It is not sufficient for 75 per cent more students simply to pay existing fees; the increase in income will not be enough. There is an existing gap between charges to students and instructional expense per student. As enrollments increase, this gap becomes an ever greater financial burden to be met by endowment and gift income and government appropriations.

Furthermore, if faculty salaries are to be increased by 75 or 100 per cent in the next decade, if we are to improve educational facilities and to provide more library volumes and educational supplies, then more income must be obtained. Even though some instructional economies may be introduced and so reduce income needs, they cannot begin to match the greatly enlarged sums of money that higher education must have. From approximately $3.7 billion spent for educational purposes in 1957–58, it is estimated herein that higher education must have some $9 billion of income by 1969–70. That is an increase of 1½ times.

The basic issue, then, which agitates the world of higher education is how much of this increase in income should come from students and how much should come from other sources such as philanthropy and government. Obviously there are two extreme positions which a person may take in answering this question. One is to say that all of the additional income should be obtained from philanthropy and government; the other is to say that all of the additional income should be obtained from students.

Perhaps there are only a few persons who will take either of these extreme positions in the next decade. Yet some of the complexities of the problem can best be understood if we examine the two extremes. There are collateral issues involved, however, which may not appear in any actual discussion of the two basic propositions. To ignore these additional factors would be to miss the eight-ninths of the iceberg submerged below the surface of the sea.

For one thing, many educational administrators, as well as others, are dissatisfied with current methods of financing our colleges and universities. It is a wearing business constantly to cultivate all available sources of philanthropic support: annual alumni giving, corporation contributions, gifts and bequests of friends, church support, foundation assistance. The college and university president must be a perpetual beggar if he is to find the current operating income and the capital funds needed to ensure institutional well-being. Some surcease from this continual solicitation would be welcome indeed to most educational administrators.

For another thing, there is the problem of how governmental funds may be distributed to privately sponsored institutions. Many persons firmly believe that governmental support, especially Federal government funds, must be provided for the instructional programs of higher education. At the same time it is realized that government subsidy of privately sponsored colleges and universities may raise troublesome issues of public policy and constitutional doctrine. Since many colleges and universities have been founded under the sponsorship of various religious denominations, and since many of these institutions are governed by and obtain financial assistance through church agencies, direct financial assistance for current instructional purpose would be subject to considerable public controversy. Such financial assistance might also run afoul the constitutional proscription against the passage of a law "respecting an establishment of religion," to use the words of the First Amendment.

One feasible means for providing financial assistance to the many different privately sponsored colleges and universities of this country is to assist students rather than the institutions themselves. A large-scale governmental program of financial assistance to students—with either loan or scholarship funds or both—can be of actual financial assistance to colleges and universities under one of two arrangements. The grant of funds to a student who then selects his own institution to attend may be accompanied by a grant of operating funds directly to the institution in recognition of the fact that tuition charges do not meet actual instructional costs. This principle has been recognized, for example, in Title IV of the National Defense Education Act of 1958 providing for graduate fellowships in new or expanded doctoral programs. The institution attended by the recipient of such a fellowship is given up to a $2,500 annual operating grant for each fellowship student enrolled.

The other arrangement by which a massive program of student aid can help finance educational institutions is for such a program to encourage institutions to raise student fees, and to raise such fees substantially. As a result, many discussions of increased student charges immediately lead to consideration of greatly enlarged programs of student assistance. Indeed, it might even be suspected that some pressures for higher student charges have as their real objective large-scale governmental programs of student aid, and perhaps also the objective of governmental financial assistance to privately sponsored institutions.

I do not wish these remarks to be interpreted necessarily as opposition to either student aid programs or governmental financial assistance to private colleges and universities. I suggest only that these issues should be clearly identified and considered on their merits as an integral part of any discussion of the desirability of increased student fees.

There is a further complication to the whole question of the desirable level of student charges. There is undoubtedly a growing concern with the tax burden of government at all levels in our country. A threatened revolt against the cost of government is especially evident in our states. Most governors and state legislators in 1959 faced the troublesome situation of rising governmental costs and a decline of governmental revenues occasioned by the recession of 1957–58. The choice was to curtail services or increase taxes. The second choice involved the further conflict between advocates of sales taxes and those favoring individual and corporation income taxes. These difficulties were not resolved in 1959; in many states the same problems will rise to plague officials in 1961.[2]

Into this situation there is inevitably interjected the question of whether students at publicly sponsored colleges and universities should not pay more of the cost of their education. One corporation official has stated his opinion thus: "It seems to me that our public institutions of higher learning should raise their tuition fees to cover the bulk of their expenses."[3] He has then given as one of three reasons for this position that "the burden of state taxes would be eased." It does not matter that many individuals may have an exaggerated idea of the proportion of state revenue devoted to higher education. (In 1957 there were only sixteen states spending more than 10 per cent of their tax revenue for higher education, and there were eighteen states spending less than 7 per cent of their taxes for that purpose.) In the years ahead a concern for state tax burdens will place great pressure upon the fee charges of publicly sponsored higher education.

Finally, we should not overlook the existence of a considerable sense of competition between privately sponsored and publicly sponsored colleges and universities. This competition is not primarily one for funds; it is in large degree a competition for good students. In considerable measure the reputation for quality in educational endeavor rests upon the quality of the student body more than upon any other single factor. It may be argued whether a quality faculty comes before a quality student body, but certainly it is difficult for an institution to recruit and retain a high-grade staff unless it also recruits a high-grade student body.

The competition in our country is keen indeed for the top 100,000 high school graduates each year. There are 70 private institutions of high prestige (out of some 1,000 such institutions) and 20 public institutions of high prestige (out of some 360 institutions) who enroll freshmen classes of nearly 100,000 persons. In other words, 90 out of almost 1,400 institutions can absorb the top 100,000 high school graduates. It does not matter that as many as 700,000 high school graduates may go on to college at the present time. The competition for the best of these students is very real.

Publicly sponsored institutions of higher education believe that some of the argument in favor of higher student charges is in reality an effort to lessen competition for the best young high school graduates. The publicly sponsored university has one major competitive advantage: its low charge to students for instruction. The privately sponsored college or university may boast of greater prestige, of closer personal relationships between faculty and students, and of larger available funds for student assistance. Undoubtedly, the competitive position of our best publicly sponsored institutions would be damaged if their charges to students were substantially increased. And the quality of the entire educational system could be adversely affected as a result. Indeed, it may be said that the educational program for the second or third 100,000 freshmen in intellectual ability is vitally influenced by the presence or absence of some of the top 100,000 high school graduates on a campus.

All of these complexities must be borne in mind in a discussion of the role of student fees in financing higher education. The direct questions of educational philosophy and practice involved in fixing particular levels of student charges cannot be resolved without some understanding of the additional issues which influence both attitudes and decisions.

Education as Public Interest or Private Desire

There are two fundamental ways in which to look at higher education. One is to regard opportunity for the educational development of youth as a social necessity. The other is to regard higher education, and indeed all education, as an individual desire. If we adopt the first point of view, higher education as a social necessity, then it follows that we shall seek the maximum necessary social expenditure to provide educational opportunity. If we accept the second point of view, higher education as an individual desire, then it follows that we should consider education as another service to be bought and sold in the market place.

American historical tradition is almost completely on the side of the point of view that education is to be regarded as a social necessity. Harvard College, founded just sixteen years after the first landings in Massachusetts, was established because the very first generation of New Englanders desired "to advance learning and perpetuate it to posterity, dreading to leave an illiterate ministry to the churches, when our present ministers shall lie in the dust." [4] The charter of William and Mary, the second American college, mentioned among its purposes that "the Church of Virginia may be furnished with a seminary of ministers of the gospel, and that they may be piously educated in good letters and manners." The third college, Yale, was founded as a school "wherein youth may be instructed in the arts and sciences, who through the blessing of Almighty God may be fitted for publick employment, both in church and civil state." [4] These were social goals.

Thomas Jefferson added another element. In advocating the establishment of the University of Virginia, Jefferson argued that it is

. . . expedient for promoting the public happiness that those persons, whom nature has endowed with genius and virtue, should be rendered by liberal education worthy to receive, and able to guard the sacred deposit of the rights and liberties of their fellow citizens, and that they should be called to that charge without regard to wealth, birth or other accidental condition or circumstance.[5]

From the very beginnings of colonial America, education was rightly regarded as a necessity for providing a learned element in society. In the young republic, learning was considered essential for a people entrusted with political power over their own destiny. Moreover, higher education should be available to youth of ability regardless of economic or family status. Thus the role of education in promoting social mobility and in opening careers to talent was clearly understood.

Such sentiments were expressed in the Northwest Ordinance of 1787, written the same year as the Federal constitution. Such sentiments were embodied in the constitutions of newly created states, and in laws making land grants available for the support of various "seminaries of learning." Such sentiments played a part in congressional action in adopting the Morrill Act of 1862, amid the darkest days of civil strife, in order to encourage further educational opportunity for youth.

Nor would I suggest for one moment that it was the publicly sponsored colleges and universities alone who were devoted to the objective of higher education as a social necessity. Privately sponsored institutions avowed the same goal. They sought gifts for buildings, and for current operation. They obtained tax exemption because they served a public purpose. It does not matter whether the support of instructional cost comes from government or philanthropy; both arrangements seek to enable youth of intellectual promise to obtain higher education as a social necessity.

Even in this day of high tuition charges by so many privately sponsored colleges and universities, the public purpose of higher education is acknowledged by scholarship programs which endeavor to ameliorate the impact of high cost. Indeed, there can be no argument in favor of large-scale scholarship programs, whether adopted by private agencies or government, except in terms of higher education as a social responsibility.

Some economists today are suggesting that the great material wealth of America has in good part been achieved by our system of education.[6] Moreover, it seems likely that education, perhaps as one among several objects of governmental expenditure, has contributed far more to the growing equalization of personal income than has progressive taxation. In fact, I am told that 80 per cent of Federal government receipts from

the individual income tax is obtained from those who pay the 20 to 25
per cent rate on taxable income.

There is no need to argue further the social necessity of higher education. The National Defense Education Act of 1958 has already expressed
a national conviction that our very survival as a nation is in large measure
dependent upon our colleges and universities.

This concern with higher education as a social necessity has not pre-
vented colleges and universities from in fact passing a substantial part
of their costs of operation on to the student. For example, the public
university which seeks to maintain a low tuition charge to the student
has had from necessity to adopt the position that the student should pay
all the cost of his room and board. Of sixty-two state universities listed
as such by Dr. Raymond Walters in 1958,[7] only fifteen were located in
cities having a population of over 50,000 persons as of 1950, and of those
only nine were located in the major urban center of their state. This
means that most young people who attend the "low-cost" state university
must actually do so at the price of meeting room, board, and travel
expenses.

The difference in cost to the student attending four different types of
institutions is illustrated in Table 1. These data are generalized repre-

Table 1. Student Expenses in College Attendance

Item of expense	Cost at colleges			
	A	B	C	D
Tuition and fees.................	$1,000	$1,000	$ 300	$ 500
Books and supplies..............	100	100	100	100
Room rent......................	260	....	275	....
Board..........................	500	150	500	150
Travel..........................	100	....	100	....
Clothing and incidentals.........	300	250	250	250
Totals.....................	$2,260	$1,500	$1,525	$1,000

A: Private liberal arts college.   C: State university in small city.
B: Private university in large city.   D: Municipal university.

sentations of four kinds of situations which a student might confront.
In actual fact, there are more choices than these for the student. Moreover, the cost estimates tend to be averages; for a particular student at
any one of these institutions might spend a great deal more on, let us
say, clothing than is estimated. Travel expense, too, might vary widely.
In practice, then, the differences would probably be greater than these

estimates suggest. Yet even with these qualifications, the hypothetical student budgets reveal interesting facts.

First of all, it is not fair to conclude that the relative costs to the student for attending various kinds of institutions can be determined simply by consulting the tuition charges. That is only a beginning. Any analysis of expense in college attendance should begin with the total cost to the student.

Secondly, it will be noted from Table 1 that a student might attend a privately sponsored university, pay a high tuition, live at home, and so find his cost about the same as that of attending a state university on a residential basis. The "cheapest" education for the student is a municipal university which charges more tuition than a state university; the difference results from reduced living costs. And it will be noticed that the actual costs to the student in attending the private liberal arts college instead of the state university are not some three times greater but rather only about half again as great.

Facts of this kind—and an awareness of pressures for increasing fee charges for both current operations and capital construction—lead administrators of state universities to worry about student charges. They realize that the expense of college attendance at a public institution can be substantial. They worry lest the public necessity of higher education may not already have been substantially sacrificed to the financial needs of their institutions. Thus it is not unusual to find state university administrators appealing to their alumni and to others to help them with scholarship funds to make sure that few worthy impecunious students are denied the opportunity of higher education.

The basic argument in favor of low tuition charges at publicly sponsored institutions is social necessity. The argument is not that higher education should be free; that position was abandoned a long time ago. The argument is only that charges to students should be kept within some limits in order to make it possible for many young people to have some reasonable hope of financing their higher education through personal earnings, loans and scholarships, and modest family assistance.

Effect of Means of Support on Institutional Freedom

There is yet another proposition from the point of view of institutions of higher education themselves which favors tuition charges to students at less than instructional cost. That proposition has to do with the institutional circumstances conducive to freedom. Most Americans today associate the concept of freedom in our society with a pluralism of social organization. Freedom to the individual, we hold, is possible when there is some choice available among professional groups, employers, unions, churches, governmental units, voluntary associations, and even schools. We abhor monopoly, and we seek security from oppression through instruments of "countervailing power."

From its own point of view, the individual college or university may expect to find some freedom in operation, usually, if it succeeds in attracting a variety of financial support. Among educational administrators and others, this is known as the doctrine of balance. The position holds that not one but a variety of sources of financial support is essential to the preservation of academic freedom.

Three different groups of citizens and educators who in recent years have examined the problem of financing higher education have come to the conclusion that there is no one best source of income. In 1952, after reviewing the various sources of support now utilized by colleges and universities, the Commission on Financing Higher Education declared:[5]

> These various sources of income are not all of the same importance. . . . All of them are valuable, however. The answer lies in developing as many of them as possible and in such balance as economic circumstances allow. . . . Out of this variety comes the flexibility, the freedom, and the originality which have contributed to the unique achievement of American colleges and universities.

A similar conclusion was reached by the Educational Policies Commission.[8] More recently the President's Committee on Education Beyond the High School has declared:[9]

> In the next ten years colleges and universities will require an enormous expansion of funds from all customary sources—besides tuition and fees, from alumni, corporations, and other private donors, and from state and local governments.

Later the Committee went on to say:[9]

> There is no one best source. . . . Only a balanced combination of total effort will serve the need without creating an imbalance in responsibility.

Finally, in projecting the sources of educational and general income for all colleges and universities as of 1969, the Council for Financial Aid to Education has suggested that 21 per cent might come from tuition and fees, 21 per cent from gifts and grants, 3 per cent from endowment, 5 per cent from miscellaneous sources, and 50 per cent from various governments.[1] This is an acknowledgment of balance.

It is surely significant of a considerable consensus that these various groups should all reach the same conclusion: the best interests of the American system of higher education require a balancing of various sources of income rather than reliance upon an exclusive source, whether that source be students, governments, corporations, alumni, foundations, church bodies, or others.

The Argument for Higher Student Charges

Two practical arguments are usually offered in favor of the proposition that higher education should be regarded as a personal desire, and hence financed by individual payment. The first is that college graduates generally obtain lucrative employment and that a college education should therefore be regarded as a personal investment. One advocate of this point of view is Mr. Devereux C. Josephs, the distinguished chairman of the board of the New York Life Insurance Company.

Mr. Josephs has noted that at the present time about 40 per cent of the tuition and living expenses of students comes from current family income, 20 per cent from long-term family savings, 25 per cent from part-time earnings of students themselves, and the remaining 15 per cent from scholarships, veteran benefits, and loans.[10] He believes that this arrangement is not satisfactory, especially when colleges and universities need more income:

> The solution to the problem is clear and simple: Colleges should raise tuition fees to charge to the student the full cost of his education, and what the student or his parents cannot pay from past savings and current earnings *they should borrow*. [Italics in original.]

Mr. Josephs goes on to observe that a number of economists have calculated that a college education is worth $75,000 to $150,000 in increased lifetime earnings. What could be a better investment?

Mr. Josephs asks also why colleges and universities should underpay their faculties or subsidize a student's education when families are accustomed to borrow for a new automobile, a television set, or other durable goods. He accuses educational administrators of being slow to see the advantages to themselves from credit financing of higher education. He concludes his case with these words:[10]

> The only sensible course is for educators to follow the practice of purveyors of other commodities: charge a fair price and encourage or help the customer in financing the purchase. Unless college officials change their attitudes and encourage students to borrow for education, many youngsters will lose a great part of the future opportunity, income and general enrichment of life that might be theirs. But if the colleges themselves would publicly advocate borrowing under appropriate circumstances, then attitudes would quickly change, and commercial lending institutions would continue to develop their own plans.

The second argument in practical terms in favor of higher student charges is the proposition that families have greater equality of incomes, and even larger incomes, than in previous years and hence are better able economically to pay for higher education. A careful analysis of the economics of student charges was prepared at the beginning of the 1950s for the Commission on Financing Higher Education.[11] At that time higher education was experiencing a decline in student enrollments after the "veterans' bulge," and fears were voiced that increased tuition charges might be contributing to the drop. The commission's study supported several conclusions. First, the higher the average income in a state the higher tended to be the proportion of college-age youth enrolled in college.[11] Second, with such variables as differences in per capita income, the educational attainment of the adult population, and the proximity of colleges to centers of population held constant, there did appear to be a tendency for larger enrollments to be associated with lower student charges.[11] This relationship was only partial, however. A large increase in charges appeared to be necessary to have an adverse effect upon enrollment. The demand for higher education was characterized as relatively inelastic, that is, as only moderately responsive to the prices charged. Third, it was pointed out that higher levels of income in the United States were increasing the ability to pay for higher education and that higher charges had not decreased educational opportunity.[11]

There has continued to be a considerable shift in income distribution within the United States. The changes occurring between 1947 and 1957 are shown in Table 2. Whereas only 17 per cent of family units had

Table 2. Changes in Percentage Distribution of Family Units by Income Classes 1947-57

Income class	1947 percentage	1957 percentage	Income class	1947 percentage	1957 percentage
$2,000 or less....	25	14	$ 6,000–7,999....	9	18
2,000–3,999.....	38	23	8,000–9,999....	3	9
4,000–5,999.....	20	25	10,000 or more...	5	11

SOURCE: U.S. Dept. of Commerce, Office of Business Economics, *U.S. Income and Output*, 1958, p. 41.

incomes in excess of $6,000 a year in 1947, 38 per cent of all families had such incomes in 1957. Even with price inflation, that is a substantial change. Whether it proves that the American population is now able to pay all the instructional expenses of higher education through student charges is another question. We should not ignore the fact that 62 per cent of American families in 1957 had incomes below $6,000 a year.

A more theoretical argument in favor of higher tuition charges has been presented recently by Dean B. A. Rogge of Wabash College.[12] He proposed that the principles of the market place should decide who should go to college. Since selection of beneficiaries on the basis of intellectual promise cannot be made with accuracy, Dean Rogge suggested that charges based upon the cost of the service should determine enrollment. Those willing to pay for the service should have the benefit of the service. He even implied that this would have a salutary influence upon the quality of instruction. Furthermore, discrimination upon the basis of price would automatically indicate those with a real motivation to achieve a college education.

Dean Rogge acknowledged that there might be a social purpose to higher education, but he held that that end should be realized by subsidy to the individual student based upon personal and family need. A general subsidy to all youth, realized by tuition at less than cost, is an unnecessary gift to young people of wealthy families and perhaps an inadequate gift to young people from poorer families. Then he admits that so radical a change is unlikely and ends his argument by advocating as a "first step" that the state-supported institutions "set up a pattern of tuition increases designed to increase the percentage of costs covered by tuition payments." Only as a "final pattern" does he expect both publicly and privately sponsored institutions to obtain revenues from tuition charges which "would be approximately equal to total costs." In the meantime he advocates an enlarged program of state scholarship grants and loan funds for students. The result of all this, he believes, would be "an increasing emphasis on private as compared to public sponsorship of institutions of higher education."

Two Further Complications of Higher Student Charges

Before we attempt some concluding assessment of the case for and against tuition charges based upon cost of instruction, let us examine two further complications. One of them is that of determining exactly what is instructional cost as a basis for educational pricing; the other is that of establishing and *paying for* a large-scale system of student assistance.

First of all, educational administrators are familiar with the fact that the instructional activities of colleges and universities vary a great deal in cost. Different institutions have different average salary levels for their instructional staff and different overhead costs. Different institutions, and different programs, have different staffing standards, expressed usually in terms of a student-faculty ratio. The variation may be from 7:1 to 20:1 or even more; the result is different costs. Some institutions use a good deal of their general income to finance their student scholarship programs; others do not. Some institutions operate extensive services to students; others do not. Some institutions have a heavy instructional load for their staff; others do not. All of these factors make for a great difference in instructional cost.

Still another cost difference arises when one university, or college for that matter, has an extensive research program and another does not. Should research expenses be counted as a cost of instruction? There is also a cost difference depending upon whether a medical school operates a hospital or not, whether a college of agriculture operates an extensive farm system or not, whether a college of education operates a laboratory school or not. Should the expenses of these "organized activities relating to educational departments" be counted as a cost of instruction? Moreover, many institutions, especially public universities, operate a number of public services such as research laboratories for small business, agricultural extension, radio broadcasting, and consulting assistance to local school districts. Should the expense of these extension and public services be counted as a cost of instruction?

Then there is also a great deal of difference in program costs. As a general proposition, it costs more to teach engineering than business administration. It costs more to teach seniors than freshmen. It costs more to teach medicine than law. It costs more to educate a student for the doctor of philosophy degree than a student for the master of arts degree.

Several years ago I reported the cost analysis of a complex university.[13] The index relationship for costs of instruction at various levels and for various subject matter areas is shown in Table 3. These data are now several years old, and they call for a good deal of explanation which need not be detailed here. The important fact is that the determination of instructional cost depends upon whether you are talking about a lower-division student in arts and sciences or a Ph.D. student, upon whether you are talking about a student of medicine or a student of law. There are great variations in cost between levels and areas of instruction.

The data of Table 3 immediately bring up the matter of differential pricing. To an important degree, with some exception for engineering and medicine, students are usually charged a standard tuition, whether they are freshmen or seniors in a college of arts and sciences, whether they are students for the Ph.D. degree in physics or students for the LL.B. degree in law. So long as charges are less than the average cost of instruction in any event, this practice is not too serious. Even so, it is probable than in many universities, if costs were accurately and closely

Table 3. Index Relationship of Instructional Expenditure
per Full-time Student, by Field and Level of Study

	Lower division	Upper division	Graduate classes	Graduate research
Arts and sciences...........	100	264	685	2,424
Business...................	67	113	284	971
Education..................	249	492	401	1,367
Music.....................	365	328	456	
Engineering................	324	286	462	2,126
Agriculture................	217	237	307	336
Dentistry..................	...	310	1,116	
Law.......................	...	...	140	
Medicine..................	...	...	1,286	

SOURCE: John D. Millett, *Financing Higher Education in the United States*, Columbia University Press, New York, 1952.

computed, most students are already paying for the expense of their instruction.

If higher educational pricing were to adopt the principle of charges based upon cost, not only would some very careful accounting be required but institutions would also have to face squarely the issue whether to engage in differential or average pricing. Under a rigorous public scrutiny which would inevitably follow in the wake of such a policy, a higher degree of standardization would undoubtedly follow. Does American higher education prefer standardization to diversity?

The second practical problem is the difficulty and cost of administering a large-scale system of governmental scholarship aid to students. I think we may take it for granted that any general policy of basing tuition upon instructional costs will be adopted only when a very substantial program of student aid becomes operative. This country is not ready, nor do I believe it desirable, to abandon the idea that higher education is just as much or even more a social necessity than it is an individual desire. This idea is now acknowledged by tuition at less than cost and by student aid programs. If the first is given up, the second will surely be greatly expanded.

It is conceivable, of course, that a student aid program might be entirely, or preponderantly, based upon student loans. There are a number of practical, and political, advantages to a system of loans, as experience under the National Defense Education Act of 1958 will probably demonstrate. Loan funds constitute a temporary and repayable loan to a college or university rather than an outright grant. Loan funds administered by individual institutions do not result in a reshuffling of students on a competitive basis among various colleges and universities, especially when such loans must be administered according to a standard practice. Nonetheless, I doubt if a loan system as such will ever be considered to be an adequate acknowledgment of the public interest in higher education.

We may then confine our attention to the intricacies of a nationwide scholarship system. First of all, such a system would no doubt be administered upon the basis of need. It would therefore be necessary to establish a nationwide calculation of how much a family should reasonably be expected to contribute to the educational cost of a dependent. Such a calculation would no doubt be similar to that employed by the present College Scholarship Service and recommended for use in handling the National Defense Student Loan program.[14] This means the establishment of support standards according to income class and number of dependents in a family. Such a calculation is shown in Table 4.

Table 4. Normal Expected Support for College Expenses from Family Incomes of Different Sizes

Annual family income	Number of dependent children in family				
	1	2	3	4	5
$ 2,000	$ 240	$ 185	$ 145	$ 120	$ 105
4,000	555	445	370	305	240
6,000	885	685	615	525	435
8,000	1,250	965	840	755	660
10,000	1,750	1,370	1,165	1,020	915
12,000	2,300	1,805	1,535	1,350	1,210

SOURCE: John F. Morse, *An Aid to Administrators of National Defense Student Loans,* College Entrance Examination Board, New York, 1959.

Secondly, a massive scholarship program must establish a general budget of reasonable student expense. We have shown the elements of such a budget in Table 1. Look at the problems that arise. Should institutions be permitted to fix their charges at whatever level they please? Suppose one university includes plant depreciation and another doesn't? How far from home should a student be permitted to travel? Should all students be encouraged to attend residence institutions rather than live at home? How well should students be expected to dress, and what social expenses are justified?

These are not imaginary questions. Some of them arose in connection with government administration of veterans' educational benefits; most of them have arisen in the management of the National Merit Scholarship Corporation. All would be bound to arise in the operation of any large-scale government scholarship program based upon a means test.

Indeed, we can establish and maintain a government scholarship system only by the creation of a new educational bureaucracy. How large this would be, how expensive it would be to operate, and how pervasive its controls would become over both family circumstances and institutional management, we can only imagine. To me, it is a frightening rather than a reassuring prospect.

Moreover, it is commonly assumed that a system of public subsidy to students based upon need would be less burdensome upon the public purse than the present system of public subsidy to state universities. Is there any basis for this assumption?

Let us look at a recent estimate of income distribution in the United States as of 1958. This estimate divides family units by income class as follows:

Income class	Yearly income
Top fifth	Over $8,000
Second fifth	$6,000–$8,000
Third fifth	$4,000–$6,000
Fourth fifth	$3,000–$4,000
Lowest fifth	Under $3,000

To be sure, we do not know much about income distribution based upon family size or age. It seems reasonable to assume that most families are at the peak of their earning power when their children are of college age. Even so, a study as of 1958–59 of the family incomes of students from Ohio enrolled at Miami University indicated that 60 per cent of all students came from families earning less than $8,000 a year and one-third of all students came from families with incomes under $6,000 a year. If this distribution were representative, and if a reasonable standard of student support were adopted, I believe that the costs of a large-scale student scholarship program might very well cost as much as $2.6 billion. The basis of these calculations is shown in Table 5. If tuition

Table 5. Possible Requirements for Support of 2½ Million Students

Number of students	Percentage of total	Individual subsidy required	Amount
200,000	8	$2,000	$ 400,000,000
600,000	24	1,750	1,050,000,000
675,000	27	1,500	1,012,500,000
200,000	8	1,000	200,000,000
825,000	33		
2,500,000	100		$2,662,500,000

were based upon cost and other expenses were allowed, these figures are by no means exorbitant.

And it should be remembered that the total appropriations from tax funds by state government for higher education in 1957–58 amounted to about $1 billion! [1]

Or let us look at the matter in a different way. I am told by the National Merit Scholarship Corporation that, by using its need formula, the average subsidy for all its scholars in 1959 will be about $750. In the state of Ohio the state appropriation from tax funds for six state institutions in 1959–60 amounts to about $38 million. But these institutions enroll only half of the students attending college in Ohio. The total full-time enrollment is about 100,000. It would take $75 million a year to subsidize 100,000 students at an average of $750 each.

Certainly a great deal more needs to be known about the magnitudes involved before there is any ready assumption that it will cost less to subsidize students than to subsidize institutions. Moreover, we might note that in many nations of the world, including Russia, higher education is supported by grants to students *and* grants to institutions!

Summary and Conclusion

It is amply apparent from the preceding paragraphs that this particular educational administrator—a student and faculty member in privately sponsored institutions and now administrator of a publicly sponsored university—entertains serious reservations about any substantial change from present financing methods. Certainly, our colleges and universities, private and public, must have more income in the years ahead. It will not be easy to extract the necessary income, whether from students, philanthropy, or government. It would be pleasant to anticipate some relief from the present struggle to finance higher education. But surely struggle is a small price to pay for a free educational system in a free society!

Because tuition is a relatively lesser part of total educational and general expenses than it was twenty years ago, it is a mistake to conclude that tuition charges to the student are not substantial. We must not forget that research and public service have now become major elements of a university budget, and that this development has changed the distribution of both educational expense and educational income. In dollar terms student charges are larger today than at any previous time in our nation's history.

It is not unreasonable to hope that many students can and will borrow funds to help meet the expense of college attendance. But it is not clear that higher education ought purposely to help swell consumer debt in the United States. It is not clear that women should be encouraged to borrow in order to attend college. It is not clear that students preparing to become college professors ought to be charged the cost of a Ph.D. education. It is not clear that students preparing to become elementary and secondary school teachers should be charged the full cost of their education.

Indeed, it is not clear that students should be encouraged to think of higher education only as a personal investment from which they should strive to obtain the greatest possible return. It is not clear that we want students channeled into high-salary professions rather than into important public service. It is not clear that we should adopt Russian methods of influencing individual behavior.

It is not clear that a government bureaucracy to determine who shall go to college and how much each student shall receive in subsidy will be a benevolent, desirable addition to the machinery of an already over-whelming public enterprise. It is not clear that a Federal government scholarship system will actually make higher education easier to ad-minister, or freer in its operation. It is not clear that a scholarship system will be kept immune from political manipulation.

It is not clear that there is something fiscally bad or morally wrong in an arrangement whereby all students receive some financial assistance in attending college. Where social necessity is involved, we do not support public service exclusively upon a progressive basis, that is, upon the basis of ability to pay. Many governmental services are supported from tariff duties, excise and sales taxes, and service charges. Why should educational benefit be apportioned solely upon the basis of family economic status?

It is not clear that a new system of pricing and a corresponding sys-tem of student subsidy will encourage 30, 40, or even 50 per cent of all college-age youth to go to college. Our achievements in encouraging youth to attend college are phenomenal; they have been realized by the joint efforts of nearly two thousand different privately and publicly sponsored institutions, existing in a variety of situations and serving a diversity of student abilities. It is not clear that such variety and diversity could survive a gigantic, central bureaucracy administering some new system of student assistance.

It is not clear that any private support, whether from alumni, corpora-tions, churches, foundations, or others, would continue to be available to higher education if some immense governmental program of student aid came into existence.

In the light of all these uncertainties any precipitate change in the fiscal practices of higher education would be unfortunate.

To be sure, I am not convinced that increases in student charges have now reached some ideal level. I believe there will continue to be modest and gradual increases in the proportion of instructional expense borne by students. But I am convinced that the best interests of our nation are served when these increases are modest and gradual.

I believe also that we must continue to experiment with a variety of financing methods to assist students in meeting their part of the costs of going to college. We need more loan funds, more scholarship and fellowship funds, more student employment opportunities.

I believe there is no one best way to finance higher education. It is too early for college and university presidents to put away their begging bowls.

Notes

1. Council for Financial Aid to Education, *Where's the Money Coming From?*, New York, 1959, pp. 6, 7, 11.

2. Cf. Robert Lubar and Charles E Silberman, "The Taxes Closest to Home," *Fortune*, p. 106, June, 1959.

3. Theodore O Yntema, "Our Long-run Internal Problems," *The Saturday Review*, p. 22, Jan. 17, 1959.

4. Cf. Richard Hofstadter and C. DeWitt Hardy, *The Development and Scope of Higher Education*, Columbia University Press, New York, 1952, pp. 3, 4.

5. Quoted in Commission on Financing Higher Education, *Nature and Needs of Higher Education*, Columbia University Press, New York, 1952, pp. 4–5, 185.

6. Cf. Theodore W. Schultz, "Investment in Man: An Economist's View," *The Social Service Review*, vol. 33, p. 109, June, 1959.

7. Raymond Walters, "Statistics of Attendance in American Universities and Colleges, 1958," *School and Society*, vol. 86, p. 429, Dec. 6, 1958. The expression five "universities listed as such" is a reference to Dr. Walters' classification.

8. Educational Policies Commission, *Higher Education in a Decade of Decision*, National Education Association and American Association of School Administrators, Washington, 1957, p. 144.

9. President's Committee on Education Beyond the High School, *Second Report to the President*, 1957, pp. 13, 75.

10. Devereux C. Josephs, "College on Credit," *Think*, vol. 25, pp. 7, 9, May, 1959.

11. Richard H. Ostheimer, *Student Charges and Financing Higher Education*, Columbia University Press, New York, 1953, pp. 83, 101, 137.

12. See the two articles entitled "What Price Education" and "Financing Higher Education," *Wall Street Journal*, May 1 and May 4, 1959. These articles

in turn were part of a larger pamphlet published by the American Enterprise Association.

13. John D. Millett, *Financing Higher Education in the United States*, Columbia University Press, New York, 1952, p. 146.

14. John F. Morse, *An Aid to Administrators of National Defense Student Loans*, College Entrance Examination Board, New York, 1959, p. 12.

9

Government Support of Higher Education

Robert D. Calkins

Earlier papers have stated the need for *more* and *better* higher education and indicated that fiscal solvency will be attained during the next decade or so at the expense of quality unless substantially larger sums are provided from all sources: tuition, gifts, and government. For over a century government (Federal, state, and local) has been an increasing source of support for higher education. In recent decades it has been a major source of funds for public institutions and a growing source of revenue for private ones. Even if tuition charges are raised substantially and philanthropy increases its contributions, more than a doubling of governmental support (from $1,752 million in 1957–58 to $3,700 million or more by about 1969–70) will be required to accommodate growing enrollments, increase salaries, and maintain or improve instruction. This increase is based on Professor Harris' estimate of much higher tuition costs. If, as President Millett proposes, tuition rates are not greatly increased, well over $1,500 million more will be needed from government to balance anticipated budgets. For the expansion of facilities an additional governmental contribution of $1,000 million annually may be necessary by 1969–70.

To gain any such expansion of governmental funds will require more of a consensus than now exists on a number of important questions. What are the commitments and responsibilities of government for higher education at the Federal, state, and local levels? What forms and amounts

183

of support are required? What is the ability of government to provide such funds? Among those especially concerned with education are other questions that relate to the consequences that may flow from a greater dependence on government support. There are differing views on what effects will follow from increased reliance on public funds and on the desirability of those effects. Beneath the differences are hopes and fears for the effect on the educational system itself, the effect on educational standards, the effect on private institutions, the possibility of political control, and the consequences for academic freedom to inquire and to teach. The argument is also heard, particularly against Federal aid, that it will undermine state and local effort. A clarification of these matters in the light of experience is essential to the formulation of sound policy.

The Responsibility of Government

State and Local Government. Since the founding of the Republic, education, including higher education, has been regarded as of such general importance for the welfare of the people that state and local governments have been empowered, by constitutional authority and other means, to pursue a positive policy to encourage the establishment and operation of schools. The early attitude was nobly expressed in the Northwest Ordinance of 1787: "Religion, morality, and knowledge, being necessary to good government and the happiness of mankind, schools and the means of education shall forever be encouraged." Ten colleges, established as private institutions during the colonial period, existed at the time of the Confederation. Under the Constitution the states accepted these institutions and encouraged further private effort. They chartered colleges, gave them tax exemption, and at times provided financial support. Many states, unwilling to rely on private effort alone, also chartered state universities and academies. Georgia, Vermont, North Carolina, and Tennessee chartered state universities before 1800. Other states followed suit. Many, especially newer states, were stimulated to do so by Federal land grants for the support of higher and common schools. The objectives in establishing state universities were to supplement the limited private colleges, furnish education under secular control, make higher education more readily available, and foster instruction in the sciences and the practical arts.

State and local responsibility was from the outset so well recognized that new educational needs prompted state and local governments to initiate new types of institutions and foster new programs. Thus state normal schools and teachers colleges were developed in the 1840s and later. With land grants from the Federal government under the Morrill Act of 1862 state universities or special state colleges undertook instruc-

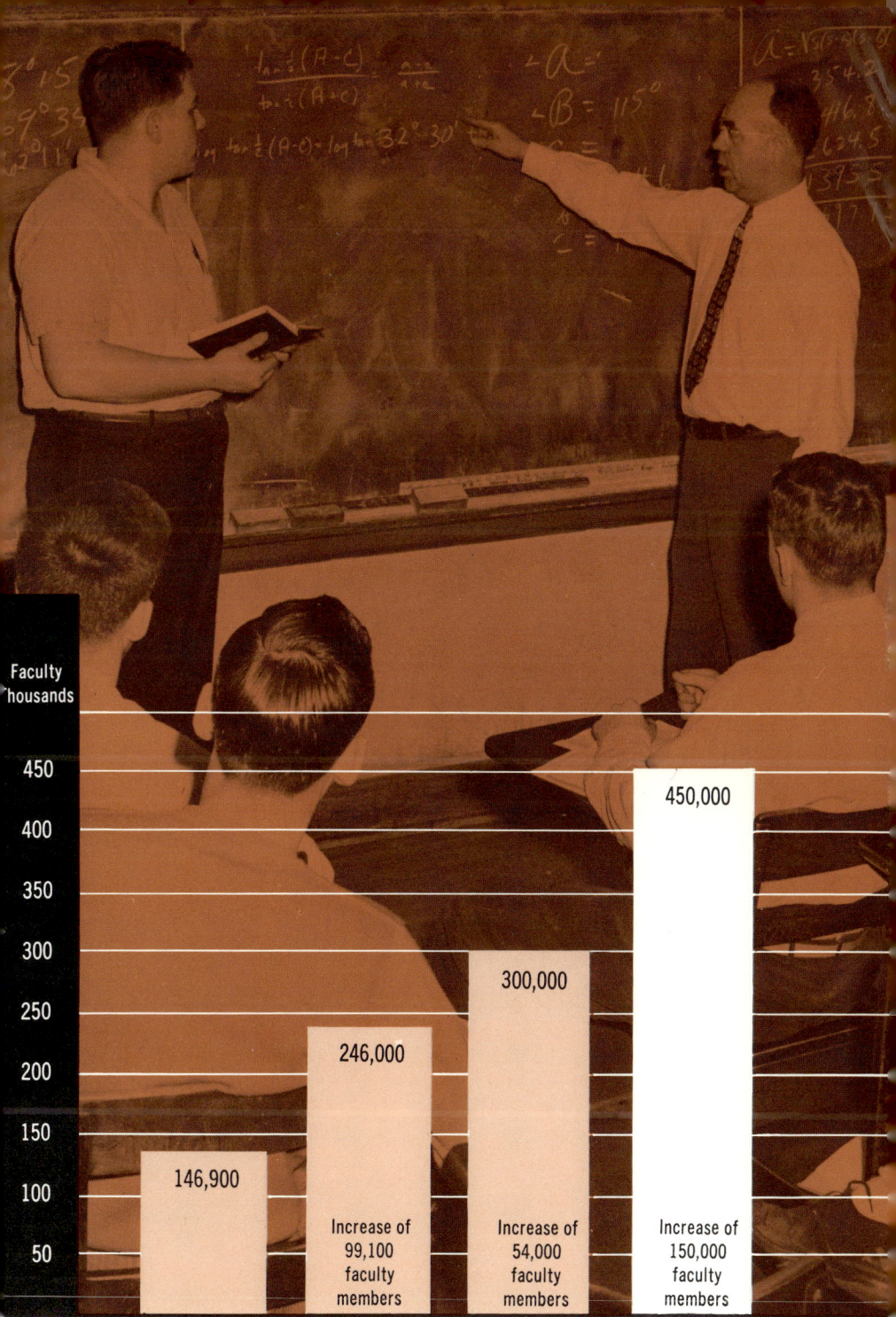

Faculty thousands			
450			450,000
400			
350			
300		300,000	
250	246,000		
200			
150			
100	146,900		
50	Increase of 99,100 faculty members	Increase of 54,000 faculty members	Increase of 150,000 faculty members
	1940	1950	1958	1970

NUMBER OF FACULTY 1940-1970

tion in agriculture and mechanical arts. Following the Civil War, professional schools and later graduate schools were developed in many public universities to match the developments in private universities. After 1910, public junior colleges and community colleges were established in increasing numbers in an effort to expand educational opportunity locally. Since World War I, numerous states have supported extension programs, adult education, special training programs for adults, and radio instruction, or more recently, educational television as means of serving the educational needs of the community. As government has expanded its effort, private institutions have multiplied, diversified their offerings, and grown, as have those receiving public support.

The resulting dual system of public and private institutions is now represented (1955–56) by 1,858 colleges and universities. Of these 81 are public universities and 60 private; 82 are public liberal arts colleges and 650 private; 168 are public teachers colleges compared to 24 private; 292 are public junior colleges and 213 private; 32 are public technological and professional schools and 132 are private, and 124 are theological schools, all private.

The pattern of education has differed regionally. In the older states of the Northeast, where private institutions had an early start, the resort to public institutions has been limited, and it is for the most part fairly recent. In the Midwest and South the state universities and other public colleges have played a larger role from the beginning. In the West, government has assumed the major responsibility of providing facilities for higher education.

During the past half century the public has turned more and more to government to provide educational opportunity. In this period public institutions have expanded in size and also in numbers. They have multiplied more rapidly than private institutions, primarily in consequence of the junior college and community college movement. Usually public institutions have offered more varied instruction at costs to the student generally below those of private colleges. They have often been more willing to accept part-time students, day or evening students, and less well qualified students. Since 1900, the proportion of college students in public institutions has risen from 38 to 58 per cent.[1] More than half of the college enrollment has been in public institutions in all except a few years since 1939–40, and the proportion has risen rapidly since 1952. Indeed, nearly three-fourths of the increment in enrollment since 1952 has gone to public institutions. The expectation is that this reliance on public institutions will increase; for the trend is toward more public colleges in rapidly growing urban centers.

Having accepted this large responsibility for higher education, most states and localities find themselves under serious pressures to expand educational support. These pressures come in part from existing institutions seeking to provide for rising costs, higher salaries, and expanding enrollments. They come also from the efforts of teachers colleges to become liberal arts colleges, of junior colleges to become four-year colleges, and of technical schools to become colleges of technology. Community leaders seeking local educational facilities press for more junior colleges, more community colleges, and more local branches, campuses, and programs of established colleges and universities. Meanwhile in leading states there are efforts to help the state university become a more distinguished institution by improving the faculty and the quality of students admitted. The rivalry for funds has encouraged some states to establish a unified system of higher education or a council of higher education in an effort to coordinate these efforts, develop a suitable allocation of functions, and create a more orderly system of state institutions. Most states provide some funds for scholarships, and several have state-wide scholarship programs for able and deserving students. The pressure for more scholarship aid is also increasing. Under such needs and pressures state and local support of higher education (excluding contributions for plant) has increased from $176 million in 1939–40 to $1,217 million in 1957–58. The funds for plant are now running in excess of $370 million a year. But these levels of support will be far from adequate for the years ahead.

Federal Responsibility. While the responsibility of state and local government for education at all levels is generally defined in state constitutions, state laws, city charters, and local ordinances, the responsibility of the Federal government has never been clearly determined. It has remained in doubt because the Constitution nowhere explicitly delegates this authority to the national government; the authority is no more than implicit in the constitutional power to provide funds for the "general welfare" and the "common defense." Proposals in the Constitutional Convention to authorize seminaries for the promotion of literature, the arts, and the sciences seem to have been lost in the proposals for a national university, the power to establish which (in the District of Columbia), it was thought, had already been provided.[2]

In his first annual address to Congress, President Washington spoke of this responsibility for education:

> There is nothing which can better deserve your patronage than the promotion of science and literature. . . . Whether this desirable object will be best promoted by affording aids to seminaries of learning already established, by the institution of a national university, or by any other expedients will be well worthy of a place in the deliberations of the Legislature.

The ambiguity has not left the Federal government helpless or entirely neutral. The authority to provide for common defense, to promote the general welfare, and to dispose of public lands and property has been regarded as adequate warrant for a number of aids to education. Most of the early leaders, no less than Washington and Jefferson, recognized the importance of education to the success of the Republic and to the welfare of the people. In various ways the Federal government took action to foster and encourage education within the states. The Congress of the Confederation in 1785, while providing for the disposal of public lands in the Northwest Territory, reserved certain lands for the support of education. In 1787 it passed the Northwest Ordinance (already cited) and shortly thereafter reserved the sixteenth section of each township for public schools and two townships for the support of a university. When authorizing the admission of Ohio to the Union in 1802, Congress set aside lands for public schools and for academies and universities, and this practice was continued when other states were admitted. In 1837 Congress distributed surplus revenues in the Treasury to the states, in part for schools. As stated by President Hoover's National Advisory Committee on Education observed in 1931:[3]

> From the Revolution to the Civil War, the Federal Government encouraged and financially aided education in the States. It endowed higher and common schools with lands, and made grants of surplus tax moneys: but it did not attempt to regulate the purposes, define the programs, supervise the teaching, or otherwise control public education in the States.[3]

Thus Federal policy from the first has been one of encouragement and support without Federal control. The Federal government has made no effort to establish a system of Federal educational institutions except in special areas beyond the jurisdiction of the states[4] and in federally affected areas where Federal installations deprive the community of tax revenues.

The Morill Act of 1862 was an important departure from the policy of general support. That act sought deliberately to foster special types of instruction by making land grants to assist the states in the establishment and maintenance of colleges offering instruction in agriculture and the mechanical arts. The land grants made no provision for buildings and were in effect grants requiring state funds. They were designed to encourage instruction for productive employment and to serve the middle and lower classes at lower cost.

Many of the land-grant colleges encountered financial difficulties in the 1880s, and in 1890 the Second Morrill Act authorized annual grants to support them. These grants were increased in 1907, and subsequently. Additional funds were provided to these colleges for agricultural experiment stations (1887), agricultural extension services (1914), and instruction in special fields such as home economics and vocational education

(1917). The present funds for these activities are in excess of $78 million per year, of which only $5 million is directly for support of instruction.

Immediately before World War II, Federal aid consisted mainly of the grants to land-grant colleges. But during the 1930s a number of public institutions had renovated or obtained new buildings through the Public Works Administration or the Work Projects Administration, which provided Federal funds as a counter depression measure. A limited number of students received partial support, including tuition in some instances, through Reserve Officer Training programs, and in the late 1930s as many as 15 per cent of all college students in some years were helped through the student work program of the National Youth Administration. Only the land-grant college funds, however, were appropriated primarily to support and improve higher education.[5]

Federal policy toward higher education entered a new phase after 1941. In World War II the government turned to the colleges and universities, as it had in World War I, for assistance with military training programs for which special knowledge was essential. The programs returned students to the campuses and made use of faculties and facilities. They were at times crucial to the institutions, especially those that suffered a heavy loss of enrollment. Nearly 36 per cent of the general and educational income of institutions of higher education was derived from the Federal government in 1943–44. This was a slightly larger share than came from the same source during the peak of the GI enrollment in 1947–48. It was important in preserving the fiscal solvency and the operating effectiveness of higher education during the war.

Immediately after the war, the nation turned again to the colleges and universities to help fill the critical educational gap created in the four years of war. The Federal government, through the Servicemen's Readjustment Act of 1944 (The GI Bill of Rights) established the largest scholarship program in history. This, with companion legislation (PL 16) for disabled veterans and subsequent legislation for Korean War veterans and orphans of veterans, has given assistance to nearly nine million persons at a cost of $16 billion. About one-third of the beneficiaries attended institutions of higher learning. Student veterans of World War II received allowances for subsistence and dependents, and payments were made to the institutions attended for tuition, or negotiated charges for costs of instruction, and for fees, books, and supplies. Korean War veterans have received allowances with no adjustment for varying tuition charges, though they have been free to attend the institutions of their choice. These payments to institutions often have not covered the full costs of instruction, but they have yielded substantial gross revenues and helped the institutions to render an important public service.

In more recent years the Federal government has shown reluctance to acknowledge a responsibility to support higher education while relying paradoxically on higher education for services coupled with the provision of various forms of support. Those responsible for public policy recognize the critical importance of these institutions to national defense and the general welfare, and individual agencies have proceeded to employ the institutions' services and facilities. Federal programs now provide specialized training of government personnel, expanded on-campus military training, and student aid for veterans, orphans of veterans, scientists, doctors, and other graduate students. They provide grants and contracts for medical education, grants and contracts for research, surplus property, and Federal loans for the construction of college buildings.

Student aid programs of the Federal government are of three broad types. First, a number of Federal agencies, including especially the Departments of Defense, State, and Treasury, are sending increasing numbers of employees to universities for special training. Next, because of the critical need for trained manpower, primarily in the sciences and related subjects, the Atomic Energy Commission, the National Science Foundation, the Public Health Service, and other agencies operate scholarship or fellowship programs for growing numbers of students. Reserve Officer Training programs and veterans' benefits furnish additional forms of student aid. Third, and of greatest potential importance, is the National Defense Education Act of 1958, which authorizes student loans and graduate fellowships in a wide range of fields with supplementary grants for the support of instruction payable to institutions attended. Most of these programs are primarily to aid students, as a means of inducing them to prepare for careers in fields of manpower shortage. They help higher education to serve the nation, but they only slightly and incidentally aid higher education. Since tuition and fees seldom cover the full costs of instruction, this form of aid is more likely to increase university commitments than offer financial relief. An important precedent has been set, however, in the National Defense Education Act, under which fellowship grants are accompanied by payments to the institution itself.

The most notable new development is the phenomenal growth of Federal grants and contracts for research. No reliable estimate of the total amount of these research funds is possible, but they have apparently risen to well over $400 million in 1959. Although few of these grants cover full costs, as detailed in the paper by C. C. Furnas and Raymond Ewell, many of them contribute funds for equipment and facilities. Both the Atomic Energy Commission and the National Science Foundation report such support. The NSF in 1957–58 made grants for basic research of $25 million, including $5.9 million for maintenance and construction of research facilities. The Public Health Service operates a diversified program of grants and contracts for both medical research and training. These programs have been welcomed as beneficial in medical schools in spite of the fact that they seldom cover full costs. The range and variety of Federal grants and contracts for research are exceedingly wide, and the participating agencies are numerous. Of greatest importance to universities, perhaps, are those of the National Science Foundation, the Public Health Service (including the National Institutes of Health), the Atomic Energy Commission, and the Department of Defense, though other agencies are important in special areas.

The effect upon higher education of these research grants and contracts is a much debated issue. The research activity may strengthen the institution as a place for graduate study or it may divert teaching personnel, misdirect instruction, and have an adverse effect on the educational program as a whole. Though the grants and contracts often provide the financial support sought, they nevertheless frequently impose additional financial burdens on the institutions for space, staff, incidentals, and overhead. As now administered, Federal research grants and contracts are not so much an aid to higher education as the partial support of additional obligations. It is clear that sound procedures and policies in the interest of higher education, government, and the public have yet to be developed for this rapidly expanding activity.

The two forms of Federal aid that have been explicitly intended to help the educational institutions meet their responsibilities are the program for disposal of surplus property and the program of loans for buildings. The former was especially helpful in the immediate postwar years and is still a source of considerable assistance. It has provided land, buildings, equipment, and other needed facilities. The college housing loan program authorizes fifty-year loans at favorable rates of interest mainly for revenue-producing buildings such as dormitories, dining halls, and student centers. From its inception in 1951 to 1957, loans of $583 million to over five hundred colleges and universities have been approved.

Of the $1,752 million operating income reported as coming from government at all levels in 1957-58, the Federal government provided $535 million, the major portion of which was for research. Additional funds for buildings were made available through appropriations, grants, and loans from Federal, state, and local government.

The power of the Federal government to support higher education is no longer seriously questioned. The government has been doing so in various ways since 1787. Yet it is an overstatement to assert that a positive policy of assisting higher educational institutions now exists, except in special and limited areas. The present policy has been aptly described as one of using and even exploiting the unique services of these institutions as essential to the national interest, but without contributing more than incidentally to their solvency, their perpetuation, or their improvement. Regardless of whether or not a Federal responsibility for the maintenance and improvement of higher education is acknowledged except in special areas, there is little doubt that the flow of Federal funds to the institutions will continue to grow, for the services of the institutions have become indispensable for the achievement of Federal purposes. But it is also unlikely that the Federal government can rely more and more heavily on the institutions and not carry its share of the burden for their support and improvement.

The present situation has been well stated by the trustees of the Carnegie Foundation for the Advancement of Teaching:[6]

> A high proportion of the federal money now going to higher education is not "aid" in any meaningful sense of the word, but rather a *purchase of services* by the government. If a federal agency needs the services of a university to accomplish one of its purposes, and enters into a contract by which it obtains those services, the money that changes hands is not "aid" any more than payment of a doctor's bill is "aid." These arrangements are often a burden for the university which undertakes, in a spirit of patriotic responsibility, commitments which are unproductive as far as the institution itself is concerned. Since the government has not always been liberal in payment of overhead and indirect costs—and since many universities have not insisted upon recovering such costs—the institution often suffers financially.

But the same trustees observe:

> Federal funds are flowing to the universities in exceedingly impressive amounts, and no one involved—federal agencies, college presidents, trustees, or faculty members—shows any concerted inclination to stop the flow. It is very difficult to find educational leaders who are willing to predict that the channeling of federal funds to higher education will decrease in the foreseeable future. Many predict an inevitable *increase*.
>
> In short, the question at issue is not whether the federal government should have a role in higher education. That question was settled affirmatively in the nineteenth century and never seriously reopened. The question at issue is *what kind* of role the federal government should play in higher education. It is not a question about which either the American people or leaders in higher education are ever going to make a clear-cut decision. But they are going to make a great many decisions that bear in one way or another on federal action, and the cumulative impact of these decisions will determine the future of federal relationships to higher education. One can only hope that these decisions will be made with a clear grasp of the issues involved.

Growing Dependence on Public Support. The acknowledged responsibilities of government for higher education have in recent decades been most effectively discharged in states where a system of higher education has been developed to serve as many of the several specialized needs of students as possible in nearby institutions, and by maintaining the state university as a preeminent center for the more able students and advanced study. California, Minnesota, Michigan, and Wisconsin are examples. No one today can accurately specify the sort of educational system that will be needed several decades hence. But it is helpful to examine recent trends, against which to consider needs of the immediate future.

The trend of recent years has been toward a growing reliance on public institutions, and a growing dependence of both public and private institutions on public funds. Since 1929–30, revenues from tuition have fallen from 30 to about 25 per cent and from other income from 15 to 10 per cent. The support of endowment and gifts has fallen from 20 per cent to about 16 per cent. Over-all, the support of government has risen from 36 per cent to 50 per cent.

Publicly controlled institutions are today more heavily dependent on government funds than ever before, except during the wartime and postwar training programs. Between 1929–30 and 1955–56 their current income from government rose from 67 to 77 per cent.

A most significant recent development has been the increasing dependence of private institutions on public funds. Prior to the war, public funds were given very sparingly to private institutions, but since 1941 many of these institutions have been used and supported increasingly by government. In 1955–56 private institutions derived 21 per cent of their educational income from government as compared to less than 2 per cent in 1929–30; much of this, of course, was for research.

Government is also an important source of support for plant and facilities. In 1955–56 government provided nearly half of the $500 million re-

Table 1. Total Plant Receipts

1955–56

(In millions)

Source	Total	Public institutions	Private institutions
Federal government	$ 13.3	$ 6.8	$ 6.5
State government	222.8	219.9	2.9
Local government	17.3	17.2	.1
Total government	$253.4	$243.9	$9.5
Gifts, grants and other	183.8	33.2	150.6
Current funds	198.0	120.4	77.6
Loans (partly government)	190.9	102.7	88.2
Total receipts	$826.0	$500.2	$325.8

ceived for buildings and facilities in public institutions and contributed $9 million for such purposes in private institutions. It also provided about one-third of the loan funds borrowed for physical facilities. Total receipts for plant in 1955–56 were as listed in Table 1.

Though many private institutions have begun to share in government funds for plant and equipment, the expansion of facilities has been considerably more rapid in public institutions. Between 1939–40 and 1955–56 the value of plant in public institutions rose from $1.26 billion to $5.39 billion, while that of private institutions rose from $1.49 billion to $4.10 billion. It is also worthy of note that as philanthropy has grown, gifts to public institutions have been increasing and that a few public institutions have acquired substantial endowments.

The issue ahead is how adequately public support can meet the growing needs of higher education and what forms of that support are most appropriate. To these questions we now turn.

Needs and Financial Requirements

Needs. The major needs of higher education for the next ten or twelve years are reasonably clear. They have been studied and reviewed repeatedly by educators and special commissions. They were ably presented in the report of the President's Committee on Education Beyond the High School (1957) under the Chairmanship of Devereux C. Josephs.[7] That report stresses, as do other reports, the national necessity to expand higher education rapidly during the next decade to meet serious shortages of trained manpower, especially in the sciences and related fields, and improve the quality of education generally. The rapid expansion of enrollment, which has already begun, is expected to continue until about 1968, when it may slacken slightly. By 1969–70 higher education will have to accommodate 6 to 7 million students. We use the estimate 6.4 million regular-session students, which compares with 3.5 million in 1958–59.

To serve this enrollment without sacrificing quality of instruction will necessitate many different actions to meet specific educational problems. The several specific needs may be summarized as follows:

1. The most pressing need is to increase now the number of able teachers for primary, secondary, and higher education and research personnel in all fields, but especially in critical areas such as mathematics and the sciences. Private and public scholarship and fellowship programs and guidance programs have been started to accomplish this result, but a considerable expansion of these efforts is necessary.

2. It is generally agreed that the salaries of teachers in higher education must be increased in order to restore the teaching profession to

an appropriate economic position in relation to other professions and draw more able minds into the field. An immediate increase of 50 per cent in teachers' salaries and a doubling of salaries by 1969–70 is considered necessary to accomplish this result.

3. Further needs include the distribution of additional students among institutions in order to use existing facilities more effectively and the simultaneous expansion of plant and facilities to accommodate growing enrollments. This calls for greater efficiency in existing institutions and the expansion of many campuses, especially those too small to be efficient. It calls for the establishment of more junior colleges, community colleges, and branch campuses of existing institutions in order to make educational opportunities more readily available at minimum cost. An expansion of adult education programs to serve the growing demand for continuing part-time education is likewise important.

4. It is highly desirable to reduce the waste of able manpower by attracting more of the brightest students into college, and by providing adequate means of financing needy students. Guidance, student loans, job opportunities, scholarship funds, and special financing arrangements are necessary now and will be even more important as tuition and other costs of going to college rise.

5. The expansion and financing of medical education present special problems that require solution. To maintain even the present ratio of doctors to population will require the enlargement of many existing medical schools and the establishment of ten to twenty new ones. A proper system of financing would relieve universities with medical schools of one of their major financial difficulties.

6. The growing reliance of the nation on research means that research for the advancement of knowledge must be expanded and better established as a regular activity of higher education. More satisfactory arrangements for the conduct of university research and more appropriate financing policies are necessary; otherwise, this growing activity will impose heavier and heavier obligations on the slender resources of many institutions.

The foregoing needs can be met if appropriate financing arrangements can be developed and the funds provided. An over-all view of the costs affords a basis for estimating whether government may be able to carry its share of the burden.

Financial Requirements. To finance the several specific needs of higher education over the next decade will require a rapid expansion of support from government as well as from other sources. For the estimated enrollment of 6.4 million students in 1969–70, general and educational income of higher education, according to Professor Harris, will have to expand from $3,600 million in 1957–58 to $9,200 million or $9,800 million in 1969–70. An additional $1,000 million to $1,500 million may be required annually for plant and equipment. (Use larger figure in these calculations.)

These estimates of educational expenditures in 1969–70 may be taken as plausible expectations. My own calculations yield a figure of $9,200 million, which, with student aid of $350 million and plant expenditures of $1,500 million, suggests a total cost of about $11,100 million. The Council for Financial Aid to Education gives an estimate of $9,000 million, which seems too low for the needs as here outlined. Throughout this paper I use the higher estimates of what it may cost, with no allowance for inflation, in order to test the feasibility of such a burden.

Although my estimates, calculated separately for public and private institutions, give totals similar to those reached by Professor Harris, they lead to quite different conclusions with respect to financing. They suggest that the problem may be more serious for public than for private institutions and that in general a much greater reliance on public funds than he anticipates may be necessary.

The calculations are presented and explained in detail in the supplementary note at the end of this paper. They are based on the assumption that 65 per cent of an enrollment of 6.4 million students by 1969–70, will be in public institutions, and 35 per cent in private colleges. Expenditures are based on 1957–58 costs per student, minus 10 per cent for economies, plus a doubling of salaries for teachers and related personnel, plus an additional $300 million for research. On this basis public institutions may have educational and research expenditure in 1969–70 of $5,733 million and private institutions $3,248 million—or a total of $8,981 million. Additional internal and outside funds for student aid bring the total to $9,561 million. In addition, plant expenditures may approximate $1,500 million per year. I have estimated the uses of these funds (in millions) as shown in Table 2.

Table 2

	Public institutions	Private institutions (in millions)	Total
Educational budget:			
Education	$5,083	$2,598	$ 7,681
Student aid	220	360	580
Organized research	650	650	1,300
Total	$5,953	$3,608	$ 9,561
Plant budget	1,000	500	1,500
Total budget	$6,953	$4,108	$11,061

In considering the sources of funds, Professor Harris postulates an increase in the tuition, per student of private institutions of $525 a year and in public institutions of $375 per year. He thus assumes that tuition and fees may yield $3,800 million, or 40 per cent, of the educational revenue needed. He expects about $1,200 million to come from private benefactors, and $3,700 million, or 38 per cent, to come from government.

President Millett believes that tuition should not be significantly increased, at least in public institutions. Though tuitions in some public four-year colleges reach $600 per year, the 1957–58 average was $90 per year, and in public junior colleges only $26 per year. These rates compare with average tuition payments in private four-year colleges of $533 per year and in private junior colleges of $464 per year. A continuation of these low charges in public institutions will throw a very heavy burden of support on taxpayers if it continues over the next decade.

My own calculations suggest the necessity of finding an intermediate course. Professor Harris assumes tuition increases for private institutions that are higher than will be necessary or likely, if present forms of public support are continued and his assumed tuition increases for public institutions are higher than seem to me feasible or probable in view of the low-charge tradition of many of these institutions. On the other hand, President Millett appears to underestimate both the ability of students to pay, if more liberal scholarship programs are available, and the necessity of increasing tuition in public institutions if the goals with respect to salaries and quality of education are to be achieved. Even a doubling of tuition in public institutions will leave a heavy burden of support for the taxpayer, and as shown later, even larger tuition increases may be necessary.

In estimating sources of revenue, I have taken a middle ground and assumed for purposes of these calculations that tuition in public institutions may be double that of 1957–58, and in private institutions 50 per cent higher. In public four-year colleges this would represent an average tuition of $180; in private institutions, an average tuition of $800. The corresponding junior college tuition rates would be $52 and $696, respectively. The former is low partly because tuition is low in public junior colleges and partly because of the large number of part-time students. Endowment, gifts, and grants are taken at their 1957–58 rate in relation to educational income, as are revenues from "other sources." Organized research, estimated at $1,300 million, is expected to be financed largely ($1,100 million) by Federal grants and contracts. Total government support (including Federal research grants and contracts) is estimated at $5,150 million. The major sources of funds appear in Table 3.

Tuition increases of 100 per cent for public and 50 per cent for private institutions may be sufficient or nearly so on financial grounds. To increase tuition by $525, as proposed by Professor Harris, would yield

Table 3

Sources of funds	Public institutions	Private institutions (in millions)	Total
Tuition (at increase of 100 per cent for public institutions, 50 per cent for private)	$ 680	$1,747	$2,427
Endowment income, gifts, and grants	225	990	1,215
Other sources	578	274	852
Federal government: Funds for education	200	50	250
Research grants and contracts	550	550	1,100
State and local government	3,750	50	3,800
Total government	$4,500	$ 650	$5,150
Total income	$5,983	$3,661	$9,644
Total expenditures	5,953	3,608	9,561
Balance	$ 30	$ 53	$ 83

perhaps another $500 million for private institutions. This would reduce the need for gifts and government support, or permit further improvements in the quality of instruction, but it would not greatly reduce the volume of government research grants and contracts. Some private institutions will be able to make larger tuition increases than are here proposed, but others are too competitive with public institutions to permit much higher charges. Unfortunately, many of the latter are unable to share significantly in either Federal government funds or private philanthropy. Unless tuition in public institutions is increased markedly, tuition increases of more than 50 per cent by private colleges will tend to divert more students to public institutions and further aggravate the problem of public support. Thus from the point of view of government, it is desirable to find ways to utilize fully the private institutions. It is equally desirable to find ways to encourage higher tuition charges in public institutions.

The foregoing estimates do not fully state the financial requirements. Over the next decade of expanding enrollment, the institutions of higher education may need to spend for plant renovation, equipment, and expansion some $11 billion to $15 billion. Many of these expenditures must be made during the early 1960s. By 1969–70 expenditures for plant and equipment may be at the rate of $1,500 million per year. The funds received for this purpose in 1955–56 were $825 million (of which $190 million was from loans), and expenditures were only slightly below

$700 million. For the period 1951 to 1960 plant expenditures (and current commitments) have averaged over $600 million annually.

More of these plant expenditures will doubtless come from public funds in the future. About two-thirds of the students will be in public colleges; Federal grants for facilities are increasing; and the practice of borrowing from government for plant is growing. My rough estimates indicate that about $250 million of the total may come from private gifts, $250 million from current funds (often for repairs, equipment, and renovations), $500 million from state and local appropriations, about $500 million from Federal grants and loans. (See supplementary note.)

Thus, the state and local burden may be expected to expand over the next decade to about $4,300 million by 1969–70 ($3,800 million for education and $500 million for plant). The Federal share may be as much as $1,850 million ($1,100 million for research, $250 million for education, and $500 million in grants and loans for plant). On that basis, state and local support would have to expand during the decade from about $1,600 million (1957–58) to $4,300 million by 1969–70, while Federal support would have to increase, under these assumptions, from about $700 million (1957–58) to $1,850 million by 1969–70, a large part of which will be for the purchase of research and other services or self-liquidating loans for plant.

Before considering the feasibility of such government support, it should be observed that these estimates contemplate philanthropic contributions of about $1,600 million per year. Gifts and grants for operating income are estimated at $915 million. Since such gifts amounted to $411 million in 1957–58, the estimate seems attainable. Most of these funds would go to private institutions. Projected philanthropic contributions for plant are estimated at $250 million and to endowment at $435 million. Such contributions in 1957–58 were about $169 million for plant and $272 million for endowment. In brief, philanthropic support must be nearly doubled (as compared to its 1957–58 rate of $852 million). If such support is not forthcoming, tuition and government will have to carry a heavier burden.

Ability to Pay

The ability and willingness of the American people to increase their support of higher education during the next decade as rapidly as the projected figures suggest may be necessary depend of course on continued economic growth, the level of taxes, and other demands upon public and private funds. Assuming a rising gross national product, no war, and no major changes in present tax rates, except in some states and localities, the expansion here projected can perhaps be attained, but not without persistent effort on the part of those who recognize the importance of higher education to the country.

The major problems seem destined to arise over public support. Increased tuition rates of 100 per cent in public institutions and 50 per cent in private institutions offer no insuperable burden in view of rising family incomes. These charges could be increased promptly over the next few years of rapidly rising enrollments, and the funds could be used for faculty salaries and increased scholarship aid. Many of the economies discussed in other chapters, if made promptly, could release funds for salaries; otherwise, they may have to be made under the compelling argument of financial pressure. The projected philanthropic contributions seem attainable, especially if industry support continues to grow and private benefactions go more largely to existing institutions for general support or special purposes, rather than to create small, independent foundations. Even the needed support of government, though difficult, is possible of achievement under favorable conditions.

To increase over-all support of higher education (including plant expansion) during the next decade from about $4,300 million in 1957–58 to $11,100 million in 1969–70 means dedicating a larger share of gross national product to the purpose. I have assumed that GNP will rise at an average rate of approximately 3.5 per cent per year and may reach about $700 billion by 1969–70. Both higher and lower projections have been made by others.[8] For a GNP of $700 billion, the task will be to increase the funds for higher education from 0.97 per cent of GNP in 1957–58 to 1.59 per cent of GNP by 1969–70. This is not likely to occur unless the public is convinced that higher education merits greatly increased private and public support.

The anticipated increase of $6,800 million for operating costs and plant is large, but when faced with the necessity of building public schools and of increasing the salaries of teachers during recent years, the public in all states responded to the challenge. They expanded the support of public schools from $5,800 million to $14,400 million between 1949–50 and 1958–59. In that period they increased the percentage of GNP devoted to public schools from 2.21 to 3.15 per cent. The comparable expansion in higher education will come between 1960 and 1969. The pressures for adequate support of higher education have begun, and they can be expected to grow over the next few years. The requests for public support can be expected to meet with some success, especially in view of the growing recognition of the essential role of higher education in the defense and progress of the country.

Increased support from government is crucial for the educational expansion contemplated. The government share ($6,150 million) of total support is 56 per cent of total requirements, as compared to 50 per cent in 1957–58. If Federal funds for organized research are excluded (on the ground that much of this money is for the purchase of special services), the remainder of governmental support would constitute 51 per cent of other expenditures. Total government support, including Federal research, represents 0.88 per cent of the projected $700 billion GNP, as compared to 0.47 per cent of GNP in 1957–58. The public funds for education and student aid alone would represent an increase from 0.40 per cent of GNP in 1957–58 to 0.74 per cent in 1969–70. In view of the fact that this ratio of government support has increased from 0.22 per cent in 1939–40 to 0.40 per cent in 1957–58, such a goal seems perhaps attainable.

The feasibility of adequate support from government depends not only on tax revenues and other demands upon public funds, but also on the methods employed for financing higher education. If Federal support is differentiated from state and local support, the problem can be seen more clearly.

Federal Support. To determine the magnitude of government support required, I have assumed no major change in existing Federal policy, but only an expansion and extension of support, on principles already approved. Such Federal support in 1969–70 is estimated at $1,350 million for operating costs and $500 million for plant. The major item in operating costs ($1,100 million) is for research services, for which full costs should be paid, as they are to industry, but with no profits. Federal funds for research are likely to increase far more than this amount, and in part this is a channeling of funds appropriated for defense, atomic energy, science, and public health into the universities in order to use faculty research talents more effectively and keep faculties in their dual role of research and instruction. It will cost the taxpayers dollars, but many of these dollars will be appropriated and spent in independent research organizations or government laboratories if they are not spent in the universities. By channeling them into the universities they can be made to do triple duty: obtain research, help the universities, and produce more trained manpower. Certainly the universities are not warranted in subsidizing organized research on any such scale out of tuition, nor are they warranted in increasing tuition further for this purpose. Research results are of benefit to everyone, and the support of research, especially in the present situation, is now recognized as an appropriate Federal function, as the support of agriculture was recognized seventy years ago.

The remaining $250 million for operating costs represents a doubling of aid to land-grant institutions ($150 million), which is likely in any event, and $100 million of income from veterans' tuition, student loans, scholarships, fellowships, and other educational grants mainly for medical education for which smaller amounts are already being appropriated. The total cost of loans, scholarships, and fellowships and grants that would yield $100 million to the educational institutions would amount to about $400 million. Thus the total cost of such a program might be approximately $600 million. Nearly $200 million is currently being provided for such purposes.

The $500 million of Federal funds for plant includes both grants for plant and equipment and loans for buildings and facilities. The grants, explained later, offer a feasible way of providing critically needed Federal aid without control. Surplus-property disposal and grants for facilities and equipment already amount to nearly $200 million annually.

If the higher estimates of $500 million for plant requirements are valid, the loan funds here stated may have to be provided by Federal agencies for a number of years. It should be recognized that, though Federal loans come from tax revenues, the college housing program is over time largely self-liquidating, and it is paid back out of current charges.

Thus, what seems at first to be a huge increase in Federal support turns out to be but a modest, and feasible, increase of funds for what is, for the most part, already being done. It is a reasonable investment in the future compared to the $5 billion to $6 billion we are currently pouring into agricultural support without a prospect of solving that problem. There is every likelihood of increased pressure to obtain such Federal support; for the states and localities have a larger and more rapidly growing burden of support to carry.

State and Local Support. The state and local portion of government support represents a considerably more difficult financial problem. It confirms the expectation that increased Federal aid, such as that discussed above, or more, will be necessary if higher education is to achieve the results expected of it. My calculations suggest that state and local support may have to be increased from about $1,600 million, in 1957–58, to about $4,300 million by 1969–70. Of the latter sum, $500 million is for plant and $3,800 million is for operating costs. The plant estimate is only about 36 per cent larger than the 1957–58 support, and it is predicated, in part, on the availability of Federal grants and loans for an increasing share of plant expansion.

The general support requirements ($3,800 million) are the serious part of the problem. They are over three times the 1957–58 rate of support. As a percentage of GNP they represent an increase from 0.28 to 0.54 per cent. Such an increase over the next decade must compete against support for elementary and secondary education, highways, urban redevelopment, and other pressing claims on state and local funds. It is difficult to estimate reliably either the revenues or expenditures of state and local governments. Several recent projections[9] seem to confirm the possibility that the necessary funds may be provided with little change in taxes, but if so, the budget battle will be close.

Many state and local governments since 1946 have been forced to increase taxes to meet the expanding costs of government. Education is the largest single expense; it formerly represented about 30 per cent of general expenditures. Because of the need to provide for the public schools, this figure has risen since 1946 to 36 per cent of expenditures and is expected by several experts in the field to rise to 40 per cent by about 1970.

Public school expenditures will continue to rise but required annual increases will be a little smaller than in the past few years. A Committee for Economic Development study on the financing of public schools shows that the states and localities have, with great effort, restored the relative position of teachers' salaries and at least avoided any worsening of the classroom shortage. It estimates that to meet the rising enrollment, expenditures must be raised from about $12,500 million in 1958–59 to about $21,100 million in 1969–70. State and local expenditures for higher education are now about $1,960 million (the $1,600 million reported as received by colleges and universities plus scholarship and fellowship funds and some allowance for accounting differences). About $26,000 million will be needed for education: $21,100 million for the public schools, $4,300 million for higher education, and $600 million for other education, by 1969–70. This sum, at 36 per cent of general expenditures, would require state and local revenues of $72 billion, or 10.3 per cent of GNP ($700 billion); at 40 per cent of expenditures it would require state and local revenues of about $65 billion, or 9.3 per cent of GNP.

To meet their expanding costs, state and local governments, since 1946, have already increased taxes and greatly expanded their debt. General revenues have increased 200 per cent (from $11.5 billion in 1946 to $34.5 billion in 1957), and state and local debt has increased 256 per cent (from $15.9 billion to $52.7 billion). General revenue has risen from 5.9 per cent of GNP to 8.7 per cent of GNP. Thus, to expand state and local support of higher education over the next decade as projected will almost certainly require additional taxes and additional debt.

If average tuition in public four-year institutions were increased to $300 per student, rather than to $180, the additional revenue would amount to only about $430 million, not enough to relieve public revenues very much. An increase of average tuition to $400 in public four-year colleges and to $100 in public junior colleges would yield about

$1,000 million of revenue and relieve the pressure on state and local funds considerably.

If GNP grows more rapidly than 3.5 per cent per year—to $735 billion, for example, the total educational budget can be met with some less difficulty. If GNP grows less rapidly, there will be real financial problems for the public institutions during the next decade.

Thus it appears that the financing of higher education may be one of our great national problems in the years ahead. There is no easy solution. To deprive these institutions of needed funds will be to deprive the nation of its own potential strength and growth. To *invest* in education even at greater cost to the public may be the only safe course for the nation to follow. But it is clear that higher education cannot achieve the new goals that are being set for it by relying solely on state and local support, without substantial help from the Federal government.

Ways and Means

The foregoing estimates may be too high or too low. Unless they are far wide of the mark, however, higher education is destined to become more costly for the student; the quest for philanthropic support will be intensified; state and local obligations will either curb other expenditures or necessitate both tax and debt increases; and the Federal government will find itself of necessity drawn more deeply into the support of higher education.

The Federal role does not imply large subsidies to the institutions; it portends no revolutionary change in Federal policy toward higher education; but it does indicate the continuation of Federal aid on a somewhat larger scale. Moreover, it indicates that Federal policies undertaken in the national interest must in the future not be so administered as to load still heavier financial burdens upon the colleges and universities and their other sources of support. Although the Federal government has assumed no financial responsibility for these institutions, it now recognizes that their strength is essential to the performance of training and research functions that are vital to the general welfare and the national defense. Yet most federal programs now rely on institutional subsidies to cover part of the costs. A minimum requirement of public policy, if the government is to strengthen and not weaken these institutions, is that most Federal programs be so financed that they can pay their way and relieve the institutions of this growing subsidy. Such a modification in Federal practice would contribute a great deal toward institutional solvency and the attainment of national objectives.

For most of the major problems confronting higher education Federal assistance is of substantial importance because the problems are of national concern. But ways and means of improving the effectiveness of this assistance are needed.

Trained Manpower. Current efforts to increase rapidly the supply of able teachers, research workers, and other trained manpower have elicited both private and public support. The fellowship programs of the colleges have been supplemented by philanthropic efforts, such as the Woodrow Wilson Fellowship Program (financed mainly by the Ford Foundation), the National Merit Scholarship Program, by fellowships from industry, and by Federal programs. The National Science Foundation offers about one thousand graduate fellowships a year for study in the sciences. It also provides fellowships for science teachers, and makes grants for summer institutes for science teachers. The Atomic Energy Commission, the Public Health Service, and other agencies of government also offer fellowships for graduate study in special fields. These efforts were supplemented by the National Defense Education Act of 1958, which made funds available to colleges for student loans, provided for 1,000 (and later more) graduate fellowships in various fields, and authorized supplementary payments beyond tuition to selected institutions for developing graduate programs.

None of these programs, except the last, contributes more than tuition to the institution to meet the cost of instruction. Although these activities are benefiting education and research by helping to increase the supply of teachers, scientists, and engineers, they need to be expanded and supplemented with payments to defray the costs of education. The surest way to increase institutional revenue from these programs is to increase tuition to levels more nearly equaling costs.

Another aspect of the trained-manpower problem is the need to attract more able youth to higher education. Here again both public and private efforts are being made to deal with the lack of information, lack of interest and motivation, or lack of funds which yearly prevent about 200,-000 most able youth from continuing their education beyond high school. The National Merit Scholarships and the efforts of the colleges are now supplemented by the National Science Foundation program to strengthen the sciences in the high schools and to provide research opportunities and scholarships. Under the Defense Education Act, the Department of Health, Education and Welfare has sought to strengthen teaching and equipment in the high schools, improve guidance, and provide student loans in college. These efforts are a good beginning, but the scope of the activities must be increased if they are to have any large effect.

Faculty Salaries. The urgently needed increase of faculty salaries will have to come mainly from increased tuition and fees, economies within the institutions, and increased state and local appropriations. Public institutions can offer to share this added cost by increased tuition and seek special matching funds for the purpose from state and local governments. Federal appropriations for the purpose of increasing salaries are in many respects undesirable, and they are unnecessary if other forms of Federal support are liberalized.

Use and Expansion of Facilities. Various measures can be taken to reduce the need for additional plant and to obtain a more effective use of existing facilities. Many institutions are far from overcrowded in particular schools and departments; others could gain a better use of their facilities by constructing buildings to relieve bottlenecks and permit a more efficient use of the entire plant. A system of interinstitutional cooperation is needed to help achieve a better distribution of students among institutions that can accommodate them. But even with such efforts a very substantial renovation and expansion of plant will be required in both public and private institutions.

There is little prospect that state and local government and private philanthropy can finance the needed expenditures on plant and in addition give the support required of them for operating expenses. Since 1951, the Federal government has been helping to meet the need for facilities through its surplus property disposal program, the college housing loan program, and grants for facilities and equipment, mainly for research, from the National Science Foundation, the Atomic Energy Commission, and the Public Health Service.

The college housing loan program has been limited to $925 million, most of which has been committed. No funds were appropriated in 1958, and the 1959 bill was vetoed twice and then revised and passed. It provides $250 million additional for loans on revenue-producing buildings. It also authorizes colleges and universities to benefit under the program of urban renewal. These features as well as others in the vetoed bills were recommended by the President's Committee on Education Beyond the High School in 1957 and were supported by the American Council on Education.

The college housing program is one of the few Federal programs designed to help meet the basic needs of the institutions. Its loans are an economical and beneficial way of providing assistance for higher education without danger of Federal control. The loans are self-liquidating and are available to both public and private institutions.

Issues have arisen over the low interest rates charged on the ground that they constitute a subsidy. Actually the interest charges are ¼ per cent higher than the Treasury has to pay on all its outstanding debt, although the rates are below current market rates. One purpose of these loans has been to provide funds at low enough rates that facilities could be built on a self-liquidating basis and thereby reduce the need for outright grants.

Opposition has also arisen against extending these loans for academic buildings, and no funds for that purpose have yet been appropriated. Such loans for 50 to 80 per cent of the cost, with matching funds from other sources, would help substantially to meet the growing need for classroom buildings, laboratories, and libraries. Unless the estimated plant requirements are grossly overestimated, such loans will be found necessary, in addition to the contributions of philanthropy and state and local government.

Proposals have also been made to substitute a Federal guarantee of college-building loans as a way of cutting Federal expenditures. There is a good deal of doubt whether the guarantee would adequately facilitate college borrowing in the open market. The guarantee might well be employed, however, for loans beyond some appropriate limit to an individual institution.

The college housing loan program is serving a useful purpose at a critical time, and it will be increasingly important during the next decade as a means of financing facilities when enrollments are expanding rapidly.

In several areas, notably for scientific research and teaching in certain fields, Federal grants, usually matching or supplementary, are already being made by such agencies as the National Science Foundation, the Atomic Energy Commission, and the Public Health Service. A more generous practice of making grants to facilitate national policy would help to relieve financial problems of many institutions. Consideration should also be given to grants for ROTC buildings on campuses that no longer have available space for that activity.

Research. Federally financed research is perhaps the most rapidly expanding activity of leading universities. The National Science Foundation, the Atomic Energy Commission, the Department of Defense, and other agencies are spending nearly $500 million annually for university research. Overhead rates on research contracts in several departments are limited to 15 per cent, which rarely covers full costs. Many research grants make little or no provision for overhead; in fact many are intended as no more than grants-in-aid. The expanding volume of this research is imposing increasing burdens upon the institutions, creating serious problems for the future. (See the paper by W. Homer Turner.)

I shall not here consider the question of whether much of this research enhances the teaching function, or impairs it; nor whether the research problems are, or are not, appropriate for a university to undertake. These are questions on which each institution must reach its own judgment as a guide to policy. The problems of research organization and finance, however, need consideration because of their direct bearing on university growth and Federal policy.

Practically every university and college regards itself as having a dual function: to advance knowledge and to disseminate knowledge through teaching. For years, however, in most institutions, research was in fact no more than a professorial avocation, and it still is in many small colleges. A generation or more ago, in leading universities, research became a part-time enterprise along with teaching. But the results were looked upon as a by-product of teaching and the activity as purely an aid to teaching. The research budget, if one existed, usually consisted of the incremental costs, determined as the costs would be determined for any by-product. For research budgets grants-in-aid that covered all or most of the incremental costs were regarded as ample financing. But as research expanded, complaints about inadequate overhead in research grants became more frequent.

In recent years research has become a major joint enterprise along with teaching. It is now big business, which in some cases overshadows the teaching function. But the concepts of research and accounting practices have not caught up with the fact that research is now a joint-product enterprise that cannot be supported on by-product cost principles.[10] As a result more and more institutions are project-poor, and neither they nor the supporters have any real understanding of the actual costs of research. The delusion is becoming too costly to be perpetuated; for teaching income or general support is going more and more to maintain an expanding research program. As tuition costs rise, this allocation of research costs to teaching budgets can no longer be justified. On joint-cost principles, staff time, space, equipment, maintenance, and overhead should be prorated to research and teaching on some acceptable allocation formula. Until these practices are followed, universities cannot know their costs, and they have no choice but to subsidize every research project undertaken.

It is not suggested that minute accounting for all research be undertaken, nor that all research grants shall cover full costs. Avocational and incidental personal research can generally be ignored in allocating costs. But more substantial research projects, organized research, and contract research must adopt more careful budgeting and cost accounting, so that the institution may at least know the extent of its contribution. Many institutions will doubtless wish to continue to subsidize research and accept grants-in-aid that defray only part of the costs, but they and the donor should be aware of the costs involved. For most organized research and contract research full costs are warranted and should ordinarily be charged. But until costs are known and the proper financing policies are widely followed, universities will be at a disadvantage in arguing for full-cost grants and contracts from the Federal government.

Nevertheless, the goal is clear. The universities face a sufficiently difficult financial future that they can properly insist on full-cost payments for all Federal contracts and a more liberal coverage of costs in Federal research grants. Though universities are nonprofit enterprises, in the present situation they are in no position to be singled out as sources of philanthropic services to government, which it neither expects nor receives from other sources. Adequate overhead and allowance for full costs on government contracts are necessary for both the welfare and future usefulness of institutions of higher education. Such policies and more liberal grants-in-aid would be among the most important contributions the Federal government could make toward the strengthening of those institutions as research centers in the national interest.

Medical Education and Research. During the past fifty years, medical education has become preeminent for its quality, cost, and budgetary problems. In recent years no other form of higher education has presented such persistent financial difficulties as the medical schools. Their obligations for the future are large and expensive.

A recent report on *The Advancement of Medical Research and Education,* by Dr. Stanhope Bayne-Jones[11] and a committee of consultants to the Secretary of Health, Education and Welfare, foresees a rapid rise in the manpower needs of medical research and medical practice. The report estimates that the number of professional medical research workers will have to double by 1970, and to maintain the existing ratio of physicians to population will require expanded enrollments and fourteen to twenty new medical schools, costing $500 million. The consultants see little hope of financing the vast training and research programs ahead except through an inevitable continuation and expansion of Federal support for medical research and education. National expenditures on medical research are expected to rise from $330 million in 1957 to $1 billion by 1970, of which about half would be Federal funds.

The Public Health Service and the National Institutes of Health are now major contributors to medical schools and universities for research and training. Both make grants for research and for instruction in specified fields. Additional support is provided by the Defense Department, the Atomic Energy Commission, and the Veterans Administration. Two-thirds ($109 million) of all funds for university medical research came from the Federal government in 1957. Federal aid for facilities, staff, and research has developed further in this field over the past decade than in any other area. Federal loans of $250 million for medical buildings were approved in 1956. An increasing reliance on Federal support with more full-cost grants is considered necessary to achieve future objectives. If Federal aid can be so increased as to relieve the drain of medical school budgets on universities, it will be a major contribution to university finance.

Special Problems

The Changing Structure. The anticipated reliance, to an increasing degree, on Federal, state, and local support creates in the minds of many people a concern about the future of higher education in this country. The concern is largely independent of worries over the economic consequences for the taxpayer. It is broader than the question of political control or interference. It relates to the difficult position of the private institution— particularly the small college that sees no adequate source of support to maintain its influence. It is a concern over the possible lowering of educational standards as a result of the prospective multiplication of local colleges and branches of colleges. It is a fear that the small liberal arts college may be on the wane.

These are appropriate matters of concern, and the existence of that concern may help to moderate the results. Thus far, no promising alternative to an increased reliance on public institutions and public support has appeared as a means of dealing with the expanding demand for education. The trend may be checked, but there is nothing in sight to reverse it. The effect on standards depends heavily on institutional policy. There are many levels of education to be provided, and the prevalence of local colleges will increase the opportunities of institutions that wish to serve only the more able students. Many weak private institutions may have to face a choice between insolvency, mediocrity, or qualifying as public institutions. But enlarged opportunities for many private and public institutions will exist, often through cooperation. The cooperation of the Connecticut Valley colleges is an example. Institutional confederation, best exemplified by the University of Toronto, is another. By pooling resources all may be strengthened. It is too soon to judge the outcome for them, but in view of the recent support the liberal arts colleges have elicited, the more enterprising ones at least have an undisputed role for future service. (See discussion by Gordon N. Ray.)

Governmental Control. Fear of governmental control and political interference is one of the principal reasons for anxiety over the changing structure of higher education. Every example of restricted freedom, or of political interference, in a public institution is a reminder that the system is perhaps becoming more and more vulnerable to political pressures. By contrast private institutions are not always more independent and free than public institutions, but they often have greater opportunity to be independent and free of political influence.

The degree of independence accorded public institutions varies greatly. Six state universities enjoy a constitutional independence that essentially establishes them as a fourth branch of government.[12] Most state institutions, however, are creatures of the legislature and have considerably less autonomy. Some are so responsible to the legislature that they have no protection of their freedom save what they can enlist from appeals to that body, or to public opinion. Many state institutions must live under legislative surveillance that involves line-by-line budget approval or the specification of educational policies, curricula, and administrative practices. In many states administrative supervision by state officials has grown in recent years. These administrative controls range from the final approval of institutional actions by state budget officers to the approval of purchasing and personnel practices.[13]

To stem this trend and to counteract the threat to institutional freedom, the recent Committee on Government and Higher Education, under the chairmanship of President Milton S. Eisenhower, of Johns Hopkins University, has urged that every public institution of higher education be given legal autonomy under broad policies of public control, and an independent board having full responsibility, and that it be subject to a post audit of its accounts, but that it be protected by positive prohibitions against interference in its internal affairs by state agencies.[13] The report suggests other practices that, if followed, would offer proper public control and yet protect the essential independence and freedom of higher education.

A good deal of the questionable control over institutions of higher education arises from a misunderstanding of their function and of the role of faculties. These institutions in a sense are not parts of government, comparable to any other department under the authority of the political executive. They are, or ought to be regarded as, autonomous creatures of government empowered to perform a function that government delegates in the public interest, namely, to seek new knowledge and disseminate knowledge and to train students in the process of seeking truth and acquiring and appraising knowledge. In their highest tradition, institutions of higher learning are intended not to inculcate popular customs, practices, and beliefs, but to develop in youth the capacity for independent thought and judgment. They are the vehicles for not only the progress of knowledge but also for the cultivation of independent thought among each new generation. Although they develop professional skills, they also develop the capacities of men to be free, to judge, to create, and to innovate. On these abilities the future of free men depends.

These institutions, or the best of them, are served by scholars who have grown up in a long tradition of which they are a part. They have faith in the powers of the human mind and in the achievements possible only through knowledge. They are custodians of knowledge from the past and transmitters of it to the future. They are trained to accept existing knowledge tentatively and to pursue the perennial quest for truth. Their loyalties are to that quest and to the republic of learning that knows no political boundaries. They are the trustees of an embattled tradition and they are dedicated to the preservation and perpetuation of the conditions by which it can serve all mankind now and in future. Betrayals of these standards occur, of course, but the cause is to employ and never to betray the greatest powers of the human intellect. Such are the purposes of true scholarship which are so often infringed by external influence, interference, and control.

It is the autonomy of institutions of higher learning, under the management of boards of able citizens conscious of their special trust, that best ensures the conditions of intellectual freedom. These institutions do not seek complete freedom from all responsibilities to society, or to the conditions of their times. Instead they seek an autonomy within broad policies and rules of fiscal responsibility under which they may operate voluntarily in the light of informed judgment and not under compulsion or threat. They seek for scholarship the independence that has traditionally been accorded the courts.

All institutions of higher learning are subjected in some degree to influence, interference, and even at times control. The test of the freedom of these institutions is to be found in the independence and voluntary nature of their response. Influence, interference, and control blend indistinguishably into one another like the bands of a spectrum. Influence, at one end, is the power through suggestion or persuasion, but without the power of authority or threat, to induce an institution voluntarily to pursue a proposed course of action. No institution is free from influence; each must deal with a multitude of influences. Many of these influences are presented as opportunities suggested or created to encourage a favorable response. Numerous Federal policies are designed to influence institutions to respond voluntarily, but they are not designed to compel a desired response.

Interference is an insistence from without, often with threats of reprisal, that an institution follow a given course of action. Political interference, and the interference of organized groups in society are not uncommon. Here the test of freedom is the degree to which the institution is able voluntarily to follow its own professional judgment, and to resist the intrusion if necessary.

Control—at least that control which violates the principles of institutional freedom—is the imposition of outside judgments by means of authority, or the threatened use of authority, over educational policies, personnel, and practices. Thus a budget practice that requires the approval of a course of instruction, or the approval of instructors, before public funds will be released to the institution is a use of control contrary to institutional freedom. The appointment of a board of trustees to carry out the wishes of a governor with respect to athletics or faculty appointments is a form of control.

Though the differences between influence, interference, and control are at times shadowy, control, whether by government or other bodies, is clearly the greatest threat to institutional freedom. The only safeguard a scholarship yet found is an assured autonomy of the institution, a governing board of able and dedicated men, and a faculty of able and independent scholars. It is the fear that we are subjecting more and more education to institutional forms that are neither independent nor free of interference and political control that worries those devoted to freedom. To them the absence of independence is the power to control, and the existence of the power carries with it the danger that it may be used.

Government Policy. The growing reliance on state and local institutions and on public support does increase the risks of political interference and of governmental control over higher education. Public funds can expand the facilities for higher education, and the tolerance of legislatures and officials can allow these institutions considerable freedom, but a truly great system of higher education, with dependable freedom, cannot be created until the institutions are given greater autonomy and are encouraged to exercise it responsibly in the highest traditions of scholarship.

The states and localities, as they increase their support of higher education, should strive to build an institutional system worthy of that support.

Federal policies, with few exceptions, have from the first been designed to encourage institutions to undertake lines of instruction or research regarded as important in the national interest. They have offered opportunities and assistance to be accepted or rejected voluntarily, and never to be adopted by compulsion. Federal assistance has also been given to help institutions accomplish their regular purposes, but again without control. It is essential that these forms of aid be continued, but in such a way that Federal control and political interference may be avoided. The increasing degree to which Federal grants and contracts must be negotiated and brought into compliance with government specifications offers some threat of control, but even that can be largely avoided by appropriate consultation with informed educators when the specifications are formulated. In the end the surest safeguard against Federal domination is a system of autonomous private and public institutions, and it is also the only final safeguard of freedom and of its potentialities for man.

Supplementary Notes on Estimated Expenditures and Income for Higher Education, 1969–70

These comments present briefly other estimates of expenditures and income of higher education during the period 1969–70. The resulting

Table 4. Estimated Expenditures of Higher Education
1969–70 (Based on 1957–58 Experience)
(In millions of dollars)

	Public institutions	Private institutions	All institutions
Assumed Enrollment[a] in Millions[a]			
Four-year colleges	3.6	2.1	5.7
Junior colleges	0.6	0.1	0.7
Total	4.2	2.2	6.4
Expenditures Based on 1957–58 Figures[b]			
Four-year colleges:			
3.6 million × $1,139	$4,100		
2.1 million × 1,158		$2,432	$6,532
Junior colleges:			
0.6 million × $362	217		
0.1 million × 795		80	297
Total expenditure estimates	$4,317	$2,512	$6,829
Less 10 per cent for economies[c] ..	432	251	683
Balance	$3,885	$2,261	$6,146
Plus 45 per cent for doubling of salaries[d]	1,748	1,017	2,765
Total	$5,633	$3,278	$8,911
Organized research[e]	650	650	1,300
Less amount assumed in above	500	500	1,000
Added research	150	150	300
Total education and research expenditures[f]	$5,783	$3,428	$9,211
Student aid:[g]			
Total student aid	220	360	580
Less amount from institutional funds (above)	50	180	230
Added aid from outside funds	170	180	350
Total net expenditures for education, research, and student aid[h]	$5,953	$3,608	$9,561

[a] Enrollment. An enrollment of 6.4 million regular-session students is assumed: 65 per cent in public and 35 per cent in private institutions. Fifty-eight per cent of present enrollment is in public institutions. It is assumed that junior college enrollment will expand from 406,000 to 700,000, and not more, because

aggregate expenditures are close to those given by Professor Harris. The distribution and the reliance on government support are quite different, in part because of different assumptions regarding tuition rates that may be charged.

The calculations and the underlying assumptions on which they are based are given in Tables 4 to 7.

---

of the upgrading of junior colleges into four-year institutions, the growth of four-year community colleges, and the expansion and establishment of branch campuses of four-year colleges, which will attract more local students.

^b *Expenditures.* Expenditure estimates are based on 1957–58 experience as estimated by the Council for Financial Aid to Education in *Where's the Money Coming From?*. These estimates are generally in accord with figures for 1953–54 and 1955–56. Since "expenditure" figures were not available, "educational and general income" estimates are used. They overstate "expenses" by about 3 per cent, for which no correction has been made here.

The expected enrollment figures for 1969–70 were multiplied by the "expenditures" per student in 1957–58 for four-year colleges and junior colleges (both public and private) to get expenditure estimates at 1957–58 rates.

^c *Economies.* Next I have deducted 10 per cent of the total expenditure estimates for economies that can be attained by a more effective utilization of staff and plant, by improved methods of instruction, and other efficiencies. This figure may be low, but in view of the difficulty of achieving such economies, it seems unreasonable to put it higher.

^d *Doubling of salaries.* It is assumed that salaries of teachers and related personnel should double by 1969–70. This cost is estimated at 45 per cent of the "balance" after economies. Total salaries in the educational budget are about 57 per cent of the total. The increase for some would probably be less than double. The staff in 1969–70 will probably contain more younger professors at salaries less than double the average for 1957–58. I have taken 45 per cent of educational expenditures as a reasonable basis for estimating the additional cost of salary increases. This does not make allowance for an average increase of 2 per cent or so per year to correspond with the increased productivity and earnings in other occupations, though such costs may well be necessary. I assume that additional economies may be sufficient to provide such further increases of salaries.

^e *Organized Research.* The foregoing estimates include an allowance for both organized research and incidental faculty research. Organized-research expenditures I estimate at nearly double the 1957–58 rates, $500 million in public and private institutions alike, and I add $150 million more for each in the expectation that government grants and contracts for research will increase faster than enrollment. The total, $1,300 million, for organized research, will for the most part not be realized as an expense if such grants and contracts do not materialize. A considerable amount of other research exists in the educational costs.

[f] Total educational expenditures. On the basis of this calculation I reach a total budget for 1969–70 of $9,211 million, as compared to Professor Harris' budget of $9,200 million.

[g] Student aid. Student aid, in the form of scholarships, fellowships, prizes, etc., has become an important supplementary item. I have estimated total student aid at approximately the 1955–56 rates plus 100 per cent for increased tuition and other costs. To determine the need for additional funds, I have assumed that public institutions will finance nearly one-fourth of its student aid out of institutional funds and private institutions will finance half out of institutional funds. These are the 1955–56 rates.

[h] Total net expenditures. Total expenditures for education, research, and student aid are net expenditures, to eliminate duplication.

Table 5. Estimated Income of Higher Education
1969–70

(In millions of dollars)

	Public institutions	Private institutions	All institutions
Estimated income[a]			
Tuition and fees (at 1957–58 rates):[b]			
Four-year colleges:			
3.6 million × $90	$ 324		$1,443
2.1 million × $533		$1,119	
Junior colleges			
0.6 million × $26	16		
0.1 million × $464		46	62
Totals	$ 340	$1,165	$1,505
Additional tuition (100 per cent increase for public institutions, 50 per cent for private)	340	582	922
Total tuition and fees	$ 680	$1,747	$2,427
Endowment income, gifts, and grants, (at 1957–58 rates: 4 per cent for public institutions, 30 per cent for private)[c]	$ 225	$ 990	$1,215
Other sources (at 1957–58 rates: 10 per cent for public institutions, 8 per cent for private)[d]	578	274	852
Total income, excluding government	$1,483	$3,011	$4,494

Table 5. Estimated Income of Higher Education (*Continued*)
1969-70

(In millions of dollars)

	Public institutions	Private institutions	All institutions
	*Estimated income*ᵃ		
Other funds needed ᵉ	$4,470	$ 597	$5,067
Government support (at 1957-58 rates, per student) :ᶠ			
Four-year colleges (enrollment in millions):			
3.6 million × $873	$3,143		$3,504
2.1 million × $172		361	
Junior colleges (enrollment in millions):			
0.6 million × $313	188		
0.1 million × $60		6	194
	$3,331	$ 367	$3,698
Funds for added research	150	150	300
Additional funds needed	989	80	1,069
Total government support needed ...	$4,470	$ 597	$5,067

ᵃ Estimated income. These income estimates are also based on 1957-58 experience. The purpose is to determine what amount of support may be required from government.

ᵇ Tuition and fees. Tuition income is estimated first on the basis of average revenue from tuition per student in 1957-58, making allowance for the differing average charges for different classes of institutions. I have next assumed tuition increases of 100 per cent in public institutions ($90 in four-year colleges and $26 in junior colleges) and tuition increases of 50 per cent in private institutions ($267 in four-year colleges and $232 in junior colleges). This yields tuition income of $2,427 million.

ᶜ Endowment income, gifts, and grants. Here (using 1957-58 rates) I have assumed income from endowment, grants, and gifts for public institutions at 4 per cent of gross expenditures (excluding added contract research) and for private colleges at 30 per cent. About $300 million of the total is expected to come from endowment income.

ᵈ Other sources of income. Other incidental sources of income are a fairly constant fraction of education and general income. I have estimated such income at 1957-58 rates, which were 10 per cent of educational and general income for public institutions and 8 per cent for private institutions.

ᵉ Other funds needed. This is the total income from foregoing items, subtracted from total net expenditures of Table 3. It is the residual to be raised from government.

SALARIES OF FACULTY MEMBERS

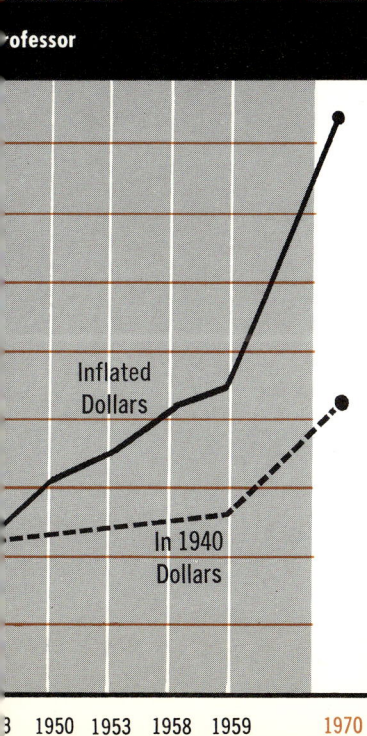

ofessor

Inflated
Dollars

In 1940
Dollars

3   1950 1953 1958 1959   1970

Dollars

$18,000

16,000

14,000

12,000

10,000

8,000

6,000

4,000

2,000

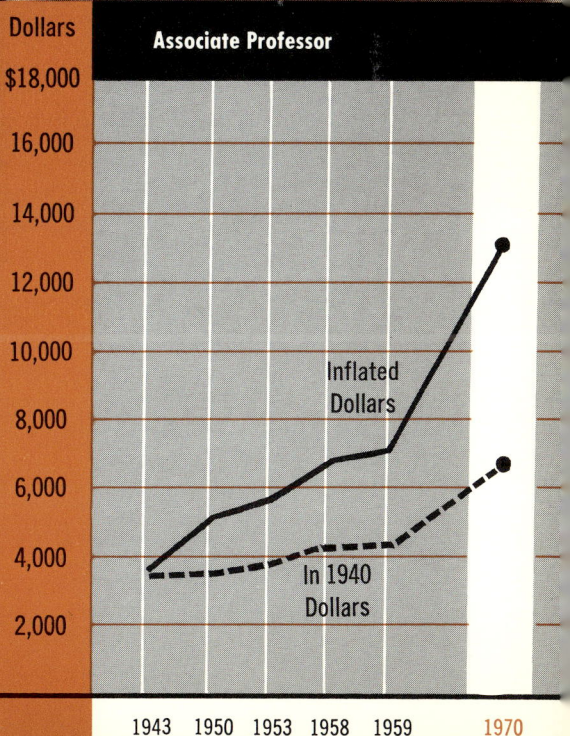

Associate Professor

Inflated
Dollars

In 1940
Dollars

1943 1950 1953 1958 1959   1970

f Government support. Government support has been estimated by calculating what support would be provided if 1957–58 rates per student prevailed and by estimating what supplementary support would be necessary to balance the educational budget. The total $5,067 million, which is $1,367 million higher than Professor Harris estimates from this source, mainly because I assume lower tuition charges.

Table 6. Summary of Estimated Uses and Sources of Income for Higher Education
1969–70
(In millions of dollars)

	Public Institutions	Private Institutions	Total
Budgeted uses of funds:[a]			
Education	$5,083	$2,598	$7,681
Student aid	220	360	580
Organized research	650	650	1,300
Totals	$5,953	$3,608	$9,561
Sources of funds:[b]			
Tuition and fees	$ 680	$1,747	$2,427
Endowment income, gifts and grants	225	990	1,215
Other sources	578	274	852
Totals	$1,483	$3,011	$4,494
Government:			
Federal grants for education	$ 200	$ 50	$ 250
Federal research grants and contracts	550	550	1,100
State and local government	3,750	50	3,800
Total government	$4,500	$ 700	$5,150
Total income[c]	$5,983	$3,661	$9,644
Total expenditures	5,953	3,608	9,561
Balance	$ 30	$ 53	$ 83

[a] Uses of funds. These estimates show the three principal uses of funds. Faculty research as distinct from organized research is included in the budget for education.

[b] Sources of funds. The first three items are taken from Table 5. Government sources are then estimated. Federal grants include support of land-grant colleges at $150 million, plus $50 million each to public and private institutions for medical education, tuition, and training fees and other support explained in the text. Federal research grants and contracts are estimated at $1,100 million. This estimate may be too low or too high. It is assumed that contracts and many grants will cover full costs and that research expenses will increase or

decrease in proportion to the research undertaken. State and local governments are assumed to provide approximately the amount needed to balance budgets for public institutions and nearly double the amount previously provided to private institutions (in 1955–56).

c Total funds and balance. The total income to be provided is estimated at $9,644 million, and total expenditures are estimated (Table 4) at $9,561 million, leaving a surplus of $83 million to be used where needed.

Table 7. Estimated Sources of Funds for College Housing 1969–70

	Public Institutions	Private Institutions	Total
Estimated budget	$1,000	$ 500	$1,500
Sources of funds:*a*			
Private gifts	$ 20	$ 230	$ 250
Current funds	150	100	250
State and local appropriations	490	10	500
Federal grants and loans	340	160	500
Total	$1,000	$ 500	$1,500

a Sources of funds for college housing. It is assumed that total housing expenditures by 1969–70 will approximate $1,500 million, divided, as students are divided, about two-thirds in public institutions and one-third in private institutions. The sources of funds are based largely on 1955–56 and 1957–58 experience. Most amounts are estimated at less than double their present or recent rates.

Notes

1. The distribution is far from uniform for different types of institutions. For 1955–56, the last year for which figures are available, the proportion of enrollment in public, as opposed to private institutions of the same class, was junior colleges, 86 per cent; teachers colleges, 96 per cent; liberal arts colleges, 31 per cent; universities, 59 per cent; technological schools, 36 per cent; theological schools, none; other professional schools, 16 per cent. Enrollment and educational income figures throughout, unless noted, are from Office of Education, *Biennial Surveys of Education in the U.S.;* financial data for 1955–56 are from unpublished figures of the Office of Education.

2. *Beneficial Effects of Federal Aid to the States for Education,* A report of the Legislative Reference Service (November, 1951; revised, March, 1958), pp. 1–3.

3. Report of the National Advisory Committee on Eucation, *Federal Relations to Education, Part I: Committee Findings and Recommendations* (1931), p. 11.

4. The exceptions have been in areas of jurisdiction, for which the Federal government has delegated powers under the Constitution, by treaties, or by

organic acts. Thus the Federal government operates military academies and colleges, provides schools directly for the education of Indians and residents of territories, the District of Columbia, outlying possessions, and other Federal areas. It likewise offers training for personnel of the Federal government, provides for scientific research, the collection and diffusion of information, and intellectual and educational cooperation of the United States with other nations. Report of the National Advisory Committee on Education, *ibid.*, p. 10.

5. Richard G. Axt, *The Federal Government and Financing Higher Education*, Commission on Financing Higher Education, Columbia University Press, New York, 1952, pp. 64–82.

6. Carnegie Foundation for the Advancement of Teaching, *Federal Programs in Higher Education, Summary of a Discussion by the Trustees*, reprint from the 1956–57 annual report, pp. 3, 4.

7. The President's Committee on Education Beyond the High School, *First Interim Report to the President* (July, 1956), and *Second Report to the President* (July, 1957).

8. Projections of gross national product over the next decade vary considerably. Projections as low as $634 billion or $650 billion have been assumed by some. Gerhard Colm's projection based on growth rates of 3.7 and 4.2 per cent indicate a GNP of $735 billion or $790 billion, as compared to a current GNP in 1959 of about $480 billion. I have assumed, for estimating purposes, a GNP of $700 billion in 1969–70 and have checked the results against a GNP of $650 billion and $735 billion.

9. For example, Otto Eckstein, *Trends in Public Expenditures in the Next Decade*, a supplementary paper of the Committee for Economic Development, New York, 1959, and an unpublished paper by Dick Netzer prepared for the National Bureau of Economic Research on *Financial Needs and Resources Over the Next Decade: State and Local Governments*, 1959.

10. This point was effectively made by Ralph F. Lewis at the Merrill Center Seminar.

11. Final report of the Secretary's Consultants on Medical Research and Education, *The Advancement of Medical Research and Education*, through the Department of Health, Education and Welfare, 1958.

12. Malcolm Moos and Francis E. Rourke, *The Campus and the State*, staff report for the Committee on Government and Higher Education, Johns Hopkins Press, Baltimore, 1959, p. 22.

13. Report of the Committee on Government and Higher Education, *The Efficiency of Freedom*, Johns Hopkins Press, Baltimore, 1959.

10

The Prospects for Private-sector Support of Higher Education

W. Homer Turner

It may be basically asserted that "private sectors" supply all of the financial resources required for higher education. The principal resources derive from (1) taxes paid by individuals and by groups in which individual efforts are joined; (2) private tuition and other payments of students and families for benefits received; and (3) all forms of private-sector benefactions, including resources from prior accumulations provided chiefly by private sources as in the case of the free-market investment of endowments. Hence an examination of the role of the private-sectors in the total financing of higher education is, necessarily, a review of the "universe of support."

There are, of course, technical qualifications to this generalization in the classifications of money flows made in economic theory and practice, and some relatively small sums arise from payments from abroad on goods and services and through use of natural-resource receipts. Even narrowly, or strictly considered, individual private payments of tuition and fees (about $1 billion) and total benefactions (about $900 million), at current levels, account for nearly 55 per cent of the operating budgets ($3.5 billion) and 42 per cent of the total budgets ($4.5 billion, including capital), of all the nation's public and private colleges, institutes, and universities. If private-sector derived endowment income of about $200 million be added, the percentages increase, respectively, to 60 and 47.

The private sectors constantly are making choices, within the democratic process, of (1) the means by which their moneys will flow, that is, through taxes or alternatively and additionally by tuitions and bene-

220

factions, and (2) the total tax and nontax funds to be applied from privately generated resources for all higher education.

America faces the certainty that direct and indirect outlays for *all* forms of education—assuming that defense expenditures continue at experienced levels—will be the largest single continuing civilian application of national resources. Higher education alone, in today's dollars, will cost the public and private purse, by the end of the coming decade, from a minimum of $9 billion to a maximum of $12 or more billion annually. And this outlay will be on top of many billions of dollars of expenditures for secondary and other forms of education.

To meet a bill of either magnitude, it appears inevitable that students and their families will have to pay more via tuition, private-sector support ought to be doubled or possibly even trebled, and conditioned by the first two elements, tax-generated resources may be heavily enlarged.

Many charged with leadership roles will be called upon to decide, initially, whether the money flows should be channeled in larger or smaller volume by the tax route or, alternatively, through the personal payment and philanthropic routes. The difficulties of decision making here are enormous. For one example, it is impossible to consider what share of the financing shall be done by student tuition without becoming entangled in the most far-ranging questions of educational policy, philosophy, and practice.

Basic Factors Determining Private-sector Direct Action

In general, the level and character of private-sector support of higher education in the United States has been, and will be, chiefly influenced by certain major developments as they affect the volume and application of financial resources. These developments are (1) the degree of growth of all forms of governmental activities, including governmental foundations, national institutes, commissions, and departments, (2) the character of income and estate taxation with their incentive consequences upon individual, corporate, and other contributions, and (3) the maturity achieved by both classical and new forms of philanthropy.

There are but three fundamental approaches to the financing of higher education. Taken in absolute terms, they are (1) funds move through tax or tax-associated channels, (2) funds move through private and voluntary channels, (3) funds arrive at end-use educational purposes through a mixture of the two channels.

Historically, the third or mixed approach has been followed since the founding of the nation. What we are witnessing now, in the midst of a contemporary crisis, are three main streams of effort. The first is an attempt to increase greatly the share of government in the total outlay; the second is an attempt to accelerate the flows of moneys from nongovernment sources; the third is an attempt to further catalyze both sources of funds. Some would have the whole task of educational finance assumed by government, through a variety of mechanisms, some existing, some newly created, some to be created. Others would hold the governmental role more or less where it is and shift greater shares of the forward needs upon other segments involved in the private-support pattern.

The volume and allocation of private-sector support of higher education, in the judgment of this observer, is forecastable by certain major inquiries. They are: What kind of education will private sectors be asked to help provide? How will such private-sector aid actually be utilized? What is the prospect of adequate private-sector response to present and forecasted needs?

The first of these inquiries is really what kind of educational product the American people will secure for the billions they are being asked to provide. That inquiry turns on a number of major considerations and is truly the fundamental—and in terms of the causative influences upon the unleashing of moneys, the cardinal—question to be examined. The ingredients of the examination are beyond the scope of discussion here; they range from principles of political economy to distinctions between instruction and education and to the identification, encouragement, and appreciation of the individual scholar. They also include accommodating soundly the great shifts occurring in science and technology, in cultural value systems, in better preparation of the educational product for an expanded age of symbols and the graduate's better positioning with regard to the nonrational part of human behavior, the greater volume factor in all social affairs, and the roles of government and voluntary groups.

The second of the initial inquiries—answering the American people are convinced that institutions of higher learning are moving in the direction of the needs of the age and are working for the central purposes of learning—relates to the precise application to be made of the funds provided as taxes, tuition, and benefactions. The American people, before releasing added resources in large volume, want to know the facts about our position vis-à-vis foreign educational advances. They want to be informed about steps to be taken as to ability and achievement factors and to be assured of sensible answers about the community colleges, interinstitutional competition, education of women, academic salaries and benefits, costs and efficient use of resources, the types of institutions needed, and scores of other matters. All such considerations are truly the antecedent determinants of the channeling and volume of future dollars for higher education.

The third inquiry is the central concern of this examination which embodies the following elements. Primary attention is given to the major sources of benefactions—what they are and the volume of assistance they now, and prospectively will, provide in relation to forecasted needs. These sources are chiefly alumni, corporate aid, general-welfare foundations, contributions of individuals, church support, bequests, and aid from labor unions. They are described in the stated sequence. The significance of entrepreneurial income of institutions follows thereafter. The remainder of the examination relates to some of the interlocks between private-sector payments and government action. Large-scale government aid occurs simultaneously with large-scale private-sector benefactions and payments. Public-sector support, often parallel to private-sector support in such areas as capital, operation, and student aid (loans, scholarships, and fellowships), heavily influences the dollar flows from individuals, philanthropic entities, and other voluntary sources. The many elements of benefactions, tuition payments, and tax-generated resources in turn interact to affect the character, volume, and incidence of taxation upon individuals and upon voluntary-enterprise groups. Accordingly, the major aspects of these interwoven matters must be noted if the total prospect for resources and their methods of channeling are to be revealed in a unified manner.

The Volume of Benefactions for Higher Education

The inquiry begins with a quick overview of America's total philanthropy, which, according to the *Philanthropic Digest,* exceeds $7 billion annually. Such benefactions represent about half the known total for the world, and the amount reflects the continuing vigor of this American tradition. Most of the $7 billion total is provided by individuals, but such groups as alumni, corporations, and general-welfare and community foundations and trusts also provide yearly outlays of many hundreds of millions of dollars. How much of the $7 billion accrues to higher education?

The American Association of Fund-Raising Counsel, in August, 1959, reported that educational philanthropy set a new record in the first half of the current year and that it expects that the total for the twelve months will exceed $900 million. After income from tuition, dormitory and other fees, governmental receipts, and such resources as come from services performed, private and, to a significant degree, public higher education is largely dependent upon a variety of private-sector, philanthropic actions.

Across the nation, gifts and grants account for ever more of the total budget. The principal gift, grant, and allocation sources, with their shares of the total financial aid provided private and public institutions in a typical recent year, are listed in Table 1. These representative, but constantly shifting ratios, are derived from studies of the Council for Finan-

Table 1. Current Annual Volume of Private-sector Aid, by Sources

Source	Total support, per cent	Est. amount, $ million	Range of estimates, $ million
Alumni and annual giving............	17	153	140–165
Corporations and corporate foundations	17	153	145–170
General-welfare foundations..........	17	153	100–200
Individuals other than alumni........	15	135	100–150
Churches and religious orders........	14	126	100–150
Bequests, trusts, and annuities........	10	90	90–110
Labor unions, entrepreneurial income, Federal aid, etc...................	10	90	90–165
	100	900	765–1,110*

* Median amount is $936 million.

cial Aid to Education, the American College Public Relations Association, the American Alumni Council, the American Association of Fund-Raising Counsel, and the National Industrial Conference Board.

Support of Public Institutions by Private Sectors

Private-sector support of public higher educational institutions is rising for all components of donor sources. A study published by the Council for Financial Aid to Education, covering the year 1956–57, reports results at an early stage of what is probably now a rising trend in the direction of private-sector assistance for public colleges, institutes, and universities. The data show that 109 of the state universities and land-grant colleges reporting received about $87 million from private sectors in 1956–57. If the trend has continued upward since 1956–57, the present total is perhaps $100 million, or one-ninth of the $900 million current total for all public and private institutions. About $10 million of the 1956–57 sum was corporate support, and alumni provided about $5 million; the remainder came from diverse sources. These institutions applied 83 per cent of the $87 million total to "current operations" and 17 per cent to "capital needs," an allocation which reflects, in part, the nature of public institutional needs. The following tax-based universities and institutes, in order of magnitude of gifts received, were among the large-scale beneficiaries of private-sector aid: California, Michigan, Delaware, Ohio State, Wisconsin, Minnesota, Illinois, North Carolina, Georgia Tech, and Kansas; each received in excess of $3 million. In the same 1956–57 study, nine municipally based institutions reported increased aid from private sectors, with corporations providing about 17 per cent out of the total.

Private Support and Educational Structure

One other factor must be noted before we examine the flows and prospective trends of private-sector assistance by the specific subcomponents of the voluntary mechanisms. This factor is the extent to which the present and prospective organization of higher education induces shifts of major support areas because of "natural constituencies" related to the functional classifications of higher education. Ten such functional classifications are as follows:

- Major private and state universities and land-grant institutions
- Public and private teachers colleges
- Private men's colleges, four-year
- Private women's colleges, four-year
- Private coeducational colleges, four-year
- Private professional or technological institutions
- Municipal colleges and universities
- Public and private junior colleges
- Public and private institutes for advanced study
- Jointly operated educational facilities, public and private

The "official classification" of the Office of Education groups a number of these categories differently for data-collection purposes, but the functional classification cited above more nearly reveals the diversity of the demands upon the public and private purses.

It is against these and other new trends in support of public higher education, and related structural and scholastic needs out ahead, that we may usefully examine past and prospective support by each of the major components of the private-sector area.

Alumni Support

Support from alumni and annual giving are currently among the largest sources of philanthropic aid accruing to both private and public institutions. Financial support of their alma maters is but one of the many responsibilities to education that bear upon graduates as educated men and women. The case for active financial support by alumni grows ever stronger, and the large-scale participation by alumni helps guarantee that no single major or monolithic source of support will emerge to dominate the future financing of America's education.

Alumni forms of aid amount to 17 per cent of all benefactions. In 1959 a public land-grant institution led the national field in alumni-support improvement, a symbol of growth in such support of public institutions. Total alumni individual gifts and annual giving plans for public and private higher education in the United States currently range between $140 million and $165 million. (A small share of this total accrues to private secondary education.) The alumni as a source of additional income for higher education hold much promise. Every graduate of every institution has had his education subsidized, to some degree, by unseen friends; tuition almost never has covered the operational cost of education, still less the capital cost.

It is estimated that there are 7.8 million alumni in America. Of these 5.4 million have been asked to give to their alma maters. About 1.2 million responded last year. In the latest year, effectiveness of solicitation rose from 20.5 per cent to 22.5 per cent. The trend is better revealed by noting the historic progression of giving. While annual alumni giving was established as early as sixty-eight years ago (Yale University), the annual total of alumni gifts in as recent a year as 1938 was only 2 per cent of the current annual total from this source. Alumni support and support by non-alumni individuals together represent about one-third of all philanthropic aid to educational institutions. The goal of the American Alumni Council is that 2 million alumni will be contributing $200 million annually by 1960, with an ultimate goal of $1 billion annually before the second decade hence.

In the years ahead, as alumni increasingly accept their personal responsibilities as educated leaders for the forward financing of higher education, many new and effective fresh approaches, as well as the tested ones, may be expected to become significant factors in college, institute, and university support.

Industry and business, which are major employers of the national educational product, have sought to encourage alumni giving by various types of incentive plans that supplement their general programs of aid to education. Most of these incentive plans are applicable to both public and private institutions, and some extend to junior colleges and secondary schools as well.

One of the most successful plans, now adopted by about seventy-five business organizations, is the so-called employer-employee matching gift plan. Under this plan the employer matches the personal contribution of his alumnus-employee to a college or university, up to a stated maximum sum. The objective is stimulation of alumni giving, as well as stimulation of more extensive solicitation by the institutions. The history of the various corporate-alumnus plans operated to date suggests that many additional millions will be generated by such methods. Thus far the maximum employee contribution matched is $2,500; the typical matched sum is either $500 or $1,000. In a single one of the seventy-five companies, within a five-year period, this plan has generated more than three-quarters of a million dollars.

A second basic plan complements and supplements the corporate-alumnus plan, or it may be adopted alternatively to the employer-employee matching method. It is an incentive-achievement approach by which an independent jury makes substantial cash awards annually, from a common pool of donated funds, to those institutions that achieve the greatest degree of improvement in a twelve-month period through alumni-support efforts. The jury-point system, supervised by the American Alumni Council, makes allotments by categories of institutions—large and small, colleges and universities, public and private—and with regard for length of alumni effort, number of alumni, and other factors, which make for equitable distribution while recognizing basic achievement in improving alumni support. It is hoped that, for every incentive-achievement dollar placed in the pool of donated fund, five to ten additional dollars may be secured from alumni.

Corporate Support

Corporations provide material financial support to large numbers of colleges, institutes, and universities incidental to contract and noncontract projects, studies, training, research, or other work that has some kinship with business operations. When so accounted for, there is either an implied, expressed, or hoped for *quid pro quo* element. Even so, the flow of dollars commonly also serves to absorb institutional overhead burdens, provide extra income for faculty, and install—at no or low cost—special equipment and other facilities usable in teaching. The sums involved, on a national basis, certainly amount to many millions of dollars, but no means to arrive at any precise estimate exist. The aggregate amount may well equal or exceed the sums provided outright by corporate contributions. The new knowledge frequently obtained—as in social or physical science research—serves both public interest and self-interest. Post employment educational activities sponsored or encouraged by business and industry involve attendance of many thousands of part-time students at colleges, institutes, and universities after working hours, in addition to significant numbers of selected employees who study during work periods under special arrangements. These activities also condition the flow of additional millions of dollars on a national basis.

There are in effect many other cooperative measures involving industry with education in addition to the industry-financed joint efforts. The latter sometimes involve trade and professional groups, as well as general-welfare foundation programs at home or abroad. All such actions add up to major impacts on the financing of higher education currently and prospectively. Here, however, attention is confined to corporation contributions and to grants made through corporate-financed foundations or trusts exclusively on a public interest and philanthropic basis, any resulting corporate benefit being a by-product.

Corporate contributions and grants to higher education are substantial and ever-increasing. Already they account for about 17 per cent of institutional benefactions. Despite the fact that the net income of all corporations in a recent year was lower than the net income for the prior year, the amount of corporate contributions to education increased. The best data suggest that approximately thirty thousand corporations are already providing some form of annual assistance for higher education. The Chicago Chapter of the Public Relations Society of America in a recent study found that, on a national-sample basis, corporate-financed foundations have been established for nearly 40 per cent of all companies with 1,000 or more employees. The study suggests also that about two-thirds of the largest companies continue to make significant dollar amounts of contribution to education and other tax-exempt entities directly, in addition to the support from their corporate-financed public-interest foundations. In addition to direct aid to education many of these foundations give indirect aid, such as support of a community hospital which may also be used as a major university teaching center.

Although corporate contributions for *all purposes* are deductible up to 5 per cent of net income before Federal income taxes, this figure has not been reached by most companies. However, on a dollar basis, direct corporate philanthropy, for the latest year for which corporate tax return data are available (1956), exceeded $400 million. A decade hence, but subject of course to many contingent variables, this total may reach or exceed $1 billion yearly for all purposes.

For what educational purposes and needs have corporate philanthropic funds been contributed? The task of estimating the flow of funds by direction and amounts is most difficult; precise data are not attainable. There is a growing trend to make corporate contributions and grants of an unrestricted character. In any event, no wholesale or finite postaudit of the use of such funds is available. More significantly, there is no satisfactory system of dividing academic interests and activities into non-overlapping categories on or off the campus. Again, interdisciplinary and interlocking uses are increasingly characteristic of institutional resource needs, in furtherance of general education, or are devoted to a particular discipline. With such qualifications, one study indicates that, among several hundred companies or their corporate-financed foundations, contributions were designated for the purposes listed in Table 2.

The fact that college administrators increasingly request contributions that are unrestricted or undesignated is reflected in the high and growing percentage of such gifts, together amounting to more than half of the total provided. If governmental scholarship aid increases, we may reason-

Table 2.

Purpose of Contribution	Percentage of total
Unrestricted use (available for salaries)	38
Unspecified (available for salaries)	13
Faculty Salaries	2
Total unspecified and unrestricted	53
Student aid	19
Capital needs	15
Basic and applied research	12
Endowments	1
Total contributions	100

ably expect the interest of many private-sector donors to shift to other forms of aid. Even so, it is expected that many already existing private scholarship programs may continue to expand; for such plans serve many desirable ends.

Among the high-priority needs of institutions of higher education are resources for basic research. Unfortunately, this area has been among the least attractive to many private-sector donors in the past, but there is now substantial indication of better nationwide understanding of the need. Leading educators have made it clear that applied research can never be successful, whether conducted in a campus, governmental, or industrial setting, until adequate fundamental research and new theory have built the base—commonly at higher education institutions—for the new applications.

Perhaps in part because of the overwhelming volume aspect of the problem, many corporate and general-welfare foundation donors do not have major capital-assistance grant programs. The fact that a foundation may in any one year have resources available for only a few capital aid grants, to be distributed among hundreds of applicants, poses an administration problem of considerable proportion, but not an overly difficult one. Such an unmet situation only serves to recall the fact that all institutions of higher education are in need of additional capital resources if they are to accommodate the enlarging student population. There is an increasing amount of imaginative action respecting plant and equipment needs now emanating from some of the institutions that are facing up to their problems. Whether a proper solution can be found short of major Federal government action, as elsewhere mentioned, will depend in part upon the caliber of leadership addressing itself to this need.

Although there appears to be wide acceptance of the absolute necessity for substantial increases in faculty income potential if we are to maintain and, hopefully, increase the quality of our educational offering during

a period when we must double its quantity capacity, the above-cited figure representing grants made specifically toward faculty salaries, demon-
strates the failure to translate understanding of this problem into need-
scale direct action. However, the fact that increasing shares of the sums
provided are "undesignated" may well mean that of the new resources
much goes toward faculty salaries, the problem which most college presidents consider to be their central concern.

Although gifts applied to it have nearly doubled in recent years, endowment continues to be one of the least interesting aid areas. While it
remains as an extremely valuable asset for some great and old institutions, it is especially difficult for young, barely solvent institutions to put
money away in this fashion when funds are needed desperately for current requirements. Today endowment is highly concentrated in a very
few institutions, although to satisfy historic concepts relating to accredi-
tation and to other factors, nearly all institutions have some resources
so classified. About fifty of the major universities and a handful of colleges, mostly "Ivy League" account for about half of all higher education
institutional endowment. As a resource, the decline of endowment may be
attributed to poor management and an earlier reluctance to move to
equity securities, among other factors. The decline of the importance of
endowment as a resource, on net balance, may be highly unfavorable for
education, particularly in regard to faculty quality and general educational leadership in key institutions, where long-range planning is most
significant. In the major public institutions, where the striving for excellence in education is an avowed policy, endowment could be of high
future value; now, of course, endowment for them is typically a minor
factor.

There are many important positive and negative considerations relating to endowment that are not indicated here. A full-scale treatment of
the subject appears in John Dale Russell's The Finance of Higher Education. In that work special consideration is given to the many implications
of support by endowment, including relationships between endowment,
social impacts, and institutional freedom of outlook. One interesting aspect of endowment is the growing relationships between equity securities markets and the funds representing the investment portfolios of
both receivers and providers of philanthropic pools of financial resources.

The current growth of corporate support for education suggests that
American private enterprise has reached a mature assessment of its motivation for giving to education. Corporations or corporate-financed
foundations are increasing the level of their support markedly. The total
volume of aid has doubled in the past four years and more than tripled
during the last six. Of total corporate philanthropy for all causes, the

share for education has risen from 21 to 34 per cent within the last two years; some expect it to reach the 40 per cent level soon. Already the dollar total has passed the $150 million annual rate. It is this observer's opinion that, if 1959 data were available, the total would be found to exceed $500 million for *all* forms of direct cash contributions. However, applying the above-cited 34 per cent share for education would yield a current rate of about $170 million for corporate aid to education.[1]

Although many corporations have had assistance programs in existence for decades, the major policy shift occurred about eight years ago, incident to the A. P. Smith Manufacturing Company litigation. Company directors acted under a statute enacted in 1950 by the New Jersey legislature specifically empowering corporations organized in the state to make contributions for philanthropic purposes. Stockholders objected to a grant to Princeton holding that the statute did not apply to corporations chartered prior to the enactment of the statute, and that such a contribution was therefore a misapplication of corporate funds. Judgment was sought in the courts in a case that carried wide significance in determining the legality of corporate giving. On May 19, 1953, Judge Stein, of the Superior Court, rendered a decision that upheld the legality of the directors' action. The stockholders appealed. On June 25, 1953, the Supreme Court of New Jersey affirmed the decision and sustained the validity of the contribution. Once again the stockholders appealed. On October 26, 1953, the Supreme Court of the United States unanimously dismissed the appeal "for the want of a substantial Federal question." Similar statutes facilitating corporate aid to education today are found in forty of the industrially significant states. The fact that the dollar volume of corporate support to education increased rapidly after this decision would indicate that a degree of motivation was already present and mainly needed to be articulated and freed of the threat of litigation. Since the year 1953, American business enterprise has conducted numerous conferences on the subject, much needful literature has been created about the problem (notably by the National Industrial Conference Board), and many thousands of corporate enterprises are in the process of creating, or have already launched, general programs of aid to education.

The most commonly stated policy justification for the use of corporate funds for support of education has been the recognition that business enterprise increasingly depends upon the skills of educated men and women and that the corporation's future is inseparable from its interest in an educated citizenry.

The matter of business support of higher education does not appeal to this observer as being based upon short-range self-interest or upon any theory that support of particular branches or functions of education will render measurable benefit to the donor corporation. Rather, he views the case as one of opportunity for constructive voluntary participation in the over-all social environment, action that looks to the strengthening of all the factors which make for a better, more open society in which every type of nonmaterial value is enhanced and thereby balances off emphasis upon a high material standard of living and provides more dignified, less onerous human labor.[2]

Corporations and corporate-financed foundations, by their activities in support of higher education in the postwar years, have shown themselves to be innovators in many respects, while chiefly avoiding narrowly restrictive and matched gifts and grants. The highly significant state group movement found its birth through corporate interest. From its beginning in Indiana in 1948, under joint leadership of Dr. Thomas Jones, former President of Earlham College, and Dr. Frank Sparks, then President of Wabash College and now President of the Council for Financial Aid to Education, and with a total of but $15,000 generated the first year, the state and regional liberal arts college movement has so grown that it now comprises forty groups which cover the nation. There are now about 500 participating colleges and universities, the program being nationally coordinated through the Independent College Funds of America in New York City. The movement soon may be generating upwards of $30 million annually for these valued institutions. The objective is to secure at least $100 million yearly. Only in this way could the many small colleges about the nation find a ready vehicle for appealing to many corporations to aid education broadly and consistently. The attractiveness of group fund raising, as exemplified by the state group movement, is also effective in many other segments of the educational world, as exemplified by the National Fund for Medical Education and the United Negro College Fund.

Another example of business leadership is found in the creation of the Council for Financial Aid to Education. This Council, organized with the support of four general welfare foundations, was established at the instigation of Messrs. Irving S. Olds, Frank W. Abrams, and Alfred P. Sloan, Jr., all of whom were then board chairmen of major national corporations. The Council since 1953 has served as a private-sector catalyst and research organization in respect to all the financial needs of higher education. Associated with the Council, in addition to many businessmen, are a number of outstanding educational leaders. The operation of the Council began under Dr. Wilson Compton, former President of Washington State University, and has continued under the direction of Dr. Frank Sparks.

Corporate philanthropy has aided many small nonaccredited colleges to serve their communities more effectively and quite often has helped them to become accredited. Many see that it is simply better economics and better social action to aid an established campus toward improved quality of educational product than to create an entirely new campus. The Council for Advancement of Small Colleges, widely aided by corporate-financed and general-welfare foundations, works to that end. College libraries, heretofore too often overlooked as a primary campus resource, have not kept pace with the increasing demands for excellence in education and the demands for quantity increases in students to be accommodated as more hard self-study occurs. Annual corporate support has been a leader in this new direction. A variety of student aid programs have frequently meant the vital difference in the withering or the blossoming of exceptional talents among our youth. It is gratifying to the corporation foundation, for example, to know that a doctoral level fellowship gave support to a graduate student in one of our great Midwestern universities, where he invented much of the instrumentation for our first two satellites. It is equally reassuring when one learns that a corporate-financed foundation grant, made a few years ago upon faith in the individual scholar who made the request, enabled this nation to gain a whole year of time and have ready the device necessary to track Russia's original satellite. Corporate support has made possible a basic study of the bottlenecks and roadblocks to unleashing a greater flow of scholarly publications in the humanities and has supplied unrestricted funds for their printing.

Our valued major universities, which for so long established a base and pattern for emulation, are now receiving aid on a substantial, recurring, unrestricted-grant basis from a number of America's leading corporations or corporate-financed foundations. At the other end of the educational spectrum these same corporations are lending their support to developmental programs for the further reduction of illiteracy and for basic education toward self-fulfillment of the less able in our society. Foreign scholars and international educational efforts are being aided in several substantial ways.

Corporations also have innovated through the establishment of their own degree-granting private institutions. General Motors Corporation, for example, expends several million annually on its accredited science and liberal arts General Motors Institute. This activity is in addition to its employee and public scholarship plans and other educational support programs. General Electric has estimated its annual postemployment expenditures for intracompany training and nonvocational employee educational assistance at $40 million annually. The Ford Motor Company, in addition to various types of contributions through the Ford Motor Company Fund, has made very large-scale resources available for both liberal arts and community education needs.

Corporations and their foundations have also recognized their responsibility to foster the humanities by direct grants in aid to these fields. The social sciences have heretofore received less than 1 per cent of the funds devoted to all fundamental research in America. In recognition of the impact upon society of human relations knowledge and skills and cognizant that research in science and technology has far outspaced man's ability to utilize this knowledge fully for the good of the social order, corporate aid is now increasingly supporting fundamental research in the social sciences. Diversified support programing is evolving for this area, with emphasis upon encouragement of individual scholarship rather than upon transitory projects.

The process by which further improvement could most likely occur would appear to include discovery, through depth development of excellence in scholarship, of the best means of advancing cross-cultural cooperation without violating cultural integrity; discovery of the most ready means to shape an effective image of man, fused from but transcending, national cultures; discovery of the ways best to utilize the vehicles of personal and public communication.

General-welfare Foundations

There are an estimated ten thousand large and small foundations that are organized under broad philanthropy charters as nonprofit membership corporations or as trusts. They include, in addition to such general-welfare foundations as Ford, Rockefeller, Carnegie, Sloan, Mellon, Kellogg, Commonwealth, Guggenheim, Hayden, Lilly, and Twentieth Century, family foundations, community trusts, and various other types. Many of them are operative in special areas, but the majority provide some assistance to higher education. The larger foundations—110 have assets in excess of $10 million each—at home and abroad devote a substantial share (47 per cent in a recent period) of their total outlays to some form of educational need. In the case of the Ford Foundation, largest of the philanthropic entities, approximately four-fifths of its grants have been for education. The major areas of grant allotments of the 110 largest foundations are shown in Table 3. The summary exhibit reveals a range from more than $100 million to more than $200 million in annual support of education. A total of more than $150 million for higher education would appear to be representative of current volume of annual grants to colleges and universities by these general-welfare foundations.

In pioneering ventures of the most significant sort, in support of intellectual life generally, in programing of institutional self-help, and in scores of other ways these philanthropic agencies are providing great material assistance. The magnitude of their grants—prospectively larger in the future than now, the understanding which they seek to evidence

Table 3. Distribution of Grants of Selected Large Foundations Chiefly 1957

Foundations	Total assets	Grants in millions of dollars								Total grants
		Health	Education	Social welfare	Scientific research	Grants to humanities	Grants for religion	Government	International affairs	
110 foundations............	$6,180,855	$203,957	$220,547	$21,740	$33,241	$10,336	$8,520	$3,986	$18,682	$521,009
Per cent by field.........		39	42	4	6	2	2	1	4	100
Adjusted 110 foundations[a]..	6,180,855	35,214	116,175	21,740	33,241	10,336	8,520	3,986	18,682	247,894
Per cent by field.........		14	47	9	13	4	3	2	8	100
Seven company-sponsored foundations............	108,000	2,401	4,014	3,553	797	290	20	884	31	11,990
Per cent by field.........		20	34	30	7	2	0	7	0	100
Eight community foundations............	211,000	1,643	3,183	2,150	334	270	246	127	25	7,978
Per cent by field.........		21	40	27	4	3	3	2	0	100

[a] Taking out unusual grants paid in 1957 by the Ford Foundation from its $500,000,000 capital appropriation: hospitals, $100,493,000; medical schools, $68,250,000; teachers' salaries, $104,372,000. Data are for 1957, or the nearest year for which information was available, often a fiscal year including a portion of 1957.

SOURCE: *Annual Report for 1958 of The Foundation Library Center.*

about the needs of higher education, and the impacts which their aggregate actions make, all justify extensive treatment not feasible in this paper.

To direct national attention to the inferior earning power of college teachers, a total of $260 million was granted in 1956 and 1957 by the Ford Foundation to help raise the salaries of college and university faculty members. These funds were distributed to all of the nation's 630 four-year, regionally accredited, privately controlled colleges and universities. Each institution received an endowment approximately equal to its 1954 instructional payroll for the liberal arts and sciences. In addition, 126 institutions received more than half again as much in recognition of their efforts to raise the salaries of their teachers.

The major general-welfare foundations have provided, for education in the United States as well as abroad, assistance to the natural sciences and agriculture, to the social sciences and the humanities, to the conquest of disease, and to the medical sciences. They have expressed concern for the needs of professional education—without neglecting the problems of elementary, secondary, and popular education—by thousands of research grants, scholarships, fellowships, lectureships. They have also financed independent permanent entities directed to the solution or alleviation of major educational problems. The Woodrow Wilson National Fellowship Foundation and the National Merit Scholarship Corporation are but two, among many, instances of the latter class of actions.

The distinguished leadership of the larger general-welfare foundations is a social asset of the highest import to the nation. The quality of leadership is revealed both in the composition of the policy-making boards and in executive direction and administration. For any social task, America has seen no greater dedication than in the conduct of these major philanthropic organizations.

In recent years, each major national political party has spearheaded an investigation of the motivation and results of the grants of these general-welfare foundations. All these investigations missed one central point about the administration of these great pools of philanthropic wealth. The central point is that, in private-sector action, there is sought to be applied that prescience and prevision which saves our society from needless errors of obeisance to tides of mass opinion while running ahead of the median point in enlightened public opinion.

Foundation actions, as history may come to appraise them from a long-term perspective afterview, might indicate wisdom or unwisdom. As to either judgment, the record would require noting also that the administrators have sought the advice, consent, and cooperation of educational leaders at each stage of their programming. It is reasonable to conclude that—with allowances for errors incident to any large-scale operation conducted under the implied and expressed mandates of the ethos of American philanthropic traditions—education at the undergraduate, graduate, professional, and liberal arts and sciences levels would be very measurably lagging in meeting contemporary problems were it not for the pioneering application of funds in a multitude of approaches to social problems through these general-welfare foundations.

It is to the matter of helping institutions to help themselves that general-welfare foundations address many of their educational programs and grants. Through grants of funds, changes which otherwise might not be accomplished can be brought about. Foundations provide institutions an extra muscle or lever as well as an opportunity to minimize or eliminate resource wastage. Yet criticism of the general-welfare foundations persists in many quarters. For example, humanist Jacques Barzun, Provost of Columbia University and Dean of Faculties, recently has provided in his book, *The House of Intellect,* an incisive indictment in describing the folklore of philanthropy.

He reasons that philanthropy (along with science and art) is the enemy —largely through ignorance—of the intellectual's needs. Those making grants in philanthropic entities, he concludes, are mistakenly dedicated to the "creative idea," the concise, objective project or survey, the socially and culturally beneficial. It is his firm contention that, when a foundation does express a desire to aid scholarship, for example, in the humanities, its actual motives may be to assuage the guilt of neglect, to project an ethical image, to associate the foundation with a respected element of good in our culture.

If the intellectual is to be served by private philanthropy, there must be strenuous efforts by leaders and followers of both camps to accommodate their disparate ways. The foundations do not appear by intention to have violated the requirements of the intellectual, nor could most of them accept the role of ignorance of the requirements. The only alternative implicit in the central thesis of *The House of Intellect,* a parting of the ways, is hardly the proper solution.

Abandoning philanthropy carries with it an abandonment of many voluntary and private mechanisms, as well as an abandonment of certain moral and ethical concepts—quite likely to the ultimate detriment of freedom. The service of this most distinguished scholar is to remind all that the intellect, freely operative, is the eternal core of social advance. The core is not ever alone the needed buildings, the needed teaching salaries and other required resources. Dr. Barzun has made a magnificent plea for a changeless central purpose of higher learning. In short, heeding his message can only be salutary, but heeding it does not require that philanthropy must be abandoned as one currently useful means to a desirable end. Corporate philanthropy, as the newest stem on the young philan-thropic tree's many branches, has a special opportunity to profit by his warning. Corporate philanthropy has been applied chiefly on an unre-stricted basis to colleges and universities and has thus served to help maintain some of the central functions of the institutions. Many feel that such modes of aid buttress the maintenance of what might be, or ought to be, changed in educational patterns. Others hold—with this observer —that such modes of giving impart strength to what has been proved to be of recognizable value at the heart of the educational process: tradi-tion and experience in the encouragement of learning.

The prospect for continued growth of foundations is positive, both as to the initial creation of new pools of philanthropy and total pay-out, be-cause investment tends to be increasing in common stocks and other secu-rities which "move with inflation." The total capital accumulation of some ten thousand foundations today is well above $7 billion, and may become much larger. The penalties applied on "unreasonable accumulations" of income earned on capital investments of foundations also tend to push annual grant outlay upward. Interrelated are possible shifts in policy with regard to invasion of original capital of foundations, the taking of capital gains on investments at periodic intervals, and associated capital-management problems. The daily press regularly records the creation of new foundations, frequently with assets in the range of $25 million to $50 million. The Hartford family, in recently creating a major new foun-dation from ownership of A & P stock valued at hundreds of millions of dollars, is illustrative of one development; the growth of funding of cor-porate foundations with resources to meet program needs for five to ten years ahead is another episodic indicator of future philanthropic capital developments. Political concern with the foundation is an unknown but potent factor which could increase or diminish otherwise freely develop-ing trends.

Support by Individuals

Another primary source of support for private colleges and universities long has been, and continues to be, the gifts of individuals who mostly are not graduates of institutions they assist. They provide about $135 million of annual benefactions. Psychologists, sociologists, anthropologists, and others have plotted the conditions and motivations that produce this re-sult. Economists and others have evaluated the income flows, the inci-dences of taxation, and other circumstances which condition the practice of philanthropy by givers to charity, science, and education. Aside from such factors as incentive taxation and availability of disposable income, the individual as philanthropist—great or small—still appears to be heavily imbued with the spirit of "community" which so astonished Count de Tocqueville. Many of our civic leaders continue to be self-made in the sense of not having been privileged to attend institutions of higher learning. Substantial numbers of individual fortunes also continue to be created despite the ravages of surtax rates on individual incomes and the inhibitions of capital gains and estate taxation. Also, many of the public-spirited community and national leaders of today are men of wide vision whose longer-surviving spouses commonly wish to emulate their examples and, as frequently, to memorialize them.

A significant element of individual giving to higher education relates to the large personal benefactions of many of the approximately fifty thousand trustees of public and private institutions. Associated with such giving are the individual benefactions made by members of advisory councils and by major civic leadership assuming responsibility for large-scale capital and operating-fund campaigns. Such individuals also affect the flows of private-sector support to the extent that they manage and supervise the financial resources of institutions by investment counsel, by determining the realities involved in proposed plant and operational programs, by ascertaining and publicizing actual costs, and by diverse other means.

The forward "ability" of individuals to contribute to higher education —assuming they are motivated to do so—is revealed in current individual income data. Whatever the complete list of complex and mutually interacting motives involved—ranging from narrowly based status seeking to the noblest impulse of which mankind is capable—the record is clear that a larger, and probably enlarging, segment of non-college and non-university graduates appreciates the financial needs of education for a growing and expanding society and for general culture. No one knows whether the optimum point has been approached in this area of support. The prospect appears strong that in absolute, if not relative terms, support of colleges and universities by non-alumni individuals may be expected to rise steadily in the years ahead.

Church Support

President John Millett, of Miami University, and his associates, in the fundamental study, *Financing Higher Education in the United States,* succinctly summarized the prospect for higher education aid as to church support in these terms:

> The essence of the matter is whether churches can tap the disposition or willingness of thousands of individuals to give to charitable and educational purposes more effectively than can the colleges themselves. If we reduce the relationship of churches to higher education to a purely finan-

cial basis—which is not and cannot be the whole of it—then we might say that many colleges veered away from their church affiliations when they found their own separate sources of gift support and that they have tended to re-establish their affiliations as their financial needs have increased.

Although about half of the $7 billion total of private philanthropy of the nation goes to the support of religion, no one knows the exact portion accruing—through religious channels—to higher educational institutions. Contributed services of religious orders, for example, are difficult to measure except on numerous variable assumptions, and the share of the faculty load taken by the religious orders—which some believe to be steadily declining—is not known.

Although the absolute dollar total provided to higher education by churches appears to reflect an increase, year by year, the total dollars involved may be less imposing than many would expect. Hundreds of our colleges and universities were founded, and in early days almost wholly financed, by the church. Today some of our great institutions identified as having religious ties receive absolutely no income from church sources. Currently, perhaps in harmony with the summary issue framed by Dr. Millett, there is a marked revival of interest, college by college, denomination by denomination, in better support of church-related institutions. Also, one new trend is that, on a national level, a few foundations have been established to make funds available for religious education.

One recent study indicates that $428 million was contributed in 1957 to the collections of only fifty-two Protestant groups affiliated with the National Council of Churches. Perhaps as much as from 10 to 20 per cent of such sums may have accrued to the benefit of selected Protestant church-related institutions of higher education. Four major Protestant communions now have formally organized offices dedicated to the generation of funds for the aid of educational institutions related to their respective denominations. Official Catholic sources are unable to supply precise data about financial aid to Catholic higher educational institutions. Of the 5.3 million Catholic and non-Catholic students attending *all* levels of Catholic educational institutions—primary grades through graduate study—some 400,000 are enrolled in colleges and universities. Calculated from the projection of an estimate of per-student-per-day dollar expenditures base, one can arrive at upwards of $30 million as the sum annually provided by Catholic sources for their church-related institutions of higher learning. About 90 per cent of these institutions are believed to be oriented toward the various orders of the mother church. There has not been made any public study that indicates the extent of financial support offered such Catholic institutions and universities by their respective orders. It is understood that intensive investigation relating to higher education assistance is now, or soon will be, underway by both Catholic and Protestant organizations. Assistance of higher education by the Jewish faith is concentrated in three or four major Jewish universities and colleges. Various indicators, inclusive of an estimate for contributed religious services, would place total current support of colleges and universities from all religious sources at about $125 million annually.

During recent decades, especially in America, there have been fundamental shifts in educational philosophy and educational structure as bearing upon higher education where operated and curricula-influenced by religious organizations—within and without the "separation of church and state" issue. The recent conference on "The State of Studies, Research, and Teaching in the History of Religions" (April, 1959, Chicago), sponsored by the American Council of Learned Societies, reached two major conclusions: that the number of competent scholars in the field is unfortunately small and that the need for properly trained teachers is great at the undergraduate level. The proceedings of the conference[3] deserve full-scale attention in connection with both the matter of educational product and financial assistance.

Bequest Support

Until recently bequest support generally has been catalyzed in a haphazard manner, except in the instances of the major universities and selected high-prestige institutions. Such universities and colleges are not now alone, however, in emphasizing this channel of fund raising. An increasing number of the more alert colleges throughout the nation are energetically pursuing this source of funds. For example, distinguished Knox College, in Illinois, expects that, over the next twenty-five years, at least 50 per cent of its total gifts will come in the form of bequests and trusts. This ratio already has been achieved for the current year. The prospect for bequest giving is, of course, associated with the trend in number of children per family and their lifetime needs, with the considerations of heavy estate taxation when residual fortunes are not given to philanthropic purposes, or with the need to reserve—until death of the family head—larger shares of resources as a partial hedge against inflation or as a means of safeguarding family interests in closely held economic activities. In the most recent fiscal year for which data are available the Council for Financial Aid to Education report, *Voluntary Support of America's Colleges and Universities,* revealed that 766 degree-granting institutions reported $89 million in bequests and estate arrangements, including trust annuities and life contracts. The latter types of instruments alone already provide at least $16 million annually, according to the same source.[4]

Many forms of new businesses, new national and international types of natural-resource investment, new fabrication, power, and communication industries, new modes of domestic and international distribution have been created in recent times. All have some tendency to make for the growth of profitable family-held businesses. Gifts to education *inter vivos* and upon death are increasingly a part of family estate planning, determined against the factors involved.

New patents and invention rights arising from the new techniques are other forms of assistance possibilities evolving through the concatenation of many influences. One of the major state universities, Wisconsin, has a major source of unrestricted revenue for perhaps decades to come because of its holding long-term patent rights donated to it by a loyal alumnus.

Out ahead, shifts in family patterns such as an increase in the number of spinsters and widows as a share of the total population, the assumption under welfare-state concepts of the care of minors and incompetents, and numerous other sociological factors including the number of marriages and the ages at which marriage is contracted could well have a net tendency to increase both the absolute and relative volume of bequests.

Directly associated with the estate and bequest problem are many ingenious life insurance, bond purchase, reserved annuity, and trust arrangements possible under existing tax laws and regulations. The intricate and complex factors involved (as in the single example of reciprocal exemption of gifts as between state jurisdictions) are not possible of detailing here. But enough experience has been gained in pioneering such arrangements to indicate that considerable promise exists for enlargement of new types of bequests and *inter vivos* giving. Bequests, while tending to be increasingly of an unrestricted character, also often assist major endowment campaigns.

Labor Union Support

Labor unions are a new source of educational philanthropy, and one which may be expanding. In many geographical centers unions have been active in higher education fund raising. Many unions have substantial student-assistance funds in operation, a number of them on a national scale. Also, the union movement has seen the creation of several large, broadly chartered philanthropic foundations, such as the Philip Murray, Sidney Hillman, and William Green foundations, from the resources of which substantial grants are made for the capital, operating, or other needs of selected colleges and universities and other forms of education. One estimate of dollar support, provided by Dr. John D. Connors, Director of the Department of Education, AFL-CIO, suggests that the sums accruing to the colleges, institutes, and universities from unions already may have reached an annual level of $1 million. Of this total, scholarship aid alone may amount to $500,000. Holding that expenditures flowing from the private sectors are inadequate to fill the need, the AFL-CIO has advocated federally financed scholarships for the best students.

The action which some believe characterized union interest in earlier years toward immediacy of concern for only selected areas—certain types of skill and training and those educational projects directly related to their current primary concerns—appears to some observers as having given way to a broader and more sustained fundamental range of activities. Such activities imply some sharing of responsibility, with other private-sector segments, for financing American higher education. Various socio-logical, scientific, and technological shifts that are occurring well may rapidly accelerate the incidence, form, and frequency of union interest in all levels of education. For example, in a major recent study of needs, programs, and approaches to labor education by Joseph Mire, on behalf of the Inter-University Labor Education Committee, special recommen-dations were made for future consideration of educational aid relating to international affairs, community relations, health, automation, general culture activities, intergroup relations, libraries, and communications.

Entrepreneurial and Auxiliary Sources of Support

Entrepreneurial income of institutions, under interdiction of rulings by the Bureau of Internal Revenue Service and tax courts cases, may not be regarded as a major future source of funds. The purchase and operation for profit of outside-enterprise businesses by colleges and universities is not allowed to stand, tax free, along with the privileges of escape from taxation as eleemosynary institutions. This public-policy position inhibits earlier efforts launched by colleges and universities to acquire profit-mak-ing businesses, as illustrated in the so-called "macaroni case" in which New York University was an interested party. Profits after taxes, where applicable, on income from operations of book stores, eating facilities, dormitories, and other auxiliary activities such as radio and television stations are substantial in dollars; they perhaps total in excess of $50 million. But inherent in these operations is not the maximum enhance-ment of income but the maximum service potential at reasonable, and usually at the lowest, cost. These entrepreneurial and auxiliary-resource avenues may be expected to increase over present dollar totals absolutely, but perhaps not markedly in relative terms, if allowance be made for price levels changes. This conclusion, of course, does not comprehend the very large-scale contract research activities which may generate major entrepreneurial resources.

Government Assistance to Higher Education

As has been noted, the flow of funds to higher education from the pri-vate sector can be decisively affected by the volume and nature of the flow of funds from the public sector. Hence, in a fully balanced survey of the potentialities of private support, account must be taken of inter-locking government financial undertakings in support of higher educa-tion. Here, because of space limitation, no more than the impressionistic outlines of such an account can be provided.

It is difficult to arrive at a satisfactory dollar-sum estimate for all forms of government aid. For private colleges alone the sums allocated to col-leges and universities from all governments—directly—probably range annually from a minimum of about $70 million to well over $100 million. Another approach to some reasonabe indication of immediate governmen-tal money flows is through examination of such survey data as are avail-able on the point from the Office of Education.[5]

All levels of government are providing $1,592 million in the year for operational budgets. Of this total, $1,524 million goes to public institu-tions and $67 million to private institutions. Of the total, Federal moneys represent $195 million (private colleges receiving $28 million thereof); local governments provide $149 million (private colleges receiving less than $4 million thereof); and state governments provide the balance of $1,248 million (private colleges receiving only about $35 million thereof).

For capital budgets, direct governmental support and taxes levied for specific application from all levels of government amount to $279 million, all but 1.7 per cent of which is for public institutions. (If bonds, fre-quently guaranteed by state and local governments, are added, then with-out regard to other forms of borrowing, governments may be deemed to have supplied an additional $187 million for capital needs, all but 4.6 per cent of which is for public institutions.)

Government versus Private-sector Capital Aid

An illustration of the clouding over of possible areas of action by pri-vate sectors is found in the capital aid programs of the national govern-ment. The Federal government, as exemplified in the 86th Congress, is considering a threefold approach to the best means of solving higher education's capital needs problems.

The first approach relates to the nine-year history of the College Hous-ing Loan Program which was thrown over by the President's veto of the 1959 omnibus general public housing bill of which the program was a part. This ended the availability of low-interest Federal loans to build college dormitories and other self-liquidating projects. The bill would have provided nearly $300 million of additional assistance.

A second method by which the Federal government would support the capital needs is the administration's proposal to elevate the issue to a position of greater importance by treating it as a problem distinct from the total national housing needs. Federal guarantee of principal and interest payment of privately arranged loans (including debt-retirement assistance to a total value of $1 billion of long-term bonds available for construction of science and engineering facilities) up to now has met with less enthusiasm in Congress than the direct-loan method of the earlier program.

A third approach, one new to the Federal scene and contained in both the original housing bill and the administration's proposals, is a provision for the *total* campus capital needs—classrooms, laboratories, etc.—and not for self-liquidating facilities alone.

Private sectors could assume at least a substantial share of the burden if they chose to create a large pool of private capital from which educational institutions could borrow at low or no interest, coupled with support from alumni and other sources. One means to encourage such pools might be to allow donors a special tax credit beyond the usual 5 per cent. Some have advocated a 100 per cent tax credit for educational construction. Such credits would allow corporations to allocate tax funds without having to pay for the right to make such decisions. (At present, donors take at least part of the responsibility by putting up part of the funds from their own profits.)

Public versus Private Scholarship Aid

An area of governmental action influencing private-sector money flows is that of scholarships. The Federal government has not entered directly upon a national policy of scholarship assistance. There have been numerous proposals—many are currently pending in Congress—to provide large-scale scholarship assistance with or without a means or needs test. One of them, proposed during the administration of President Harry Truman as a rider to the then current so-called Oil Tidelands Bill (offered before the Supreme Court acted), would have utilized royalties therein involved to provide upwards of 200,000 Federal scholarships As inflation continues, as tuition or other elements of educational cost rise, the political pressures for action on this front may be translated into definitive measures, which will further involve the national government in financing higher education. Other proposals would involve joint state-Federal scholarship efforts. Most of the states of major population and economic import already have large-scale scholarship programs, chiefly based on competitive ability, political sponsorship, and means-test eligibility requirements.

At the state government level, action representative of the new trends in scholarship aid is that currently taken in New Jersey. A state scholarship commission is about to begin operation of a plan to provide $400 of assistance to "needy freshmen," with an estimated 5 *per cent of all New Jersey high school graduates* becoming eligible. This program replaces an earlier plan for assistance to students entering the state university and the six state teachers colleges. *The new scholarships may be used at private, public, and religious institutions.*

Private scholarship plans have been a feature of private-sector national life from the earliest phase of the colonial period. Until very recently private plans have been increasing steadily in number, diversity, and volume of benefit. The private scholarships of all types provided yearly are estimated to total 265,000 at present. The annual benefits from them are estimated at $84 million, including those made available chiefly from originally supplied private-sector voluntary resources. The magnitude of proposals for governmental intervention in the field appears to have slowed private-sector scholarship expansion, but with significant qualifications.

When attention was turned to devising the most effective methods for conducting a private-sector nationwide selection of able students, and for developing a program offering maximum stimulation for all who participated, the National Merit Scholarship program was developed.

Since the inception of the Merit Scholarship program—originally sponsored by the Ford Foundation and the Carnegie Corporation and now participated in by scores of other donors including many corporations and corporate-financed foundations—more than 1.5 million high school students have been tested. Participation now extends to some 15,000 of the nation's high schools. Approximately $16 million in scholarship aid has been committed. Over three thousand of the nation's most able students hold scholarships at some four hundred colleges. Tens of thousands have received the necessary encouragement to continue their education.

Government versus Private-sector Loans

The National Defense Education Act of 1958 authorized the expenditure of nearly $300 million over the succeeding four years in student loans. Although it is too early to conclude whether this step in Federal action is a permanent feature of the landscape, it already serves to pronounce a current national policy on the loan side of the picture. The Secretary of Health, Education and Welfare, under whose jurisdiction the program operates, stated on July 28, 1959, that nearly 121,000 college and university students in 1,372 participating institutions were expected to seek loans (averaging $500) under the Act during the next academic year. This will represent about 5½ per cent of the anticipated full-time enrollment. Against these estimates, the institutions will supply, as their required participation share, the outlay of 10 per cent of the total loaned;

the latter is estimated to aggregate about $60 million for the ensuing academic year.

Private loan funds, the future of which may be heavily conditioned by governmental student aid ventures and numerous proposed state and Federal scholarship aid plans, long have been significant. These private plans in 1957–58 already were providing in excess of $100 million in assistance. Various long-term loan plans of religious organizations, business and professional organizations, commercial banks, fraternal orders, and others, have made it possible for more than 100,000 to remain in college and complete their education.

Many banks throughout the nation have loan plans, and the number is growing. For example, Massachusetts banks that are participating in the Massachusetts Higher Education Assistance Corporation loan program have loaned approximately $1.3 million to 2,000 students within the twelve months ending April, 1959. An even larger sum was loaned in New York under a somewhat similar plan. A like program exists in Maine, and other plans have been authorized in Connecticut, Rhode Island, New Jersey, and Indiana. Despite the action taken at the Federal level, many feel that private long-term loans could become the major vehicle through which educational opportunity is extended to all economically handicapped high school graduates with the ability and motivation to attend college. A study by the College Life Insurance Company, of Indianapolis, reveals the recent growth and strength of this movement for private loan fund resources. Dr. W.W. Hill, Jr., director of educational research for that company, predicts that in less than ten years the annual borrowing, in all forms and under all plans, for college education will exceed $1 billion and be maintained at a high rate for a long period.

In addition to the other programs indicated, hundreds of colleges operate their own loan plans. At Harvard, loans increased from an annual rate of $10,000 in 1949 to a rate of $400,000 in 1959. The College Entrance Examination Board estimates that in the future from one-fourth to one-third of all students will be involved in loans.

The present national policy on Federal loans is, of course, a route chosen to honor the idea of self-help, but it is also a current political means of avoiding what many consider to be a serious "separation of church and state" issue in connection with the major effort of many groups and leaders to obtain various forms of Federal aid to education. All Federal and state aid programs of whatever character make the institutions, in ultimate economic aspects, semipublic. This is true because all participating institutions receive public aid through the student payments. Stating the matter another way, such plans may be said to provide education at a lower unit cost to taxpayers while keeping certain institutions from bankruptcy.

Government versus Private-sector Fellowships

As with scholarships and loans, private-sector action in the fellowship field is related to the impact of various governmental aid plans for graduate study fellowship support, chiefly at the master and doctoral degree levels. Government agencies at the Federal level already have expended or committed hundreds of millions of dollars in this area. In a recent year, for example, an aggregate in excess of $25 million was expended by but four Federal offices in support of pre- and postdoctoral graduate study. Within this group were the National Institutes of Health, supporting nearly 1,500 fellows at a cost of about $6.5 million. The Office of Education, under the provisions of the National Defense Education Act, was authorized to award 1,000 predoctoral fellowships costing $4.9 million annually. The Atomic Energy Commission sponsors some 300 fellowships worth nearly $1 million yearly. Most significant also is the current $13 million annual expenditure of the wholly government-financed National Science Foundation, which, within its seven programs, will assist 3,670 pre- and postdoctoral students in their studies in American and foreign universities during a single year.

Much greater in coverage is the indirect support to higher education students and their facilities through Federal research contracts with universities. The Bureau of the Budget estimates that 22,000 to 25,000 research assistants benefit from these contracts annually. In addition, one of the above-cited agencies devotes $50 million in a year to trainee programs.

The large-scale infusion of these Federal programs has enormously expanded the national higher education establishment, even though the fellowships are for the most part confined to relatively few disciplines—chiefly the natural and physical sciences—and notwithstanding the repeated claim that many of the research contracts impose an undue, and sometimes not cost-recouped, financial outlay upon the institutions.

Positioned against this all-Federal effort, which is mostly of quite recent origin, is the complex of fellowship grants developed slowly over a period of two centuries, initially by individual donors to the institutions and more recently expanded by business, corporate foundation, and general-welfare foundation support. Of institutions offering graduate work, 406 recently reported the annual availability of nearly 25,000 such private fellowships with an aggregate worth in excess of $18 million.

Tax Incidences and Private-sector Money Flows

A central danger to the successful assumption of reasonable and adequate shares of the total financing problem of higher education by private sectors would be dominance of a view that government should be the chief supporter of the national educational budget and that, in any event, higher educational financing is merely a simple, straightaway choice in the incidence of individual and business taxation. What is centrally required is a clear demonstration that the democratic process may best function if private sectors adopt whatever policies and practices are feasible to ensure an enlarged and continuous flow of resources to all forms of higher education. The alternative is a direct invitation to full absorption of responsibility by political means.

Dr. Clifford C. Furnas, Chancellor of the University of Buffalo, recently proposed that Federal taxpayers, corporate and individual, be allowed to deduct a certain amount from their tax bills and contribute the money directly to public and private colleges and universities. On the simplest level, this would mean that an individual with a Federal income tax bill of $100 could give $5 to a college or university and pay the remaining $95 to the Bureau of Internal Revenue Service. Corporations likewise, under this plan, would be allowed to contribute 5 per cent of their tax bills directly to institutions approved by the Office of Education. Dr. Furnas estimates that this would promptly quadruple the amount now raised by private voluntary contributions. He also advocates a kindred policy by each state. Otherwise, to meet the cost of education, he estimates that private philanthropy would have to reach, for education alone and without regard to other philanthropic needs, the figure of a minimum of $2 billion by 1970, and that tax support for higher education would have to rise by 257 per cent.

He argues that, while this plan amounts to letting individuals and corporations distribute what would be tax money to education as they might see fit, the method is in the spirit of private enterprise and would lower the direct tax burden for education.

Under the present Federal tax law individuals can deduct 20 per cent of their adjusted gross income (and under certain conditions 30 per cent) for charitable and educational contributions and corporations get a similar deduction of 5 per cent of their taxable income, before Federal income taxes, in any one year. Such deductions do reduce an individual or corporate tax bill, but they are partial rather than full tax credits. As an example, $1 given to education by an individual in the highest income group still costs that person 9 cents.

Some hold that dependence of educational institutions on corporate-derived support, stimulated by the present 5 per cent contribution tax provision or by other incentives, may develop a vested interest in a tax structure that is burdensome to society.

Many believe it would be better policy to work for revision of the present onerous system of high corporation and individual tax rates and thus gain funds through the increased gifts—and incentives therefore—by individual donors. There have been studies which suggest that tax revenues would not be reduced by a repeal of the corporate tax and might even be increased, because of the gain in receipts from individual income taxes.

The habit of giving by individuals is well established, and the gain either through increased incomes and dividends or increased retained earnings, which enter into the individual expenditure calculus, would provide, many believe, the stimulus for larger private contributions. Higher tuitions then could be charged against this higher income. The decision to pay the cost of education would then lie with the individual families.

The most common objection to approaches which provide individual tax allowance credits is that it is not politically feasible, particularly in the next decade, which is one of especially heavy crisis in higher educational finance. The more fundamental objection to this and other plans is that they further erode the tax base with no immediate provision for offsetting the loss of Federal revenues.

A tax credit for tuition-paying families is resisted on the ground that it would give tax credits to families without regard to their needs and therefore cause a wasteful diminution of the tax revenues.

Families facing the cost of college education for a child must expect to run into a sudden heavy expense of about the same magnitude as that of buying a house. Unfortunately there is no mortgage market in college education, nor is there fully balanced and adequate consumer credit, despite the indicated value of private college loans.

What may be needed is a combination instrument which will provide for savings, hedge against inflation, insure to some degree the income earner of the family, and provide a penalty for discontinuance and afford substantial reward. A special Treasury saving bond has been proposed as one step in this direction. Alternatively, perhaps what may be needed for educational financing is something like the private savings and loan associations which did so much to effect the financing of housing.

Tuition Payments within the Private Sector

The largest single element of resource for private college and university financing is student tuition. Tuition also is a small but increasing factor in the over-all financing of tax-based institutions. Educators and administrators are sharply divided, along with various educational finance experts, on the issue of whether tuitions and fees can be, or should be, markedly increased. But subsidies can end only with pricing at or near full costs!

A few over-all conclusions appear reasonable. With inflation, tuition costs in both the public and private institutions will rise. With the rise in tuition cost, the residual sums required from public sources and private sectors could be altered on a short-term basis, but with the prospect that because of a series of associated variable social factors, there could result a net long-term increase in additional money flows required.

The Forward Total Needs

This summary of the support record and prospect by the various sub-components of major moment in the total private sector, covering alumni, corporate aid, foundations, individuals, churches, bequest gifts, labor unions, and government, seeks to bring together an answer to the question raised at the outset. What is the prospect for the adequacy of private-sector aid? A final means toward discovery of the answer to this question is through a brief examination of the magnitude of the forward budgetary requirements in the years ahead, that is, balancing out the support prospect against the needs of the nearly 700 publicly controlled, and 1,300 private and church-related colleges and universities, now serving about 3.5 million full- and part-time students.

The 1958–59 budget estimates of the Office of Education as to income and unmet financial needs of the approximately two thousand institutions are some evidence of the needs. From these data it is seen that for the year *the unbudgeted current operating deficit and unmet capital needs* account for $824 million of the $5,140 million of *total* expenditure for all institutions. (It should be recalled also that there is a *backlog* of unmet capital need, accumulating since World War I, which has been estimated at $1.6 billion.)

The uses of the 1958–59 budgeted income for operation and capital purposes are suggested by major categories in data also compiled by the Office of Education. Of the operating expenditure total, about 60 per cent is scheduled to be spent for higher education in public, and about 40 per cent in private, institutions. This distribution parallels rather closely the distribution of students between public and private colleges, but the minor difference in ratio may also indicate that private colleges, in general, are supporting their operations less well *per student* than are public institutions.

A detailed examination of the above-indicated data would reveal that the chief reliance of private institutions is upon tuition and fees paid by students and that the second most important means of support is philanthropy. Conversely, it is seen that public colleges and universities rely largely on tax sources. The long-term trend of sources of income for both public and private institutions is shown in Table 4.

Other data indicate the estimated 1958–59 amount of money budgeted for capital purposes. Examination of such facts reveals that private col-

Table 4. Long-term Trend of Sources of Income

Year	Tuitions and fees	Support from governments	Gifts and grants	Endowment earnings	Other sources	Total, $ million
1943–44	17.9%	59.0%	5.8%	8.7%	8.6%	864
1949–50	21.5	58.8	6.5	5.2	8.0	1,834
1953–54	23.5	53.4	8.2	5.4	9.5	2,357
1955–56	25.2	51.6	8.6	5.1	9.5	2,859
1956–57	25.3	50.3	9.9	4.9	9.6	3,194
1957–58	25.3	48.9	11.5	4.6	9.7	3,580

NOTES: The data relates to educational and general income of colleges and universities. With the exception of the projections for 1956–57 and 1957–58, the figures in these tables are taken from the biennial *Statistics of Education: Receipts, Expenditures and Property*, published by the Office of Education. Data are for continental United States only. Projections for 1956–57 and 1957–58 are based on average rates of growth in the years 1949–50 through 1955–56, with adjustments based on factors determined by surveys. Data are for both public and private institutions.

SOURCE: Council for Financial Aid to Education, *Where's The Money Coming From–?*

leges and universities are receiving from the American public a proportion of capital funds for plant development smaller than the proportion they are receiving from the same source for current support purposes, namely, 38 per cent of the capital budget as compared to more than 40 per cent of the current operational support budget. This may indicate that private colleges and universities are losing the race for plant resource development more rapidly than they are losing the race for current operating resource support. Further examination of the major sources of support for capital purposes reveals the chief reliance of public institutions upon governmental appropriations and of private institutions upon benefactions. Private colleges and universities plan to issue bonds (or otherwise borrow funds) for less than 29 per cent of their budgeted capital needs as compared to about 36 per cent for public institutions. The trend of investment in plant, by types of institution, is shown in Table 5.

One may project the cost of operating the American system of higher education in terms of children (along with various other assumptions) who have already entered the elementary school and who will be seeking entrance to college in the decade ahead. All projections, although necessarily highly qualified, do assist in visualization of some of the financial answers. Over the next decade, assuming a nonfluctuating dollar, along with numerous other variables, it is estimated by the Office of Education that the total cost of meeting building needs and other *capital* requirements will approximate $15.3 billion, three times the current annual outlays. It also

Table 5. Trend of Investment in Plant, by Types of Institutions
(In millions of dollars)

Type of institution	Total cost of new construction, Sept. '54–Aug. '57	Cost of buildings constructed 1957–58	Cost of buildings constructed or contemplated, 1958–59	Average yearly plant outlay	Index: current ratio to 1954–57 taken as 100	Estimated needs for new facilities, Sept. '57–Aug. '67
Major private universities (48)*	$ 200.8 (45)	$ 76.3 (34)	$ 220.9 (39)	$ 5.7	381	$1,030 (48)
State universities and land-grant colleges (55)	411.2 (51)	198.0 (48)	644.4 (53)	12.2	352	2,483 (52)
State colleges (102)	136.2 (78)	62.7 (54)	187.1 (84)	2.2	283	740 (96)
Private men's colleges (44)	33.5 (34)	24.9 (26)	42.1 (38)	1.1	338	115 (42)
Private women's colleges (100)	44.4 (52)	21.8 (30)	50.5 (50)	1.0	353	243 (89)
Private coeducational colleges (276)	163.2 (208)	74.8 (143)	154.5 (179)	.9	329	779 (269)
Private professional and technical schools (56)	22.4 (25)	14.5 (17)	22.9 (23)	1.0	334	211 (49)
Municipal colleges and universities (12)	29.5 (10)	16.6 (8)	34.0 (10)	3.4	351	67 (7)
Junior colleges (192)	53.5 (94)	36.4 (57)	101.6 (95)	1.1	563	373 (168)
	$1,093.5 (597)	$526.0 (417)	$1,458.0 (571)	$ 2.6	347 (Pr.) 387 (Pub.)	$6,041 (820) †

* Numbers in parentheses are the number of institutions in survey sample.
† If projected to 1,889 institutions, the estimated total is $11.4 billion for the period Sept. 1, 1957 to Aug. 31, 1967.
SOURCE: Council for Financial Aid to Education, *Nearing the Breakthrough*.

estimates that, in the year 1967–68, the total budget of higher education institutions for educational and general purposes will approximate more than *three* times the budgeted expenditure for 1958–59. Various others have made more conservative, and some believe, more realistic, estimates. Economist Dr. Seymour Harris, of Harvard University, for example, arrives at expenditures of $9,800 million for only educational, general, and student aid needs, or expenditures which only double current levels. His estimate includes allowance for substantial reduction in total outlays arising from efficiencies to be gained in operations and management.

The Future Shares of Support within Private Sectors

From what sources may we expect to receive large-scale sums for future operational support and additional heavy outlays for capital improvements, assuming the lower estimate of needs? No one can see far enough into the future to predict with certainty that the major sources of current income can be expanded to provide for the greatly increased financial needs of higher education. Certainly it is not safe to assume that a decade hence these sources will be providing the same percentages of income that they provide today. The future holds too many imponderables to permit estimates whether tuition and fees may be doubled or tripled, whether individual and corporate philanthropies will contribute a larger share than at present, and what shares Federal, state, and local governments will contribute. The Council for Financial Aid to Education has estimated that in the year 1969–70, individual and corporate philanthropy will be contributing $1.9 billion to the *current and capital* support of higher education in the United States. This would be more than twice the 1959 contribution of $900 million, if the Association of Fund-Raising Counsel estimates be taken as a base. Certainly, annual private-sector support to *private* higher education would have to be at least doubled by the end of the next decade if all such institutions are to succeed in expanding their physical plants, improving their programs, and maintaining faculty salaries at a realistic level, while retaining its current relative position in the total educational structure.

A failure of private sectors out ahead to provide their appropriate shares of education could contribute to a possible serious deterioration of educational quality. The public opinion consequences of this probably would bring about the necessary readjustments in financing but perhaps only after a period of low-grade higher education might have been experienced. This is neither needful nor inevitable.

What role will government have in this situation? The character and volume of future governmental support of higher education contain ingredients of fundamental import to the future of our society. Commingled with government action are the consents as to tax flows derived from private sectors, private-sector tuition payments, and private-sector benefactions. The social policies at issue are focused in University of Illinois President David D. Henry's statement in the *Educational Record* (July 1959) and by such differing approaches as these:

> It is not necessary to take a strong, entrenched position on either side of this doctrinal battle. A clear grasp of the issues leads one to accept certain arguments from both sides. American higher education is in desperate straits with respect to its financial future. This is a matter of national importance. If it is to be solved, all of the groups which have an interest in solving it must play an appropriate part. A healthy pattern of financing will involve contributions from many sources—students, alumni, the states, the Federal government, business corporations and philanthropic sources.[6]

> An increase in government activity is not necessarily evil in itself—the central question is whether the government activity actually provides a needed and constructive service for the people. The absence of wise and prudent government action can be more costly in the long run. Sumner Slichter, of Harvard, has spoken persuasively on the theme that our government is not merely an expense—it is a service-rendering organization that repays its costs many-fold in the services it renders![7]

Businessmen and economists, polled about the central thesis of John Kenneth Galbraith's long-time best seller, *The Affluent Society*—that we need to deemphasize material motivations and enhance the public affairs interests correspondingly—generally disagreed with him. But one aspect of the poll taking is significant for financing higher education. Asked if there should be increased opportunity for education of the economically less privileged and if more emphasis is needed upon the cultivation and education of America's human resources which stress the development of applied intelligence and creativeness, a clear majority of the several thousand businessmen and the hundreds of economists interviewed unqualifiedly *agreed*. This observer considers such an attitude to be a portent of the directional movement of the American people in the period ahead as the great debate on the educational "what," "how," and "amount" moves into a definitive action stage. Whatever the quantitative dollar-support and participation outcome, the vital share underwritten by the private sectors will serve to protect freedom, encourage diversity, add strength, and undergird the other essential elements of American higher education.

Notes

1. Such estimate excludes the administrative costs of corporate philanthropy which, for thirty thousand or more companies, may aggregate some millions of dollars.

2. For a differing concept see "Corporate Giving: Theory and Policy," by Richard Eells, *California Management Review*, vol. 1, no. 1, 1958. See also "The Emerging Pattern of Corporate Philanthropy" and "Next Steps in Community Leadership," both by W. Homer Turner, U.S. Steel Foundation, 1958.

3. American Council of Learned Societies, *Newsletter*, vol. 10, no. 5, June, 1959.

4. The Bureau of Internal Revenue Service reported in 1956 that there were more than 400,000 estates and trusts, of which some 12,000 claimed deductions for contributions.

5. No one knows the full amount of Federal government aid to education. One recent Office of Education publication describes 137 Federal educational activities costing approximately $2 billion annually; the same publication states there may be as many as 300 programs if *all* Federal activities in *all* forms of education, at *all* levels, be counted.

6. Carnegie Foundation for the Advancement of Teaching, *Annual Report, 1956-57*.

7. Former Secretary of Health, Education and Welfare, Marion Folsom, *Proceedings of the American Philosophical Society*, August, 1958.

11

Potentialities of Educational Establishments Outside the Conventional Structure of Higher Education

Harold F. Clark

In simple agricultural societies one can obtain a fairly satisfactory education by growing up in the community. In early commercial and trading societies a limited education for some part of the population is almost a necessity. Some of this education may have to be provided by formal educational institutions. In the early stages of industrial societies formal education becomes necessary for larger and larger fractions of the population. This education is normally provided in the early years of life. We customarily say people need to go to school from six to eighteen, or possibly twenty-two or twenty-five years of age. In addition to this education of the young, in highly complicated and dynamic industrial societies continuous and fairly systematic education must extend through essentially the entire working life of very large fractions of the population, or from ages twenty-two to sixty-five.

The United States is now in the process of moving from the earlier stage of industrialism, involving primarily the education of the young, to the highly technical industrialism that is increasingly involving the continuous education of much of the working part of the population.

There was a time, even in the early part of the twentieth century, when you got an education, then you went to work. No more inaccurate statement could be made today. Any campaign to encourage people to get their education before they start to work is likely to mislead people. Such an idea misses the very nature of our modern industrial society.

The education of the nineteenth century—elementary, high school, college and university—has clearly become inadequate to deal with the modern technological world. This statement does not mean that the earlier type of education has become unnecessary or unimportant—it has, in fact, become more necessary and important—but such a conception of education has become totally inadequate to deal with the world into which we are now rapidly moving. The old, historic type of education has become only one part of an extraordinarily complicated and complex procedure. Some parts of these new procedures are developing so rapidly that it may be another generation or two before we can get any very satisfactory picture of how the total educational program will look over the longer period.

This new type of education could be classified in many different ways. As one method of trying to gain some picture of our total educational development, it may be helpful to group the education around four large methods of organization. We might be justified in calling them four major systems, or ways, of carrying on education. It might be technically somewhat more accurate to say they are four parts of the total educational process now going on in the United States.

The first educational system would be the regular historic system of education composed of the elementary school, high school, college, and university. The second educational system would be the elaborate programs that have grown up in the course of dealing with research, development, training, and education in business and industry. The third is the educational program that is carried on by an extremely large number of organzations of all types in the United States. Some estimates indicate that perhaps as many as five thousand organizations carry on some type of educational program. The fourth system would be the elaborate procedures that have been developed by which people go on with their own education after they leave what we have called the historic formal system.

An extremely brief description will be given of each of the three systems other than the regular historic system of education.

Education Offered by Industry

Business and industry have set up a system of research, development, education, and training that rivals in size and complexity the regular system of higher education in colleges and universities. A brief discussion of the program of research and development in industry may give some faint indication of what is happening.

Program of Research and Development in Industry. Industry is spending $7 billion to $8 billion on research and development. Some 200,000 engineers and scientists and some 200,000 highly trained technical workers are involved in the work. It is interesting to keep in mind that the total staff of all the colleges and universities for all purposes is of the order of 200,000. It would seem to be reasonable to state that business and industry are using about as many scientists and engineers in research and development as the colleges and universities are using staff for all purposes.

Both the figures reported each year by McGraw-Hill and those given by the National Science Foundation would indicate that the colleges and universities are doing something of the order of 8 or 10 per cent of the total research and development in the country and are providing from their own funds roughly 2 or 3 per cent of the total amount of money spent on research. The recent report of the National Science Foundation indicates that the equivalent of perhaps 16,000 full-time people are concentrating on research and development in the physical, biological, and social sciences in the colleges and universities. It would seem as though the comparable figures for industry would be approximately 200,000.

We only have to go back to the beginning of the century to see what a revolution these figures indicate. Two generations ago, if one had been asked where research was being done in the United States, the colleges and universities would undoubtedly have been mentioned. There were individuals who were doing research on their own. (This, of course, has been true for a very long time in Western Europe and in the United States.) The number of such people would have been extremely small.

In 1890 few, if any, people would have mentioned industry as a source of systematic research. Even by 1900 only a very occasional person would have mentioned industry as a source of research in the United States. The situation was changing rapidly before World War I, and by the time the war started, expenditures on research and development in industry were approaching the size of the expenditures of the colleges and universities in the same areas. By the early 1950s the expenditures of industry on research and development had equaled the total expenditures of the colleges and universities for all purposes.

It is probably true that the expenditures of the colleges and universities have been directed in a larger degree toward fundamental research than have the expenditures of industry. It has been pointed out that for this reason the gross figures may overemphasize the importance of industry in the research and development picture. That may be true. Recent figures by the National Science Foundation estimate that in fundamental research the colleges and universities are still spending about as much money as industry. One of the very great problems here is to find some means by which industry can step up its expenditures on fundamental research.

The best figures available indicate that the salaries in industry are very substantially larger than the salaries in the colleges and universities. The net result of this, if continued over a long period, will be to pull a very high fraction of the extremely able people into research in industry rather than the universities. Unless a substantial fraction of these people can be kept in fundamental research, the results could be serious.

Range of the Education and Training Program of Industry. Business and industry have developed elaborate programs in the field of education and training. As would be expected, these programs are strong in the highly technical fields. Many of the large companies hire highly trained people from the colleges and universities, and then proceed to give them elaborate and expensive additional training. Sometimes this training is fairly concentrated for a year or two or three. In a much larger number of cases it is a continuous program that goes on indefinitely after the person starts to work. Advanced courses in physics, chemistry, electronics, and many other fields are covered in these programs.

The total research and development programs paid for by all sources are above the $10 billion a year level. Thousands of people are involved in them. This much money and this many people will almost certainly bring about a great acceleration in the rate of change in almost all technical fields. It is no longer possible for one to get his technical training in the colleges and universities and expect it to be satisfactory throughout his working life. Many of the most successful companies have found that most of their technical personnel must go on with their education throughout their working careers.

There is every reason to assume that the expenditures on research and development will continue to grow very rapidly. If that is true, technical change will doubtless speed up much above the present level. It is also necessary to keep in mind that the most startling increase in research and development expenditures has been during the last ten years. These expenditures have not yet had time to have their full effect upon changes in the technical fields. Sometime in the 1960s or 1970s the rate of change is likely to step up well above the present levels, which will put a greater strain upon the educational programs of industry to keep their personnel up-to-date by means of their training programs.

Education at the Scientific and Engineering Level. A good many companies, particularly those with very large research expenditures, are getting close to the point of expecting almost all of their technical personnel to go on with their education fairly continuously. One of the major problems will be how industry will proceed when essentially all technical workers must continue their education throughout their entire working life.

Education in Management. As industry has become larger and also more technical, management problems have increased greatly. All kinds of technical experts have increased in the scientific fields, in accounting, finance, taxation, law, and many other areas. As the workers in these fields increase their technical competence, the people who are making the general decisions of management must also increase their competence. Most large business concerns have consequently set up elaborate programs in the field of management.

These programs start at the lower levels of management, go through middle management, and in some cases reach high up through top management. The strong tendency is to increase the range and the quality of these training programs. Some of these programs are run by professional organizations. The American Management Association provides many courses of this type. The American Bankers Association runs almost the entire range of banking courses. In some individual banks perhaps as many as 25 per cent of all employees will be taking courses run by either the bank or the American Institute of Banking. There are probably a good many industrial and business concerns in which the percentage of personnel involved is of the same order, or higher.

Courses at the Technician Level. Another point of very rapid expansion in the training programs of industry has been at the level of training technicians. Modern industry requires increasingly large numbers of highly trained technicians below the engineering level. The junior colleges and technical institutes have performed a major service in training these people. The military establishment has also provided a massive educational program at this level. In fact, some reports indicate that perhaps half of all the technicians in the electronics field have been trained by the military establishment. But with all this help from other agencies, industry has had a very large job to do at this level.

Almost all major industrial companies in the United States offer elaborate training programs at the technician level. Almost anyone who has demonstrated high skill and willingness to learn on the job can ultimately work himself into a training program of this type. With the further development of automation in industry, the number of people required just below the engineering level will probably continue to expand very fast. The repair and maintenance of complicated machinery takes people of at least this much training.

General Education. Some industrial concerns have found it effective to offer fairly broad programs in general liberal education. Sometimes this is at a high level. Some further liberal education is offered to management, and many of the courses that might be offered in a liberal education are found scattered through the education and training programs of industry.

Educational Programs of Organizations

There are many thousands of organizations in the United States that run educational programs. Some of these organizations, such as The American Association of University Women, church organizations, and labor organizations are extremely large, the membership in some cases running into millions. At the other end of the scale there are small local organizations that have only a few hundred members.

The educational programs of all of these organizations put together would overlap a large part of the program of the colleges and universities. The labor unions would cover in their educational program much of the material covered in the field of labor, and some general economic and social science material. The League of Women Voters would cover some of the material in the field of government or political science. Church groups would probably overlap almost completely the material dealing with religion, ethics, morals, the study of comparative religions, and much of philosophy and some psychology.

Some of the art groups would overlap most of the material in the fine and applied arts. Some of the groups interested in the field of languages would cover much of the field in the courses in English literature. There are large numbers of organizations interested in foreign languages. There are specialized groups in every one of the sciences. In many cases they carry on educational programs of one kind or another. At this point, of course, it is difficult to separate the work of scientific organizations from the educational or business organizations to which the scientists belong.

Even in an organization such as the American Chemical Society, the overwhelming proportion of the members are no longer members of college and university faculties. Most of them are professional chemists working in places other than colleges and universities. The meetings and publications of the organization are a substantial factor of the program in chemical education that goes on in the country.

There is an almost unbelievable range in the program of these organizations. Almost all technical and professional fields have a variety of organizations, many of which carry on educational programs. Thousands of strictly voluntary organizations more closely connected with the leisure-time life of people than their work also carry on educational programs.

In the effort to find some organization that did not carry on an educational program, an investigation was made of one of the major yacht clubs of the country. After being assured that it did not carry on an educational program of any kind and under no circumstances would consider doing so, we were told by the same people that it had one of the finest courses in navigation in the country! The course in navigation closely paralleled the course taught in one of the famous academic institutions on the same subject.

The educational programs of the churches are an illustration of another large class of programs. These educational programs, of course, are voluntary, and are run in large part by volunteers. Seemingly something over a million teachers are involved in the programs, and somewhat more than a million classrooms are used to carry it on. The number of people enrolled in the church schools seems to be about three million larger than the number enrolled in the elementary and high schools in the country. The number of classrooms and teachers are about the same number as in the elementary and secondary schools. The number of adults involved both as teachers and as students is also extremely large.

The educational programs carried on by these thousands of organizations are a major factor in the total educational program of the United States. The development of these programs is another indication that education must continue through the entire life for a very large number of people. The educational programs of business and industry naturally have a strong bias toward the working aspects of life; the educational programs of a very large number of the volunteer organizations have a strong bias toward the other aspects of life. The latter are particularly strong in the artistic, moral, and religious fields and in the emotional life of the country. They provide much of the continuing education in these fields. In fact, in many of these areas their educational programs completely overshadow the programs run by the colleges and universities.

Educational Programs Carried on by Individuals

For a long time much education has been carried on by the individual working alone. A case could be made for the position that the education that counts most is what the individual does for himself. It is perfectly clear that in our highly technical society the individual has to find methods of continuing his own education through most of his life.

The individual uses many means to assist him in this process. About a million people are taking correspondence courses each year. Some of these courses are undoubtedly at a low level; on the other hand, some of them are probably at a high level. A wide range of fields is covered, with a substantial emphasis on the technician level and some work on the higher scientific and engineering level. In any one year this program does not look large compared to the program in the colleges and universities. But over the lifetime of a generation of people, it can provide a substantial addition to the total higher education of the country.

There is another large source of continued education in the 18,000 schools, other than colleges and universities, that take high school graduates. At first thought it may not seem reasonable to include these 18,000 schools under the heading of individual education. Some of them closely parallel the colleges and universities in structure, methods of organization, and teaching. Most of them, however, are much more closely geared to the student who wants a particular course, or a particular subject or activity. In most of them a person can work on a problem or a field of study for a short time at high intensity and stop at almost any time he desires. These schools together cover a great range of educational activity.

A large part of the advanced education in the fields of music, art, and dramatics is carried on by these schools. In all three of these fields, of course, the most advanced instruction is given after one has gone through such schools and moves into private work with the great artists and musicians. Needless to say, in the fields of art, music, and dramatics the combined educational programs of the specialized schools and private instruction overshadow all the work offered in the colleges and universities in these fields. A problem in the field of higher education is whether regular colleges and universities should expand in a major way in these fields, or whether the specialized schools should continue to do most of the work.

The members of almost all the professional fields face an increasingly difficult problem of keeping up in their areas of specialization. Individuals will be looking for better methods of doing this indefinitely into the future. As knowledge continues to expand even faster in the future than in the past, the problem will become more difficult. The development of professional and highly technical books and magazines in almost all fields is some indication of its importance.

It is entirely possible that the majority of highly technical books are now used by people in their continued education, and not by the colleges and universities. Increasingly, business concerns will be interested in the chance that a worker will continue his education, and this may become more important than the amount of education he already has. Probably the most economical of all ways for a person to continue his education is to do it himself. The person who has the knack and facilities for doing this will become not only an extremely valuable worker, but an unusually valuable member of society as well.

The necessity for continued learning may force a major change in the colleges. As long as there was some reasonable chance that a person could learn a major fraction of what was known in his field, the colleges could concentrate heavily on making sure that the student knew the information available. The colleges should still provide as much information as they can in the time available.

In most fields, however, the student is going to leave college with a very slight mastery of even present knowledge, and in many fields his information will quickly become outdated. The colleges may well have to consider spending a great deal more time making sure the student has the competence and desire to go on with his own education. That could easily mean that he will have to work on his own in college much more than he now does in order to develop the necessary skills for continuing his own education.

The Program of Education and Training of the Military

It is difficult to estimate with any high degree of accuracy the size of the educational program of the military establishment. All people who have tried to do so, however, come up with the opinion that the amounts of education and training are extremely large, even if the basis of comparison is the entire regular, college, and university system.

A few statements from the Air Force Blue Book may give some indication of the extent of the schooling in one part of the Defense Department.

All men, when they enter the Air Force, are given classification tests. The high-scoring men are sent to special technical schools for the critical fields of electronics, radar, jet engine, weapons system, fire control, armaments, and missile training. After terms of various length in these schools, the men are sent to the using commands, and undergo further training. More than 50 per cent of the men move on to technical schools. This would run into hundreds of thousands of men per year.

The Air University is an indication of a school at a very high level within the military system. Some indication of its size is given by the fact that 130 men at the level of colonel, 600 men of the rank of major and lieutenant colonel, and 700 lieutenants and captains are studying at one time. The kind of training they are undergoing is to seek solutions to complex problems; some of the problems require as much as three typewritten pages to present. Among the subjects discussed are the strengths and weaknesses of the socialist and democratic systems, case studies of the major countries before and during World War II, and the future role of the United States in world affairs. These schools are concerned with education, general and professional, rather than with training in technical specialties.

Another part of the Air Force's advanced educational system includes basic studies in cosmic rays, the problem of weightlessness in flight, and psychological problems arising in space travel. At another advanced school more than two thousand officers and airmen are trained each year in aviation medical services and specialties. At still another of the Air

Force's advanced schools officers with outstanding engineering and scientific talents are now studying aeronautics, astronomics, nuclear engineering, and related subjects.

The policy of these advanced schools is stated to be truly to educate, rather than merely train and instruct. Some 215,000 persons in the Air Force are taking correspondence courses in such subjects as mathematics, electronics, and jet engineering theory. For whatever the figures are worth, the Air University is credited with 15,000 officers and airmen, the Air Training Command with 137,000, and the Air Materiel Command with 200,000. A very large fraction of these men are concerned with giving or receiving training or education, or with research and development. Even the operating commands say they do a large amount of training and substantial amount of education. A careful reading of their material and some very slight acquaintance with their practices seems fully to support this position.

The Meaning of the Research and Development, Education and Training Expenditures of Industry

What are some of the problems raised by the large expenditures of industry in the field of education? Probably the easiest place to trace some of them is in the field of research. Almost everyone would admit that the number of people who can do highly creative research in any society is extremely limited. One important scientist writing about the problem says that the important advances would probably come from a group no larger than 2500, and possibly as small as 200 or 300 people.

Two generations ago if a person wanted to go into the field of research in the physical or biological sciences, almost his only opportunity was to work in a college or university. Now the colleges and universities are spending less than 10 per cent of the money that is being spent on research and development. It would seem as though this has clearly complicated the problem of the colleges and universities in obtaining their reasonable share of first-rate talent in the fields of research.

All the evidence we have indicates that the salary scales in research in industry are higher than the salary scales in the colleges and universities. This is bound to pose one of the major problems as far as the support of the universities is concerned. How are the colleges and universities going to get the money to obtain their reasonable share of the high-grade ability in the field of research? Other important questions remain: What kinds of problems should be investigated in the colleges and universities; what types of problems can reasonably be turned over to industry for investigation?

The questions become extraordinarily difficult at this point when applied to fundamental research. How much in the way of economic resources should society turn over to the universities for fundamental research? The evidence in answer to this question is not as good as we would like. However, the opinion of almost all competent people in the field is that the resources devoted to fundamental research should be expanded very greatly. This holds true particularly as far as the colleges and universities are concerned, and it may be almost as important as far as industry is concerned.

At least one advantage in getting industry to do more fundamental research is that the method of financing would be fairly obvious and easy. The third alternative, of course, would be to have the states or the Federal government sharply step up their expenditures to the universities for fundamental research. A fourth possibility might be to expand fundamental research in some of the great nonprofit laboratories, and to establish many more such laboratories. Probably all of these methods should be seriously considered, and possibly all of them used.

Meaning of the Educational Expenditures of Industry

The expenditures of industry on education and training in the technical fields have expanded very rapidly in recent years. Looking back at it, this seems like a very obvious development and one that is likely to continue. However, it does raise all kinds of questions as to what types of technical training shall be provided by industry and what kind by the regular educational institutions. It would be difficult to conceive of the aviation industry operating in the United States in anything like its present form if it relied entirely upon the colleges and universities to do its education and training.

Hundreds of courses are provided by the industry in almost every technical field affecting the occupation. This goes back into developments in metallurgy, into mathematics, problems affecting stresses and strains, into the fundamental chemistry of certain kinds of materials, and literally hundreds of other fields. It would be difficult even to imagine the kind of development that would have to take place in the colleges and universities to deal with these problems on the scale that would be necessary.

It is almost as difficult to imagine the modern chemical, electrical, or electronics fields or the oil industry operating without elaborate education and training programs of their own. The most obvious meaning of these programs is that industry has become so highly technical and changes come so fast that much of the education and training program must be closely geared to the industry and specific occupation. Single companies in some of these industries will have many hundreds of courses, and their educational and training expenditures will equal the total budget of even the largest universities in the United States. The total research, development, education, and training budgets of many of these companies will be far larger than the total expenditure of any university for all purposes.

Clearly a whole host of problems arise in trying to get any solution to what kinds of courses shall be given by the colleges and universities and what kinds by industry. Will the overlap be almost complete, or will the colleges and universities try to limit themselves largely to the fundamental background or theoretical courses, leaving the practical courses largely to industry? Industry already seems to be deep into fundamental theoretical courses in many fields. Is this a development to be encouraged? Is it so important to get additional fundamental and theoretical courses that they should be offered at all levels to every possible person in the colleges, and after the people go to work? Do these changes relieve the college and university budgets of large expenditures in the practical fields?

New machinery and equipment in many fields is becoming so expensive that it may be impossible for the colleges and universities to buy it. Is the proper solution to work with industry in these fields, to allow industry to use the newest possible equipment, as it would be inclined to do, and see if some method can be worked out to use some of this equipment for instructional purposes?

If education has to continue through the entire working life of the person, then the problem of what shall be learned before one starts to work has to be opened up all over again. It looks as though the technical worker in many fields will have to be prepared to go on with his education and training throughout his entire working life. In other words, education and training have become a normal part of job activity in a great many fields, the number of which will probably increase very rapidly in the generation ahead.

The sharp separation between going to school and working that has existed in the past may become very much blurred. The figures would indicate that the percentage of people who are taking courses in a regular college while they are working has risen greatly. There is nothing in sight that is likely to stop this development for a very long time. People who are going to school already are, in very large numbers, working; people who are working are already, in very large numbers, going to school. Both groups may continue to increase in number.

We may be moving toward the time when practically all workers will also be going to school, as a part of their job or as a part of their advancing general education. The shortening of the work week makes this entirely feasible. A worker could work thirty-five hours a week, go to school five or six hours a week, and still not have an excessively long working week. Many young people, particularly in their late teens or early twenties, could well afford to go on with their education after they start to work, to great advantage to themselves and to the community.

The whole discussion of who shall go on with their education after high school, and how many, may change its form because of this development. It may be that essentially all young people will go on with their education after they finish high school. The real question probably is going to become this: What percentage of them should start to work at the same time they go on with their education, indefinitely?

Perhaps even more important questions are these: What percentage of the students and what type of person should attempt to go through school very rapidly? If we assume that practically every worker is going on with his schooling after high school, then probably the most important question becomes the percentage of the population that should undertake highly concentrated forms of schooling.

Financing the Four Systems of Education

As other sections of this volume have clearly shown, the problem of financing the colleges and universities is an extraordinarily difficult one. It may well become more difficult in the years immediately ahead. Some of the difficulty stems from the fact that people are buying something on which the return may be postponed a very long time. Another important part of the difficulty lies in the fact that we have not found particularly good methods to advance the money to buy the article to many of the people who will profit most from it. An additional point of difficulty lies in the fact that some of the return is probably widely diffused over society as a whole.

The three newer systems of post–high school education succeed in evading all three of these difficulties in large part. This may be one reason why they are expanding as rapidly as they are and why they will probably continue to grow during the foreseeable future.

The research, development, education, and training financed by industry can be reasonably related to the expected return. The one big exception might be in the field of pure research, and this is the field in which the problem has been least adequately dealt with as far as industry is concerned. The applied research and development programs of industry can be as closely geared to returns as industry cares to make them. Industry might undertake projects on which they expect a return in a very short period. As management becomes more sophisticated, the tendency is to lengthen greatly the period over which the return is expected. This, of course, is partly a function of the amount of resources available; the larger the resources the longer business can afford to wait for a return.

The expected return in industry from education and training must, of course, be an estimate, but it can probably be a fairly sophisticated estimate. Some of the very largest industrial concerns estimate that they are still getting five dollars of return for every dollar they spend on research. Clearly, as long as any such figures hold, the amount spent is likely to advance very rapidly.

Business probably cannot estimate with complete accuracy the return it gets on a given amount of training. However, management seems to be fully convinced that the present expenditures on the training of management, technicians, and operators are paying a satisfactory return. As long as management feels that the return is high, the only sensible thing to do is to continue to expand the expenditure. This is the situation, and it gives promise of continuing for the foreseeable future. The wisdom of this decision is in part tied to the rapid technical changes that are being brought about by the extremely large expenditures on research and development. Because there is every reason to assume that these expenditures will advance, there is every reason to assume that the rate of change will continue to increase. As long as this continues, we can expect the education and training expenditures of industry to rise.

The costs of the research and development, education and training programs of industry can be, and are, added directly to the products produced. In other words, these expenditures are a normal cost of operation of the industry. That is exactly as it should be. The cost of improving telephone service should be added to the cost of telephone service. The same should be true of products in the chemical or electrical fields or in the oil industry. Over the long run, of course, expenditures on research, development, education, and training are expected to, and undoubtedly do, both improve services and reduce cost.

The important thing from the standpoint of this volume, however, is that a method of financing these expenditures is immediately available, and as far as anyone can see, the method can provide for enormous additional educational expenditures. In fact, there would seem to be no reason why the expenditures could not expand to such point that the estimated return from them would drop down to the return of other expenditures of money that management makes. On the basis of any information that is now available, we can look forward to further extremely large expansion by industry in the fields of research and development, education and training.

Financing Education Provided by Organized Groups

I am sure the thousands of groups that provide educational programs in this country think they have great difficulty in financing the organizations themselves as well as their educational programs. However, such educational programs have advanced very rapidly and will doubtless continue to do so. One very good reason is that a person can join an organization that has an educational program in which he is interested. The labor unions run educational programs of interest to the members in the union. The same is true of the churches, the large women's organizations, and specialized and technical and professional groups of all kinds.

The fact that these organizations can provide programs especially geared to the interests and needs of their members is a very great advantage. If an individual finds one of these programs of sufficient interest, whether for vocational, cultural, or recreational reasons, he can easily pay for it. From the financial standpoint, there are other major advantages of this way of providing certain parts of the educational program.

There would seem to be about 100,000 people who use a major part of their time in running the educational programs of these organized groups. They probably involve something of the order of five million people on a part-time basis. These part-time people may be paid workers or volunteers, depending upon the organization. Normally, some already-constructed building and administrative framework is used to carry on these educational programs. This means that at least the reported costs of the programs are fairly modest, and it may very well be that the actual economic cost is low.

If the teachers are providing their time from what would otherwise be nonproductive time, society may have a net gain. If buildings are used at odd hours when they would not otherwise be used, this also might be a net gain to the community. There may well be important differences of cost here as compared with the formally organized educational programs.

The American people have at least a $100 billion of discretionary spending; the amount may well be considerably larger. As much of this discretionary spending can be devoted to education as the people are willing to so spend. If voluntary organizations can provide many kinds of education that individuals want, and also provide it at a price they are willing to pay, that would seem to be a net gain so far as education is concerned.

Although evidence is far from what one would like, in regard to both the programs of education offered and the willingness of people to pay greatly increased amounts for the education, what evidence there is would indicate that people are willing to expand their expenditures at this point. Until much better evidence is available, it would seem reasonable, then, to expect a major expansion of education through organizations of all types. It is important to keep in mind that the fundamental problem of financing education is to persuade people that it should come higher in their list of either tax or discretionary expenditures. Possibly because of the favorable cost and price situation, and possibly because of a favorable personal interest in some of these programs, organizations seem to be well placed to get large additional amounts of money from their members for educational programs.

Financing Self-education

A large number of ways of enabling a person to continue his education after leaving formal schools have been developed in the United States. A million people are taking correspondence courses; other millions are reading technical, scientific, and professional books and journals. Individual study goes on by a large fraction of successful business and professional people today. Museums and art galleries provide education in many fields, and even listening to radio and television are becoming important factors in the continued education of the American people. In many professional fields what evidence we have indicates that one must go on learning at an extremely rapid rate to keep up with the technical field.

All of these efforts combined make a major addition to the educational program in the United States. In almost all of these cases the person is using his own money to pay for something that he wants to buy. Within practical limits the amounts could be extended almost indefinitely. Even the low-income families in the United States have some discretionary spending, and some of it could be used to buy more education, if the individual so wished. For almost all families above the very lowest level of income, the amount of discretionary spending increases very fast; consequently, the amount that could be spent on various forms of self-education quickly becomes very large.

To the extent that it is possible to persuade people to substitute more expenditures for self-education for some of their present expenditures, we could tap a large additional source for educational support. Self-education in many of its aspects probably can be highly efficient at very low cost. One of the reasons for the low cost is the relatively small staff necessary to operate such a program. A fairly good case could be made for the thesis that self-education may well be not only one of the most important goals of education, but also one of the lowest-cost methods of adding to the total amount of education.

Meaning of the Additional Programs of Education

It has frequently been stated that the United States is a nation of ninth- or tenth-graders. For the people now going through school, the average amount of formal schooling is substantially above twelve years. If the educational programs provided by industry, organized groups, and self-education are added to this, a very great increase is obvious. It might not be unreasonable to assume that 15½ years of education would be closer to the real situation in the United States today.

We have also been told many times that the United States is only spending 3 or 4 per cent of its national income on education. If we add up the total cost of the various systems of education, it may very well be that the total figure is nearer 9 or 10 per cent of the national income. If complete figures could be collected, it is at least possible that the percentage would go substantially higher.

Greatly increased amounts of money should be spent on the formal system of higher education in the United States. Almost certainly the expenditures should be doubled, and possibly tripled, fairly quickly. In order to use this additional money most wisely, however, it would seem essential that the total program of post–high school education be considered. If this is not done, it would seem to be impossible to make intelligent decisions on what agency should expand what part of its total advanced educational program.

The colleges and universities will doubtless play a far greater part in our future than they have in the past. However, they have been supplemented by other powerful institutions that provide large amounts of research, education, and training of people beyond high school age. Without a doubt other agencies and institutions will arise to add to the ways of attaining advanced education.

It is extremely important that efforts be made to look at the entire program before decisions are made regarding what agencies shall do what particular part of the total program. The American public will undoubtedly be willing to provide an adequate amount of money for post–high school education if all of the facts, opportunities, and advantages are presented to them.

Notes

1. Harold F. Clark and Harold S. Sloan, *Classrooms in the Factories*, Institute of Research, Fairleigh Dickinson University, Rutherford, N.J., 1958.

2. Homer Kempfer, *Adult Education*, McGraw-Hill Book Company, Inc., New York, 1955.

3. National Science Foundation, *Proceedings of a Conference on Research and Development and its Impact on the Economy*, 1958.

4. National Science Foundation, *Scientific Research and Development in Colleges and Universities Expenditures and Manpower—1953–54*, 1958.

5. National Science Foundation, *Science and Engineering in American Industry, Final Report on 1953–54 Survey*, 1956.

6. John Walker Powell, *Learning Comes of Age*, Association Press, New York, 1956.

7. Paul H. Sheats, Clarence H. Jayne, and Ralph B. Spence, *Adult Education*, The Dryden Press, Inc., New York, 1953.

12

Probabilities and Possibilities

Willard L. Thorp

This paper is written after sitting for two weeks at the head of the conference table at the Merrill Center. The conferees had before them preliminary drafts of the earlier papers in this book, and much of the interchange
is now reflected in the papers in their revised form. However, the fifty
hours of talk around the conference table plus continuing debate in the
dining room and banter on the beach could not but produce illumination
ranging from the momentary brilliance of pyrotechnics to the steady light
of the bull's-eye lantern.

This paper is an attempt by one person to present his impressions and
recollections of the more interesting points in the discussion. It cannot
be called a summary or a report of any recorded consensus. Little time
was spent in discussing points on which there seemed to be agreement,
and no time was devoted to trying to measure degrees of concurrence or
variance. Since the conferees are personally involved in the problems of
higher education at different points and from different angles, much seeming disagreement turned out to be more a difference in emphasis than of
purpose. This brief chapter can do little more than suggest the multi-
formity of higher education and point up the complicated character of
its problems.

Educational Quality: The Variable of the Future

Some time during the late 1960s the number enrolled in institutions of
higher learning will pass 6 million; the 1959 figure is 3.6 million. Some
put their estimates much higher, even to 9 million, but no one expects

the number to be smaller than 6. Roughly, this means something like doubling the numbers in a decade.

These youngsters are not hypothetical; they are already solid bodies in primary and secondary schools. They are the product of the great postwar rise in the birth rate and represent an enormous population increase after about fifteen years during which the Depression and war held the birth rate down. Not only is there this great increase in these age groups, but a higher percentage than ever before will continue into higher education. Decade by decade, an increasing proportion of high school graduates have gone to college, and no slackening of this trend is yet in sight.

The improved economic position of families, the increased availability of education with low tuition payments or scholarships, and the lack of a tempting demand in the labor market have all served to enforce the personal as well as social ambition to continue one's education as far as possible. Moreover, there has been considerable pressure on certified teachers without a B.A. to return to school to get the degree or to proceed further. Industry also is encouraging many to return for degrees in related fields at the B.A. and M.A. level. Whether the objective be prestige, social position, earning power, social service, or merely imitation, the fact is that more and more of the eligible age groups are entering colleges and universities.

The problem is not whether or not a number in excess of 6 million will be enrolled in institutions of higher learning at some point during the next decade. It seems clear that they will. The problem is what kind of institution will handle them and what that will do to the quality of higher education. If quantity is fixed, then quality becomes the variable. Will present forms of higher education expand along familiar lines, or will the added numbers be enrolled in large evening classes in high school buildings? Will the ritual of education be completed by means of a great shift to fringe-type institutions of the most checkered form? Will higher education consist more and more of sitting in front of television sets or sitting alone while engaged in loosely supervised independent study? Will the demands which can be clearly foreseen be met by a series of improvisations as emergency succeeds emergency, or will we find ways of influencing the shape of the future on a more rational basis?

Nor is the area known as higher education a constant. Some of the more advanced high schools are now covering certain college subjects, and students are more and more entering college on an advanced placement basis. At the other extreme, the expanding area of knowledge poses a problem both as to the appropriate scope and depth for college and graduate work and the creation of new ways for keeping graduates up to date.

The amount of post–high school educating done outside the colleges and universities probably exceeds that done in the accredited institutions of higher learning. This includes not only the lonely music teacher with her procession of students, but specialized private schools for training jet pilots, artists, accountants, foreign-trade experts, and people in a host of other occupations. In addition, and probably larger in scope, are the training and education programs in business and industry, ranging from training for routine duties to courses in the highest levels of mathematics for the scientists. These activities are not so much a substitute for the college and the university as they are an actual addition to the provision of more specialized higher education. To a considerable extent, they are able to call upon individuals and draw upon financial resources which would not otherwise be available for higher education. However, to some degree, these programs do compete with the universities for manpower.

Still one added dimension in higher education is the rapid expansion in refresher courses aimed at keeping the person already trained abreast of new developments in his field. With the rapid expansion of knowledge, technical skills learned years ago become obsolete, and the need for the updating of one's knowledge is becoming increasingly serious. Much of the responsibility for providing the opportunity for intellectual renovation falls upon the colleges and universities, especially the medical and business schools, and must be taken into account in considering the probable future demands upon the system of higher education.

Problems of Evaluating Student and Institution

What can be said about the quality of the raw material—the student— ten years from now? Presumably, the potential capabilities in a larger population will be distributed in the same way they were in the smaller group, so there should be the same proportion of "bright" students, or the same proportion with high IQs. One might anticipate that the increased proportion going on would necessarily mean a lowering of the average capability, but there are several forces at work here. One is the effort through various means such as the National Merit Scholarship program to make sure that the promising youngsters do go on to college. (The actual figures are misleading, since perhaps as many as 15 per cent of the brightest youngsters continue their education outside the framework of the conventional colleges and universities—in music and art schools, for example.) The unfortunately large number of girls of high capability who drop out may tend to diminish. In addition, there are various submerged or isolated elements in the population where the feasibility of higher education is not realized and where much of promise is never developed, including urban slum dwellers and those in depressed rural areas. There are other cases in which the primary and secondary education is so inadequate that almost unpassable barriers to higher education are created. In other words, there still are many high school graduates who do not go on in spite of the fact that they have capabilities above the present entrance requirements.

While these forces may tend to raise the average, the greater pressures will be to provide some kind of post–high school educational experience for a larger share of those in the middle group of intelligence, so far as this is measurable. For such, the appropriate training, at least within our conventional forms, may be an advanced vocational school or junior college. Furthermore, an increasing share of the future total will probably be students who will live at home and also work. Some may attend the local college only part time, others will work a limited amount during the week but do most of their earning on week ends. Incidentally, this group will provide an added pressure for an academic five-day week in addition to that coming from those who dedicate their week ends to other nonacademic purposes.

Just as there is a wide variation among the abilities and conditions of students, so there is a wide diversity among educational institutions. At one end, certainly in prestige and probably in quality, are a limited number of private institutions and a few public institutions. Here the applications for entrance are so numerous that the opportunity for selection assures a superior student body. At the other extreme are a great many small institutions, mostly private, which are struggling for survival with such financial difficulties as to limit their faculties to those of either little competence or little economic motivation. Then there are the great state institutions, often with many branches, and the municipal institutions, often with large evening enrollments. In fact, classification can be between large and small; urban and rural; college and university; publicly or privately sponsored; men's, women's, or coeducational; four-year or two-year; profession- or occupation-oriented; residential or commuter; sectarian or nonsectarian. These various groupings produce a great variety of institutions. In economic terms, higher education is a highly differentiated product.

While the four-year residential institution has provided and will probably continue to provide the bulk of higher education, the most rapid growth during the next decade is likely to be in the junior college and the urban university whose students can attend on a part-time basis. Able to live at home and to earn enough to meet his costs, the student who is not scholarship material will solve his problem in this manner. This need not be the terminal point of his education, though it undoubtedly will screen out many for whom something less than four years is appropriate. The drive for general vocational training in these institutions is in part a reflection of the demand by small business for the kind of trained personnel which the larger enterprise can train for itself.

If one visualizes the situation as one of students with varying capacities
and institutions with varying requirements, it might seem that the problem is simply one of working out the appropriate disribution so that the
most perfect matching is achieved. To a considerable extent, that is true.
It is unfortunate when a poor student has to be flunked out of an institution to which he should not have been admitted in the first place, and it
is equally unfortunate when a student of high potential is not challenged
and loses interest in intellectual development because he is surrounded
by less able students and exposed only to tedious teaching. Fortunately,
there is some tendency for the students with the higher potentials to go
to the institutions which are considered the better. In fact, about two-
thirds of the resources spent on higher education benefit about one-third
of the students. That might be the appropriate relationship, if one could
feel that the sorting-out process had been well done. Such is probably not
the case, although the situation does seem to be improving steadily.

Achieving the best allocation of students is exceedingly difficult. We
still cannot make very accurate judgments concerning the potential of
an applicant, nor can we be certain what forces, in addition to potential,
make for achievement. Those who go to college at all probably tend to
try to enter institutions at or above their capabilities, because of the
insistence by parents that their children have a better education than
they, and also because of the competitive relationship among youngsters.

Nor is it easy to evaluate institutions. Nine-tenths of all students go to
colleges or universities near their homes, or at least in their own states.
A few states, like New York and New Jersey, have a net student emigra-
tion, and others, like Massachusetts, have a net student immigration.
While judging institutions would be difficult even if one had all the facts,
the information which is available to parents and prospective applicants
is inadequate, to say the least. While it is true that the experiences of
students within any one institution probably vary much more widely than
the averages between institutions, there are important differences of character, emphasis, and atmosphere. Reputations tend to exaggerate differences and to change exceedingly slowly. The matching of student to institution might be happier if more objective and complete information about
each institution were available. Surely a four-year investment deserves as
responsible a prospectus as the type required in the securities market.

To add to the confusion of rating institutions, there is a persistent urge
for upgrading among institutions. There is little prospect for many new
institutions except at the junior college, urban commuter level, but the
two-year college may want to become a four-year institution. The school
which gets no National Merit scholars wants one and then two. The college with a local constituency wants students from other communities.

Under the pressures of increased demand for higher education, standards will be both raised and lowered at the same time. Certain elements of the system will raise requirements and quality and add depth to their programs as they become more selective. Others will be forced by social demands to expand to such an extent that quality cannot be maintained.

It is important that there be variety. Automobility would suffer greatly if there were only Cadillacs and Corvettes, and the same is true of education. The junior colleges take some of the pressure off the four-year institutions, and the good four-year colleges take some of the pressure off the better institutions. Educational institutions can improve vertically and horizontally. They can try to move up in function level and they can seek to function more effectively on their given level, but it is important that many of them stay on the lower levels.

There still remains the difficult problem of matching student to institution. If for no other reason than to reduce social and personal tensions, it is important to improve the present admission process, and for both student and institution to realize that there is a proper place for him and it. The conflict over college admissions does have certain merit. It requires a school to clarify and emphasize its quality and uniqueness. It rapidly educates the boy in college values, though it probably gives him quite an imperfect picture. But the conflict is costly. Scholarship funds are wasted in the process of bidding for the best students, and administrative costs are high because of the large number of multiple applications. The public concern over the strains on students and parents is rising as black-market conditions increase. Concerted action between the preparatory schools and the colleges and universities is needed to resolve this situation. The objective clearly is not to bring every rung of the ladder up to the top, but to make each rung as strong as possible. Quality must be thought of in terms of each level; for example, junior colleges must function on their own terms, not those of a four-year college.

Problems of Supply: Facilities and Faculty

A college or university requires many things. Essential elements are facilities and faculty. Doubling the student body will require substantial increases in both. Whether or not the present national plant and equipment in institutions of higher learning is adequate for present enrollments is largely a matter of one's standards. While there are many places where crowding is excessive and equipment antique, there also are some institutions which actually are operating at less than capacity, but they are chiefly small liberal arts colleges whose contribution to the total cannot be anything but small. In most other institutions, while dormitories are full and libraries are often much too busy and too small, classrooms and laboratories are underutilized on any time-study basis. On many campuses, the traditional practice is to use classrooms in the morning and laboratories in the afternoon. So long as present enrollments persist, there is no compulsion to change, but with increased enrollments, there is a distinct possibility of getting along satisfactorily with a less than proportional increase of new buildings in many institutions. On the other hand, the institutions of most rapid growth, the urban commuter institutions, are already putting their space, both day and evening, to very high utilization. While they have no dormitory problems, their educational facilities are already inadequate. Furthermore, their land and construction costs are often on a high urban base.

There are special problems in increasing the educational capital investment in that a capital market for borrowing by educational institutions is only beginning to develop. It is possible to get help from the government for the construction of certain types of buildings, and some of the publicly sponsored universities have been able to enter the bond market to borrow for self-liquidating structures. Already developing is the practice of setting up a complicated set of fees for the use of libraries, laboratories, etc., such as to bring them within the income-producing category. Incidentally, that device increases income without disturbing the tuition charge.

Although the Federal government has concerned itself somewhat with the problem of the capital part of the educational budget, there still is an opportunity for private capital in this area. A large revolving pool of private capital, possibly contributed at a low or no interest charge, might be one way of meeting the problem. Such a pool could subject borrowers to matching agreements to stimulate further contributions.

The capital problem is not limited to private institutions. Difficulty is now faced by many of the public institutions which have received funds until recently from the dwindling World War II surpluses in state treasuries. About one-third of the states allow borrowing by state universities; another one-third may borrow on referendum approval; and the final third may not borrow at all. In most cases there must be a self-liquidating basis for the loan. Financing capital expenditures from general revenue funds presents major difficulties in view of the pressures of other demands on state funds. By borrowing as a university obligation, the costs can be spread over time and, if self-liquidating, never place a burden on the taxpayer. This will clearly be the solution in some states, but others may find it increasingly difficult to get capital funds for expansion.

An even more difficult supply problem is that of faculty. The essential resources of brick, limestone, and mortar exist for buildings. The increased student enrollment is already in existence. Even available funds are in existence within our unprecedented national income, if they can only be properly allocated. But a sufficient supply of qualified teachers to meet the expanded demand simply does not exist, and teachers are not easily found or made. The present flow through graduate school is far from adequate to meet the estimated requirements. One helpful aspect is that junior colleges do not require faculty with as high qualifications and, since this is one area of rapid expansion, their requirements may be met satisfactorily, although the general average of faculty training will fall.

To some extent, the existing supply can be augmented by using people not presently employed in the academic world. Undoubtedly, the largest number are to be found among women, who have been discriminated against except in women's colleges, teachers colleges, and small coeducational liberal arts colleges. Vestigial Depression rules and antinepotism regulations have prohibited faculty wives from serving in some institutions. It may be possible to attract some individuals away from industry and research agencies if salaries increase sufficiently, but movement in the opposite direction is likely to be the stronger. A more likely relationship with other sources is the borrowing of such personnel on a part-time basis, an arrangement already in practice by many urban institutions. There also is a noticeable tendency for colleges and universities to raid the high schools, a development which shifts the problem rather than solves it.

While the short-run problem can be eased by borrowing and raiding, the long-run requirements for full-time faculty personnel suggest the need for finding ways and means of increasing the flow of new teachers into higher education. Higher teachers' salaries, the inevitable result of shortage, will be an important factor here, although it is doubtful if colleges and universities will ever be in a financial position to outbid industry and research institutions. Something more like a national market for highly trained personnel is developing, and competition for faculty will be felt in all institutions. The usual forecast is to say that salaries will double, based on some sort of parity with the professions of law and medicine, although this is not clearly a relevant basis for forecasting. Actually, the justification for salary increases is simply the tremendous shortage of teachers. However, since the composition of faculties may change, with many more added near the bottom than the top, the average salary paid in all institutions will probably not double.

One important development, for which some omens have appeared, would be the opening of pay scales to a much wider range. Until recently, the salaries of instructors were advancing much more rapidly than those of full professors, who were losing ground as compared to living costs and not participating in any way in the general rise in real incomes. To many who are selecting a lifework, the immediate salary is less important than the prospect of advancement. The push for higher salaries at the top is coming from outside demands in certain fields, and this will be accentuated by interinstitutional forays.

While this development will unquestionably increase the costs of higher education, it is an expression of the normal market process whereby an excess of demand over supply is corrected. It leads to a more careful use of the valuable resource and also contributes to increasing the supply. Some high salaries may be a relatively inexpensive way of encouraging people to enter the field. It may be noted that many colleges have disregarded these possible strategic gains by making indiscriminate across-the-board salary boosts.

But teaching has other appeals, and in spite of the fact that salaries did not keep up with the rising cost of living during the years prior to 1955, the number on college and university faculties increased steadily. The low salary may have actually attracted some as offering an evidence of social dedication, but in the greater number of cases low salaries are probably a deterrent. However, in addition to higher salaries much more effort must be made in higher education itself to persuade a larger group to enter the teaching profession.

In spite of every effort to increase the number of qualified teachers, there will still be a shortage, particularly of senior faculty. This will inevitably raise the problem of how to use them so as not to impair the quality of education. Some help might be obtained by raising the retirement age. But it seems inevitable that the student-teacher ratio will rise. This may affect the last two years in a different manner than the first. The much smaller number of courses usually offered in freshman and sophomore year than in the later years means that there is a much larger number of students per course, and thus teachers are used more nearly at capacity. In the last two years, in most institutions, a multitude of courses are offered to meet the wide variety of student (and teacher) interests. This may mean that a course may be given even though the enrollment is only two or three students. Since the number of these specialized courses need not increase further, and in fact should be reduced, the result will be more students per class, even though the classes may still be only of seminar size. When the scarcity is particularly pressing, television and reduced class hours may contribute. Experiments seem to suggest tentatively that students can make substantial progress under a wide variety of techniques which fly in the face of many established educational beliefs. As an absolute minimum, professors should not be required to spend time and energy on activities connected with their work which can be done by less skilled individuals. In fact, in many situations, the provision of secretarial and research assistance might result in a substantial increase in the contribution made to teaching.

Any review of the future supply of teachers must concern itself also with the effectiveness of graduate schools. Here program and practice both need review. For example, an important segment of scientific literature is now printed in Russian, yet the language will not be accepted in most institutions as meeting the foreign language requirement associated with advanced degrees. Another development which slows down the flow of new teachers is the fact that the period spent in graduate school seems to be stretching out more and more. Potential graduate students, outside the fields of medicine and law, are all too often faced with an indefinite and undefined future, an almost complete lack of information about where they may be going and how they are to get there. The graduate schools must take much more responsibility for encouraging and developing teacher resources.

For certain institutions and faculties the rapid expansion of research has created problems for the educational operation. One of the purposes of the university has always been the advancement of knowledge, so research has been a legitimate activity of faculty members. In relation to education, it has presumably kept them more alert as teachers and has provided projects upon which graduate students could serve their apprenticeship. However, the rapid expansion of university research in the form of massive projects under contracts with the government and to a less extent with industry has led to such a degree of separation that many individuals in a number of university communities now are active on research exclusively. This has an impact upon teaching in three ways: it may divert the energies of high-level talent and the supply of facilities away from education; it may cause the administration and the community to downgrade educational responsibilities; it may disturb the budget by contributing to increased salaries through enhancing the demand for high-grade individuals and by incurring added costs for which there is not adequate recompense, particularly in overhead.

As a further form of diversion of manpower, there is the increasing demand from outside for various types of service from the academic man. It may be lecturing to nonacademic audiences or consulting with private or governmental agencies. Some of this activity is likely to be of real value in revitalizing and informing the professor and may augment his income; a considerable part of it must be regarded as community service, may not contribute to professorial development, and is uncompensated. In either case the diversion is of time and energy away from teaching and research.

The increased demand upon individuals in certain areas of crucial talent also leads to more leaves and absences, which may have a falling-domino effect as one school seeks a replacement by hiring someone away from another, which then has recourse to the same method to fill the vacancy created in its own staff. Staffing requirements may have to take these requirements into account, and the problems created may call for an improved market which might provide some sort of pooling of replacement needs and available individuals.

In addition to facilities and faculty, there are other factors which bear upon the quality and cost of higher education. Of tremendous importance is the nature of the education which has gone before. Any step in the direction of strengthening the high school contribution to the student's development is sheer gain, and today some of the more advanced high schools are actually giving some college-level instruction. The colleges and universities could certainly set certain performance standards with respect to reading and writing and possibly mathematics. The elementary foreign language work which seems so out of place as a part of higher education ought to be done before college, or in special summer schools. The attrition rate, an expensive element in education, should be reduced as student preparation and counseling improve.

Another step which might affect quality would be to review the motley programs which often have accumulated under one aegis and determine whether or not it may be possible to transfer some of them elsewhere and thus upgrade the institution generally. There is a genuine value in differentiation, and judgment about an institution is too often not sufficiently focused upon whatever part of institutional activity may be relevant. An excellent medical school does not necessarily imply a good business school.

In general, it seems clear that there has been both a rise in and multiplication of costs in many institutions, particularly the stronger ones. Administrative and admission cost, public relations and fund raising, and student service expenditures have risen drastically. Particularly in the latter case there is some question whether these services should be part of the bundle which every student receives or there should be some choice on his part. Although there has been a rapid expansion in institutions which do not offer many of these services, colleges and universities featuring them continue to experience high enrollment demand. In terms of total cost to the student it should be noted that an automobile constitutes a heavy lien on a student's resources.

Undoubtedly, substantial economies can be made by changes in educational methods and by increasing the student-teacher ratio. Other reductions in cost can be achieved in some institutions by operating on a stripped-down basis. Another source of potential savings may lie in greater interinstitutional cooperation, particularly in those cases in which several institutions are in the same locality. Several recent developments in this direction seem rather promising. One other management practice which might contribute to the efficient operation of educational institutions is more exact and complete forward planning.

The trends in the immediate future seem to be such as to permit some economies of scale and to give increasing weight to lower-cost institutions, namely, the junior colleges and the urban commuter colleges. Nevertheless, the probable increase in the level of faculty salaries will make total operating costs increase as fast or faster than enrollments. The requirements for new capital may not increase at quite such a rapid rate, but they will be sizable.

Problems of Finance

If one starts with the two propositions that higher education should be available to all qualified students and that many families have such limited incomes and resources that they cannot meet the full cost of such education, there obviously must be some arrangement to meet the individual's or the institution's financial deficit. The growth of these many and varied institutions of higher education in the past has been made possible by contributions from many sources.

There are four basic patterns of solution, plus many variants. The first is to reduce the cost by stripping the educational process to its bare bones. The urban commuter college comes nearest to this ideal. The residential college with health services, psychiatrists, athletic fees, fraternity charges, university presses, and the like may require payments of quite a different order of magnitude. The second is for the state or private contributors to pay much of the cost so that the charge to the student is reduced. The third is to have high tuitions but to sort out the students according to some kind of means test and provide scholarships in appropriate amounts to those who cannot pay their way. The fourth is to put the responsibility upon the student and his family. If adequate funds are not in hand, the payment is spread over a longer period of time through some banking or loan arrangement in the form of a variation of the installment-purchase technique. In actual fact, these various approaches are not as antithetical as is sometimes argued, and some elements of all four appear in most institutions.

One complication in thinking about placing the responsibility for payment on the family is that much of the increase in numbers is the result of larger, rather than more, families. The one-child family has largely disappeared, while four children are a not unusual number. This means that the family may still be able to finance two children through college, but that is no longer all there are. The final outcome may be that the boys go to college and the girls stay at home, or at least that fewer girls go to high-cost institutions. This phase of the problem might be complicated even further if one included as a cost of education the loss of earnings during academic life.

The new system of National Defense Act loans seems to place the Federal government on the side of financing students, provided they are willing to accept future obligations. Perhaps similar emphasis might be placed upon anticipatory saving, if there were some inducements such as a special bond with a premium interest rate or an employer-employee plan of the kind used in pension plans. While such a plan does not take inflation into account and does not meet the problem of extremely poor or persistently spendthrift families, it does take advantage of compound interest and could be included in existing automatic savings plans. Present evidence indicates that, although most families expect to send their children to college, the actual saving for the purpose is extremely small. The use of student loans seems to run into a special difficulty in the case of girls, who feel that it is unfair to their future husbands for them to become committed to long-term loan payments.

In part the choice among the various patterns of financing is likely to be a matter of expediency. But certain more basic implications are suggested by them. How should responsibility for education be distributed between individual, government, and other institutions? Is higher education so important to the nation that it should be regarded as a social cost, or is it primarily a means for increasing the earning power of the individual so that he presumably can afford to and should pay for the investment from his added capacity to earn? How much and what do the parents get out of it? Is higher education a method of providing basic vocational training and of inculcating "the rules of the game" so that other existing institutions have an interest in it? Since higher education has some part of each in its objectives, the philosophical approach does not resolve the issue but instead suggests that there is a place for variety and that the student certainly should not be made to bear anything like the entire cost.

One development which is important is the appearance of tuition differentials. This is clearest in the publicly sponsored institutions which have higher tuitions for out-of-state students than for their own citizens, presumably on the theory that the tax subsidy is collected only from state residents. While this may be dubious tax theory, it is politically attractive, although it will encourage the trend toward provincialism in higher education. Luckily, the idea has not extended to the point of requiring the graduates to remain in the state and thus pay off their debt to the taxpayers. Another form of differential is one set in accordance with the level of education, although few four-year colleges relate their charges to the lower cost of the first two years as compared to the last two. But costs do rise as students climb the ladder, and graduate training is the most expensive of all.

Perhaps the most important characteristic of the publicly sponsored institution is the low level of tuition charged. There are some evidences of increases, particularly against the out-of-state student, but the probability is that general increases of tuition will be self-limiting. Tuition increases based upon an economy, low-taxation argument will occur from time to time, but the increase will generate its own political reaction. The combined insistence of the public for higher education for more people and for low-cost education will mean either a serious deterioration of quality or a failure to meet the objectives. This is a welfare issue which will be decided by political response and not by economics. It will inevitably work in the direction of increasing appropriations and, if not forcing tuition down again, at least checking any further increase. After all, taxpayers are always in revolt, but the welfare argument has a high record of success. Certainly, any thought of raising tuition substantially in the publicly sponsored institutions appears to be contrary to the present political winds, though small and gradual increases may be feasible.

As to the private institutions, the situation differs greatly between the strong and weak. The strong have application lists longer than their admissions potentials. Their high tuition is regarded in part as a measure of excellence. They can readily raise tuition further, so long as it is accompanied by an increase in scholarships for the low-income students. But the weak institutions are the ones in trouble. For them, the handwriting is on the wall, unless they have angels handy. They must either improve quality along with increased tuition, so that they can compete with the publicly sponsored institutions, or enroll themselves for public support, either municipal or state. It seems quite improbable that their facilities, if of any value, will go unused in the face of the pressures which will develop. But it stands to reason that few parents will, or should, pay a considerable tuition for an education inferior to one which could be obtained at substantially lower cost.

Relationship of Business to Higher Education

The relationship of business to higher education has changed dramatically in recent years. In the 1920s there was real fear of improper business influence upon education and even free pamphlet material was regarded with suspicion, let alone consultation fees. Today, not only has business developed its own means of higher education for its own personnel, but teachers and research persons move continually back and forth. The volume of private research contracts is growing. But perhaps the most important new development is the rise in corporate contributions to educational institutions.

As might be expected, business support takes many different forms. It is most likely to center on the localities in which the firm operates. It may be special support to the development of the technical fields which relate to its operations. But it also may make contributions to education budgets based upon a broad interest in the national educational base.

The colleges themselves have made some efforts to obtain more business contributors, but here again, as in the case of admissions, the notion of an adequate prospectus is not widespread. Contributions might react to a much more careful setting forth of a development program covering five to ten years in the future. And in turn, it might be useful to contributors, as well as encourage improvement, if there were some system for publicizing distinctive developments by various institutions, possibly even some form of annual award. In this decade of exceedingly rapid expansion, it may be helpful to record in some way the most significant evidence of achievement in self-improvement. One other opportunity not as yet exploited is that of the employee of the corporation which is willing to match his gift as an alumnus. Since many institutions have alumni records only of home addresses and not of place of employment, they cannot follow up this opportunity with appropriate exhortations.

Gifts and grants are made largely to the privately sponsored institutions; they represent more than 20 per cent of the income for educational and general purposes of such institutions as compared to less than 3 per cent of similar income for publicly sponsored ones. The combination of accelerated efforts and the high level of taxes has made this a rapidly growing element in the financial picture. There is substantial evidence of a wider interest on the part of business in contributing to education, but there is also the perennial danger that contributions from any source—alumni, corporations, or government—may create a proprietary attitude with assumed rights of interference. It is extremely important that contributions from whatever source be made in such a way as not to impinge on academic freedom, using the term in a very broad sense.

Relationship of Government to Higher Education

The estimates of future enrollment suggest that the greater increases in numbers will be in the publicly sponsored institutions, as in recent years. Since the prospects are not bright for substantial tuition increases in this area, the implication is clearly one of increasing state support. However, any generalization must start with a reference to the variety of performance in the fifty states. This in turn depends upon tradition and attitude, upon economic resources, upon the weight of other claims upon the state's revenues, and upon the expansibility of tax receipts—which is a function of the nature of the tax system.

While the state contribution to higher learning is over 17 per cent of total revenue in Utah, Nebraska, and South Dakota, it is only 2.3 per cent in Massachusetts and 2.5 per cent in New York. Although the states claim to be hard pressed for funds, it should be possible to double the contribution to education in many states without causing a financial crisis. The states are perennially worried about their increasing expenditures, but that is not an insuperable obstacle in most cases, although the argument that higher tax rates will discourage industrial growth is a powerful one. It is more likely that interstate comparisons in higher education will, at least within comparable areas, initiate a sort of ratchet effect, with each state trying to match its neighbors' provisions for education.

Those who automatically bristle at the notion of further Federal aid to education should recognize how much the government has done in the past to encourage higher education. The land-grant colleges date back to 1862. Aid to agricultural colleges is of long standing. The use of campuses during World War I and the financing of higher education for veterans under the GI Bill of Rights constituted massive government action in the field. The rapid increase of government contracts for research has overshadowed all other financial relationships with the Federal government.

There is an indirect influence of major importance to the financing of education in the tax exemption of gifts to educational institutions. It seems a fair assumption that at least one-half of a gift made to an educational institution is costless to the individual or corporation and consists of Federal tax reduction. In fact, educational institutions have acquired a substantial vested interest in the maintenance of high personal and corporate income tax rates. Similarly, while state and local governments appropriate huge sums for the publicly sponsored colleges and universities, the exemption from property taxes constitutes a less-evident but important form of assistance to privately sponsored institutions. Some of the suggested tax concessions, such as providing a tax reduction equivalent to tuition paid, would not be effective where they are needed most: among the poorest families, who pay so little in taxes anyway.

The more recent developments in Federal aid other than research contracts, which should not be considered as aid because they are part payment for services rendered, have taken scattered forms, chiefly in extensive scholarship and loan programs and in aid to building construction. These programs straddle the issue of whether aid should be given to individuals or to institutions. If aid is given to individuals, there is less opportunity for interference with academic freedom. On the other hand, this tends to increase the pressure upon the better institutions and not give much support to those down the ladder. The use of Federal guarantees of loans for dormitories and other buildings is a growing practice. However, both public and private institutions have sometimes run into ideological or legal difficulties in using such funds. Some trustees appear to feel that it is appropriate to force a student into debt for his education but improper for the institution to improve the quality and quantity of the education offered by borrowing the necessary funds. More certain and effective methods of capital financing are clearly a requirement of the future.

At the present time, the picture of the relationship of the Federal government to higher education is most confused, something like the experiments in modern art that involve unplanned spots of various colors. There is neither any statement of general purpose, like that in the Full Employment Act, nor any apparent coordination of the various bits and pieces of government policy relating to education. To pretend that larger government expenditures on diverse and even undefined principles means that the system will not be affected is unrealistic. Any large government contribution is certain to interfere in one manner or another. Through the land-grant colleges, for instance, the government forced an educational expansion away from the purely classical curriculum to one which seemed more appropriate to the country's needs.

The Multiple-source Approach and Its Virtues

The total picture appears to be that the great variety of institutions and the variety of individuals who desire to enroll in them will engage in a process called higher education. How good the process will be will depend to a large extent upon the resources available. One need worry not about these resources being excessive, but about their being too little. Somehow the total costs must be met from tuition and other payments by the student, return on past endowment and current gifts, and contributions by the state and Federal governments. Not only will the products and costs vary from institution to institution, but the relative contributions from the available sources will differ.

It seems clear that, during this period of rapid expansion, every source will be needed. One danger is that it will be assumed that some one source, such as increased tuitions plus a loan fund or contributions by the Federal government, will be regarded as having final responsibility for whatever the deficit may be, in which case other sources will tend to dry up and quality may suffer. The actual fact is that the level of contributions from the various sources will probably be largely determined independently, and the quality of higher education will be as good or bad as the total makes possible. There is a positive value in the multiple-source approach; for such a condition strengthens the position of academic freedom in the institutions.

The problems as outlined are large and difficult, but not staggering. The main drive to meet them will come from parents and applicants who will provide an insistent demand. Institutions themselves must be responsible for maintaining and improving quality. Another source of added motivation will be increasing information about educational developments in the Soviet Union, where tremendous emphasis is being placed upon selecting the more promising and making certain that they work hard in educational institutions. It is of course true that an educational system appropriate to the Russian scene, with its controls and requirements, would be out of place in America. While we may feel confidence in our own system with its wider choices and greater freedom for both individuals and institutions, the Soviet experiment does provide one further inducement for us to increase our efforts to provide quality in higher education.

Nevertheless, it must be realized that there is a prejudice against change in many educational enterprises, as there is in all established institutions. This is augmented by the dispersion of responsibility among faculty, administration, and trustees. Even the faculty cannot be regarded as a unit, and it is often better described as a loose federation of rival departments. The faculty is responsible for the curriculum but not for the budget; the trustees must be responsible for solvency but cannot interfere with the structure of costs; and the administration has few prerogatives in either of those fields except to act as stimulant and lubricant. Perhaps there should be some form of insurance, or unemployment compensation, for college presidents who endeavor to move mountains! To cast this situation in terms of class struggle among faculty, administration, and trustees —the usual approach to the problem—is misleading. The fault lies with none of these groups but instead flows from the system in which there are too many checks and not enough incentives. What is needed is not polemic but invention and innovation, particularly of a political nature. There must be some means of arriving at decisions with the total picture in mind.

The number and types of institutions result in a real form of competition among them, not merely on the highly publicized football field, but in their search for students, for faculty, and for added financial support. Nevertheless, they have certain things in common. The requirements for expansion will be so great that all institutions should welcome the expansion of all others, since thereby the problem of each will be somewhat eased. In addition, there are many situations in which, because of propinquity or common problems, cooperation among institutions which leads either to economies or to a fuller use of resources can develop.

The conflict which has received the most attention over the years is that between public and private institutions, based largely on the spread in tuitions. At present there is no serious conflict among the better institutions, but it is to be found among the financially frantic, weaker institutions in both camps. Much of the publicity of this conflict arises from statements by persons only loosely connected with higher education who have an ideological bias against or in favor of government action. Working to strengthen the weak in both camps would put an end to most of the conflict.

The Challenge and the Way It Will Be Met

The discussion has centered upon the problems of the next decade. It seems clear that they will be met in a variety of ways, some of which will clearly be makeshift. At the same time, the forward drive of our society will increase the body of knowledge enormously, create dependence more and more upon the use of higher skills and abilities, and provide a stronger economic base for expanding expenditures, both private and public. If we look beyond the next decade, it is difficult to forecast what the image of higher education will be. It will likely be for a longer period of education on the average rather than shorter, with much greater scope and depth. Many of the commuting students of the next ten years will come from families which have no tradition of higher education. In the next generation, they will want to give their children a better education than they had. The ideal will continue to be the four-year residential rather than the commuter institution.

The years spent in the colleges and universities will be but a part of the process of education. At one end, the necessity for extraordinary specialization and the rapid expansion of knowledge will require a tremendous expansion in on-the-job education and in postgraduate refresher courses. At the other end, we may find valuable forms of post–high school educational experience for students with a relatively low potential. The American image of itself has always included the notion of a well-educated people, and the present system of higher education has grown in response to deep-set human aspirations in a free society. From time to time and place to place progress in higher education has been achieved by the effort and contributions of many individuals. The next decade will clearly be an unusual period of pressure and strain. The inevitable increase in numbers in the institutions of higher learning will make it difficult to maintain quality, let alone improve it to meet the requirements of transmitting man's growing knowledge to future generations. It will require the efforts of many individuals to meet the challenge. Our rich economy can and, in fact, must make these developments possible. In turn, the enhancement of our human capabilities by more and more investment in education will contribute to further technological, economic, and social development.

Appendix

The McGraw-Hill Book Company's 50th Anniversary Seminar
on
Financing Higher Education: 1960–70

Papers to be prepared on the following topics:

I An over-all view—a general, broad-stroke statement, setting the stage for the discussion and highlighting key issues which would:

1. Block out the economic position of higher education in terms of:
    a. Present deficiencies.
    b. Prospective requirements over, say, the next decade.
2. Sketch in the institutional framework of higher education in the United States now, stressing the great diversity of affiliation, sponsorship, etc.
3. Lay out key problems and issues involved in attaining solvency for higher education. Examples: the balance to be maintained between tax-supported and privately supported schools, Federal financing, the maintenance of open avenues to higher education for all those mentally capable of taking it, and adequate provision for the pursuit of excellence, etc.

II A detailed analysis of how higher education is financed today, how the system developed and what is required.

This paper would deal with the support of higher education, both in terms of:

1. Sources of funds such as tuition payments, endowments, taxes, etc., and
2. Demands upon resources as measured by share of the gross national product, national income, etc.

III Cooperation or conflict in the pursuit of solvency?

This paper would include:

1. A look at the subject historically.

2. Discussion of the potentialities for economically effective cooperation with:
  a. Joint research and development in educational and business operations.
  b. Comparative studies as guides to improved performance.
3. A flagging of danger of a disastrous interinstitutional conflict between tax-supported and privately supported institutions in their
search for adequate financing.

IV   Potentialities of better institutional management for improving economic
position.

This paper would include:
1. An arraying of tools for good educational management, including
those bearing on:
  a. Effective use of teaching facilities.
  b. Effective use of plant.
2. Examples of notably competent use of tools for good management.
3. Suggestions of new avenues to be explored in getting better institutional management.
(Note: This paper might well get into the problems of:
1. Making efficient selection of students for the type of education
provided.
2. Measuring success in providing the type of education offered, i.e.,
productivity.)

V   The present, potential and prospective role of the consumer (the student).

This paper would deal, both historically and prospectively, with the part
played by tuition payments, scholarships, grants and loans in:
1. Meeting the financial costs of higher education.
(Analysis of changing capacity to pay would be involved here.)
2. Making socially effective use of the nation's educational potential
in meeting the needs of educated people.

VI   The role of government—local, state and Federal.

Where paper No. II would provide an account of how higher education
is actually financed today, this paper would concentrate on:
1. Different methods of providing support of various states and localities.
2. The relative pros and cons of different methods of supporting
higher education.
3. The adequacy of governmental support of higher education at
present.
4. The prospect for governmental support of higher education, with
particular reference to the Federal government and the issues involved in Federal aid to higher education.

VII Private (as opposed to tax) support—by foundations, business and religious organizations, and college and university alumni.

This paper would include:
1. Some account of the magnitude of this type of support, historically and presently.
2. Some speculation about the probable future magnitude of such support,

but would be concerned primarily with:
1. Techniques for mobilizing such support, with emphasis on those that are notably successful.
2. Issues and problems involved in support of this kind. Example: appraisal of danger of business control as a result of business support.

VIII The role of the production of knowledge (through research).

This paper would include:
1. An account of the importance of research contracts in the financing of higher education.
2. An appraisal of the effects, positive and negative, which research contracts have on the teaching performance of the institutions concerned.
3. Methods, if any, by which benefits of research contracts now concentrated in relatively few institutions might be diffused.

(Note: It may be desirable to have a paper on the contribution of income, other than that for instruction, toward the financing of higher education. This would presumably include such things as:
1. Income from hospitals.
2. Rental of campus facilities.
3. Providing community entertainment with athletic exhibitions, dramatic presentations, etc.)

IX Potentialities of educational establishments outside the conventional structure of higher education.

This paper would include:
1. Examination of what educational establishments such as those maintained by industry and the Army do in or near the field of higher education.
2. Ways and means by which the educational activities of these establishments might be more effectively mobilized to get ahead with the total task of higher education.

Index

297